REPRESENTING
Popular Sovereignty

SUNY Series, American Constitutionalism
Robert J. Spitzer, Editor

REPRESENTING
Popular Sovereignty

The Constitution in American Political Culture

Daniel Lessard Levin

State University of New York Press

Published by
State University of New York Press, Albany

© 1999 State University of New York

All rights reserved

Printed in the United States of America

"Let Freedom Ring," by Barry Manilow, Bruce Sussman, Jack Feldman.
(c) 1990 Careers-BMG Music Publishing, Inc. (BMI), Appoggiatura Music
and Camp Songs. All rights administered by Careers-BMG Music Publishing, Inc. (BMI). All rights reserved. Used by permission.

"We the People," by Edd Kalehoff and Victor Sonder. (c) 1987 Maxrex Music. All rights reserved. Used by permission.

For information, address State University of New York
Press, State University Plaza, Albany, N.Y., 12246

Production by Diane Ganeles
Marketing by Anne Valentine

Library of Congress Cataloging-in-Publication Data
Levin, Daniel Lessard, 1963– .
    Representing popular sovereignty : the Constitution in American
political culture / Daniel Lessard Levin.
        p.   cm.— (SUNY series, American constitutionalism)
    Includes bibliographical references and index.
    ISBN 0-7914-4105-9 (hc : alk. paper) 0-7914-4106-7 (pbk.: alk. paper)
    1. Constitutional law—United States. 2. Political culture—
–United States. 3. Representative government and representation—
–United States. 4. United States Constitution Bicentennial,
1787–1987. I. Title. II. Series: SUNY series in American
constitutionalism.
KF4552L476   1999
342.73'02—dc21   98-27368
                                                            CIP

10   9   8   7   6   5   4   3   2   1

For my parents

Contents

Acknowledgments

This book has benefitted from the kindnesses of numerous colleagues, friends, relations, and public officials during its evolution from an unformed idea for a dissertation at the University of Wisconsin to its current state. In Madison, Donald Downs, Joel Grossman, and Richard Merelman provided me with the ideal mixture of freedom and criticism required of a dissertation committee; their cautious optimism about this project gave me both the encouragement to continue and forewarning of potential dangers. Stanley Kutler and Bert Kritzer were provocative and helpful additions to the committee at the dissertation defense. While I wrote the dissertation, I was supported by a community of sympathetic readers and listeners who included Lisa Brush, Chris Burke, Chuck Epp, and Eric Gorham. The University of Wisconsin provided financial support in the form of a Detling Trust Dissertation Fellowship, and I am greatly indebted to the Institute of Legal Studies and its associate director, Joy Roberts, for both the use of its facilities and its wonderful comraderie.

In Philadelphia, I am indebted to Mr. Ward Childs, Archivist of the City of Philadelphia and to the staff of the City of Philadelphia Records Center, and to Dr. David Dutcher, Chief Historian at Independence National Historic Park, who was an invaluable guide to the celebration and its players. Fred Stein and Craig Eisendrath generously provided me with many helpful insights during interviews. Tom Davies of Independence National Historic Park provided videotapes of the celebrations. I am immensely grateful to my brother, Michael Levin, who supplied me with a home, away from home but near Philadelphia, and copied many of those videotapes.

In Washington, Ronald Swerczek and the staff of the National Archives guided me through my work with the often incomplete records of the Commission on the Bicentennial. I owe great thanks to the staff of the Commission. Kent Larsen and Bill Hamilton were especially helpful; Barbara Hanrahan, Louise Brunsdale, Barbara McMahon, and Max Andrews were particularly generous with their time, as was Mark Molli of the Center for Civic Education and Sheila Mann of Project '87. I am greatly indebted to Leon and Marianne Levin, who furnished me with lodging and made my time away from Madison much more pleasant.

This manuscript had a long journey from the finished dissertation to its new form; I have accumulated additional debts along the way. Although I sojourned there only briefly, Ripon College was a community in the fullest sense; I am particularly indebted to Robert Melville and Marty Farrell. My current home at Boise State University has allowed me to both complete this project and move well beyond. Greg Raymond and Stephanie Witt have been supportive department chairs; I am also grateful for John Freemuth's guidance through the publication process. Tricia Trofast cured the many computer-related infections that afflicted the manuscript, while Kelly McColly served as a strict proofreader and editor. At SUNY Press, Clay Morgan has been both helpful and respectful of my judgment, while Bob Spitzer's enthusiasm for the manuscript was much appreciated after the long process of revision. Needless to say, all of the manuscript's remaining faults are my responsibility.

My greatest debts are to three people who supported me throughout this endeavor. Gabrielle Levin Lessard has been my companion and partner for as long as I have worked on this project; her encouragement and patience have been constant. My parents, Simon and Judith Levin, provided both personal and material support long before I began this project; their contribution is without measure. I dedicate this book to them in profound appreciation.

Introduction: Constitutionalism as Culture

"To live in the United States," writes Herve Varenne, "is to participate in a unique historical process that has solidified into a set of laws, customs, habits, and rules for behavior and the interpretation of behavior—that is, into what we call a 'culture,' *American* culture."[1] The set of social phenomena that Varenne defines as "culture" might equally well be defined as the American "constitution," the principles and practices that define, and which underlie, the proper relationships that exist within the United States. While this broad definition of the term "constitution" has fallen out of use among Americans, so fond of describing four scraps of paper stored in the National Archives as "our Constitution," it is this constitution which underlies many of the most important issues in our constitutional politics.

Understanding American constitutionalism rather than constitutional doctrine requires that the *image* of the Constitution as received in popular culture be given as much attention as the document itself, and that the central concern of any study of constitutionalism be the "composite representation of the historic [document] and of the ideas and ideals, policies and sentiments, habitually identified with [it]."[2] Studying the Constitution as a cultural artifact is, however, quite difficult. There are relatively few concrete

1

examples of the public's orientation toward the Constitution as a political symbol. To place the Constitution in the still larger universe of American culture is even more difficult. In the late twentieth century, public symbols like the Constitution have become elements of a fragmented political culture through the larger cultural process of postmodernism, a poorly defined but analytically important category. Whereas modernism was distinguished by the way in which cultural categories, such as religion, science, and politics, were seen as distinct practices with independent value systems, postmodernism is typified by the way in which economic, cultural, political, and scientific realms become intermixed and citizens' assumptions about what is factual and what is fictional become confused.[3] The most obvious examples of postmodernism occur when two or more different social spheres overlap, such as when prominent politicians or journalists appear in television comedies as themselves, thus breaking down putative distinctions between televised fiction and social reality.[4] Postmodern discourse uses images rather than narratives and words rather than sentences to create a disjointed discourse that reflects the hyperkinesis of an over-developed media.

In a postmodern culture, constitutionalism is characterized by political principles that are simply unfathomable from the perspective of the Constitution's authors. A postmodern Constitution relies on forms of authority which are incompatible with an interpretation of the Constitution as solely a political document from the Federal period. Instead, the Constitution serves many important functions within our political and popular culture. Beginning with the words, "We the People," the Constitution is a collective representation because it signifies the unified body of the nation, fusing that nation into a single text in which all members can find themselves represented. The Constitution's use of the first person plural symbolizes the new nation's capacity for unified collective action. The Constitution created a union of semi-sovereign states, allowing local identities to exist within a greater, unified identity that is most graphically represented through the geographic arrangement of the Framers' signatures.[5]

The traditional understanding of the Constitution as a political and historical text also leaves us without an analysis of the importance of the original copy of the Constitution which—unique, handwritten and irreproducible—lies at the heart of the Constitution's aura.[6] This original copy is ensconced in the National Archives in a display known as the Shrine, where, shielded in a bullet-proof canister, it may be instantly lowered into a subterranean vault and thereby protected against all danger including nuclear holocaust.[7] These precautions, taken because of the document's singularity and permanence, serve as visible reminders of its value as an authoritative text, which is kept sacred through its separation from the profane world. As a messenger from another time, the Constitution symbolizes a permanence and order that cannot be found in daily life.

While the Constitution as a political and historical document is often the subject of media attention, the Constitution is not often presented as a sacred text which animates our political and popular culture. Sacred texts rarely enter the profane realm of popular culture, but when they do they tell us much about our own civic religion. Thus, the Bicentennial of the Constitution's creation and ratification that took place from 1987 through 1991 was a "dynamic spectacle" which provides insight into the Constitution's meaning in modern popular culture. As an event, the Bicentennial was a fascinating glimpse of a mass society attempting to reach back into its civic republican past. To use a single example, the popular mass market newspaper *USA Today* ran special articles on the Constitution and the activities commemorating its anniversary throughout this period; it also interviewed the chairman of the federal Commission on the Bicentennial of the United States Constitution, former Chief Justice Warren Burger.[8] Gannett, the corporate parent of *USA Today,* cosponsored an essay contest on the Constitution for high school students,[9] contributed funds to the Bicentennial celebration in Philadelphia,[10] and during the

opening ceremonies in Philadelphia, *USA Today* included a
special pull-out section on the Bicentennial's meaning for
contemporary Americans.[11] The newspaper even promoted
its own capacities as a device for civic education by distributing free copies in Vermont schools as part of a Bicentennial lesson plan.[12]

In postmodern culture, even the sacred and durable
Constitution may enter the profane, disposable world of the
daily newspaper without much comment. That national
elites pursued the goals of civic commemoration and education through private, commercial media was scarcely given
a thought, and the responsibility of the larger public for celebrating the origins of the American state was rarely noted.
Instead, the possibility of introducing the Constitution into
the private world of the breakfast table made the marketing
of the document both attractive and necessary. By packaging the Constitution as a commodity to be consumed in
much the same fashion as news, sports, or comics, the Commission and the Bicentennial's other celebrants made the
text real and part of Americans' lives as a cultural icon. Yet,
cultural representations of the Constitution cannot substitute for Americans' alienation from the Constitution as a political and historical document.

Thinking about Modern Constitutionalism

The United States Constitution is now over two hundred years old. That simple fact requires Americans to ask
themselves whether it makes sense to link their contemporary national and political identity with a two-hundred-
year-old document. Most answer this question in the
affirmative. A poll conducted during the Constitution's bicentennial year of 1987 discovered that many more Americans believed that the Constitution had been effective in
"making Americans think of themselves as one nation"
than believed that the Constitution "treat[ed] all people

equally" or thought that the Constitution "establish[ed] a fair system of justice."[13] Yet, if one examines American library shelves, periodicals, or news accounts, the Constitution is far more commonly discussed as a legal document than as an important symbol of national unity and solidarity. Rarely, moreover, do scholars examine how the Constitution operates as a patriotic icon and symbol of the political system or consider the implications of constitutionalism for the political identity of Americans.

The Constitution is far more than a legal document defining the powers and limits of a particular system of political institutions. At the same time, the Constitution itself is less important than all of the other values which are associated with it; it only makes sense in the context of the larger culture in which it endures. To declare something "constitutional" is not merely to assert its legality or political legitimacy, but also that it accords with American character and values. Although polls regularly demonstrate that Americans are ignorant of the Constitution's contents or history,[14] and that few Americans follow the Supreme Court,[15] their assertions regarding the constitutionality or unconstitutionality of laws or government policies are a staple of talk shows and letters to the editor.

From time to time, scholars have written of this popular fascination with this little understood document. In the 1930s, Edward Corwin wrote of a "cult of the Constitution,"[16] while Max Lerner described the contemporary "fetishism of the Constitution."[17] These themes were revived in time for the recent Bicentennial by Sanford Levinson who explored the document's role as a sacred text in his *Constitutional Faith,*[18] and by Michael Kammen, whose *A Machine That Would Go of Itself* is the only systematic historical survey of the Constitution's role in American culture.[19] Of these authors, Levinson has been the only one to focus on the document itself in attempting to explain its special role within American culture. However, all of these authors have taken a cultural approach in attempting to assess the significance of the Constitution to American political culture. They have distinctively treated the Constitution as much as a product of history and sociology as of political theory, and, in doing so, drew upon a tradition as old as Aristotle and continued by Montesquieu, the philosopher favored by many of the Framers.[20] More commonly, however, students of the American Constitution have modeled their work on Montesquieu's "rival," John Locke, whose inquiry into first principles and a mythical social contract is mirrored in their emphasis on the political thought of the Federal period.[21]

Overemphasis on the Federal period encourages the study of a society which has long ceased to exist, while neglecting contemporary culture and political thought. Our historical understanding of the cultural meaning of the U.S. Constitution no longer accounts for the character of contemporary American society. This study combines political theory with empirical research in an attempt to revive "sociological constitutionalism," and to better understand the modern life of the Constitution outside of courts and political institutions. By broadening the area of constitutional interpretation beyond the forms practiced in academic, legal, and political institutions, American constitutionalism may be interpreted as a practice that is both structured by its place within American political culture and is an important source of political and cultural values. Such an interpretation is essential to any analysis of the Constitution's meaning in a diverse, postmodern, and thoroughly capitalistic culture.

This attempt to analyze the Constitution's place in contemporary American political culture is based largely on an examination of the events that comprised the Bicentennial of the Constitution. The existence of a bicentennial celebration may prompt the question of whether the Constitution celebrated was, substantially the same document ratified two hundred years ago. However, the purpose of this study is to mine the celebration itself for clues regarding the character of modern constitutionalism rather than to compare the contemporary interpretation of the Constitution with the "original understanding." Because the Constitution is largely absent from the uniquely modern phenomena of popular culture, the Bicentennial was a gift to anyone interested in modern constitutional culture for it was, in David Procter's terms, a "dynamic spectacle," through which scholars "may study the process of establishing, maintaining, and unravelling culture by examining the way community rhetors transform some dramatic event into enactment of their culture."[22]

The Bicentennial offered a relatively formal setting for the expression of public and elite attitudes towards the Constitution, making it a useful case study for understanding the Constitution's role in American political culture.[23] That public culture is by no means unified; many institutions and social practices, including mass media, advertisements and consumer products, the educational system, the arts, and community organizations, create a common identity. The combination of political and popular culture in bicentennial events and programs provide a unique opportunity to understand both the rhetoric and symbolism of contemporary American constitutionalism as well as the institutions and practices through which it is preserved and transformed.

Studying Constitutionalism as a Contemporary Ideology

Understanding the process by which American constitutionalism evolved and is today expressed requires both an interpretation of the cultural system surrounding the Constitution and an analysis of the actors and institutions which shape it, and are shaped by it. American constitutionalism results from conscious choices made by actors within cultural institutions who produce, reproduce, and transmit the public culture. This does not mean that a nation's political culture can be easily manipulated without regard for coherence and internal logic.[24] While constitutionalism does not contain its own explanation or justification, those actors and institutions who perpetuate and modify American constitutionalism are themselves constrained by the meanings already associated with the Constitution.[25] As Michael Schudson notes,

> social power is required to enshrine a work but . . . once enshrined, the work accumulates a self-perpetuating rhetorical power. It gathers partisans, partisans beget schools, schools beget cultural authority, cultural authority begets an established tradition, the tradition embeds itself not only in formal institutions but in our very language.[26]

In more formal settings, such as the Constitution's Bicentennial, those individuals and institutions who articulate constitutional norms are presented with special opportunities to present their messages. They also present us with a special opportunity to examine the assumptions and predispositions underlying American constitutionalism as a cultural form.

The ideological contradictions of constitutionalism are more apparent in public discussions and popular representations of the Constitution than in the academic and legal discourse that normally surrounds it. This contrast reflects the distinction between a "lived ideology," the beliefs, values and practices that pervade the lives of all of society's members, and an "intellectual ideology," which is a formalized set of propositions used by those who are in the business of constructing or maintaining ideologies.[27] Nonetheless, the great number of disparate portrayals of the Constitution in public culture is not the result of the public's incapacity for coherent thought, but results from the multiple demands placed on such an important symbol. Clifford Geertz has argued that many of the contradictions of an ideology result from its role as a system of symbols. Symbols often express different and contradictory ideas through such mechanisms as metaphor, oxymoron, and personification. Ideologies are built from a multitude of symbols, which may include many different meanings.[28] Because of the multiple associations between the Constitution and other symbols, ideologically informed representations of the Constitution are particularly dynamic.

The Conscious Creation of Constitutional Culture

Trying to discover the Constitution's meaning in popular, political culture is further complicated by the relative scarcity of images provided. For a central symbol of the nation's political traditions, the Constitution is strangely peripheral to much of American public culture. While politicians often invoke the words of the Declaration of Independence or the Gettysburg Address, and patriotic displays often include depictions of such nationalistic symbols as the Statue of Liberty or the Liberty Bell, the Constitution is generally neglected during patriotic celebrations. Unlike unifying symbols of national identity, the Constitution represents a complex political system that is internally divided. While the Constitution works well as an embodiment of social integration, the complexity of the political relationships it describes overwhelms the Constitution's ability to communicate any single, well-defined set of ideas.

The mass media and bureaucratic organizations structuring much of contemporary American life are necessarily part of the form of modern constitutionalism insofar as a nation's constitution is shaped by the all of "the institutions, roles, or symbols which are thought by their members to be characteristically constitutive of, and therefore central to, the 'inclusive' or 'larger' or 'whole' society."[29] And these institutions are essential mechanisms by which constitutionalism may be communicated to a large and diverse public. The Bicentennial was largely coordinated by a federal agency, and by the marketing departments of major corporations. Yet, these mechanisms were often underplayed through the official portrayal of the Bicentennial as a spontaneous, grassroots celebration in which the people, and not the government, saluted the Constitution. By categorizing these corporate contributions to the celebration as "private," rather than public, activity, commemorators attempted to communicate the idea that the Bicentennial was a popular celebration, planned and implemented without state activity.

The Bicentennial's meaning as a dramatization of popular sovereignty was also furthered through more obvious forms of public commemoration. Such customary means of collective representation as parades and historical reenactments assembled representatives of different occupational, racial, religious, and ethnic groups in scenes which compressed complex social realities into neat tableaux. The portrayal of contemporary Americans as embodying constitutional values also included their participation in historical reenactments in which they symbolically became ratifiers of their nation's charter. Such ritual exercises condense social relations in much the same way that historic preservation condenses history, by bringing representatives of different social groups together in a way which eliminates contradictions, tensions, and wrong turns. Social distance was eliminated from the Bicentennial's collective representations in a way which dramatically reduced the alienation and conflict which necessarily exist in a two-hundred-year-old republic with a diverse citizenry. Historic reenactments strove to make the past more "real," and better establish the past as a normative standard against which to judge the present.

Like liberal democracy, historical observances and community celebrations are forms of self-representation. Representation is itself a process by which communities make that which is distant present again. Rituals of representation are occasions to erase the historical and social distance between citizens, civic heroes, and the larger social order, and to reconnect citizens to what is "real" and "authentic" in the national culture. By invoking the images and forms of the Federal Period, commemorators presented the modern Constitution as the natural result of that mythological past and erased much of conflict characterizing the political and social development of the United States. Such a presentation of our constitutional history allowed Americans to imagine themselves as the authors of the document under which they govern and are governed.

The written nature of the U.S. Constitution also makes it possible for the document to bridge past and present and to make that past tangible. As a text, the Constitution is more easily disseminated throughout society through such media as advertising, educational materials, and "pocket" copies which are easily delivered to citizen-consumers. The document's written properties provide contemporary citizens with an opportunity for a direct encounter with the words of the Constitution's authors, and thus provide further evidence of the document's "authenticity." Yet, the textuality of the original document stands in an ambiguous relationship with the idea of community and deliberation, both providing a common referent for diverse readers and also creating the false promise of an authoritative reading.

The Constitution's written form does not, however, preclude opportunities for symbolizing the process of democratic deliberation. Small group discussions in which citizens considered the strengths and weaknesses of the constitutional system were promoted as educational exercises that would involve citizens in processes of deliberation and consent. These deliberations also had a symbolic component because of the dramatic way in which citizens revisited the decisions of the Constitutional Convention and relived the original ratification of the Constitution in 1788. Ironically, such educational exercises lacked the singular feature of a democratic process—the opportunity for the practice of sovereignty. Instead of political issues subject to local democratic control, such as community schools or snow removal, the discussions focused on questions the Constitution placed outside of the democratic process—free speech, the right of privacy, or the rights of criminal defendants. Issues which might be more properly or effectively addressed through electoral politics were often excluded from these simulations of the democratic process as too political.

The small group discussions were intended to remedy what organizers saw as a crisis in citizenship perceptible in low voter turnout and other forms of political participation. That same perception of crisis also underlays a large number of civic education programs funded and implemented as part of the Constitution's Bicentennial. The Bicentennial's organizers used the rhetoric of educational crises to describe citizen alienation from the political process in a manner which insulated the political process from criticism. Where social critics might find students' alienation from that process proof of students' capacity to understand their own interests and position, the diviner of educational crises perceives a failure to teach students to appreciate the social system. Responsibility for any failures within the political system are, by implication, located in the citizenry rather than the political system itself.

The central question which animates this work continues to be whether it makes sense for Americans to link their contemporary national and political identity with a two-hundred-year-old document. Both of America's constitutions have changed over the past two hundred years with, and because of, technological, cultural, and economic changes within American society. "The incorporation of America" no longer refers to the unification of popular sovereignty through a document and a government, but to "the emergence of a changed, more tightly structured society with new hierarchies of control, and also changed conceptions of that society, of America itself."[30] Instead of a republic governed by virtuous citizens, an ideal that has never existed, contemporary America has been shaped by the growth of a national economy, media, and welfare state that has brought all of American life under their dominion. How that state, social institutions, and media represent themselves to the people is the story of modern constitutionalism. Whether the values implicit within these modern institutions are in accord with the traditional principles of American constitutionalism, including popular sovereignty, is worth contemplating.

CHAPTER ONE

The Problem of an Abstract Constitution

A central irony animates any book devoted to the Constitution's significance in American culture. It is not the abundance of the Constitution's representations within that culture that must be explained, but their paucity. To put it plainly, constitutionalism lacks sex appeal in the competitive world of American popular culture. Commemorations of the Constitution's longevity have been eclipsed in popularity as occasions for patriotic celebrations by the anniversaries of such events as George Washington's birth and the signing of the Declaration of Independence.[1] Among recent celebrations, the Constitution's Bicentennial looked particularly lackluster when compared with the centennial celebrations of the Statue of Liberty in 1986 and the bicentennial observances of the American Revolution.[2]

As Michael Kammen notes, there are relatively few representations of American constitutionalism and popular sovereignty, especially "when one considers the centrality of constitutionalism itself in American culture."[3] Howard Chandler Christy's painting "We, the People" is the only artistic representation of the Constitution that compares with all of the famous depictions of the Revolution in American political culture,[4] and the Christy painting became famous primarily through the exertions of the federal Commission celebrating the Constitution's Sesquicentennial.[5] As Wilbur Zelinsky has observed, the number of local governmental units named "Constitution" is exactly one, compared with three hundred and twenty-four for "Union," one hundred and eighty-two for "Liberty," twenty-nine for "Freedom," and an even two for "Equality."[6] Similarly, the number of streets named "Constitution" is dwarfed by those named after other patriotic ideals.[7]

The Constitution's weakness in American ceremonial culture can also be seen in the lack of popular support for even a single day set aside for the celebration of the Constitution. Constitution Day, the seventeenth of September, when the Constitution was signed by the remaining thirty-nine members of the Constitutional Convention, is celebrated with much less fanfare than the Fourth of July, commemorating the signing of the Declaration of Independence.[8] Constitution Day was first proposed in 1916 and was first observed nationally in 1919; it was remade as "Citizenship Day" by Congress in 1952, changing the focus of the holiday from the history of the document to the duties of the American people.[9] Both We the People 200 in Philadelphia and the federal Commission on the Bicentennial lobbied Congress for over a year to designate September 17, 1987 as a one-time federal holiday, giving all federal workers the day off, and encouraging the states and private employers to do so as well. The national holiday was essential to the commercial success of the parade and gala, a fact understood by all involved in creating the events.[10] The historical neglect of Constitution Day continued even during the Bicentennial; the bill authorizing the holiday was defeated as legislators found the economic cost of a national holiday greater than the commemoration's historic significance.[11]

That the Constitution is a difficult document to understand has been demonstrated by the difficulty that promoters have confronted in gaining greater publicity for it. Sesquicentennial organizer Sol Bloom attempted as early as 1926 to secure governmental funding for a movie about the

Constitution; when faced with indifference, Bloom began to defend the Constitution against charges that it was "dry," even exclaiming that "[i]ts content can be made as vivid as some of the most thrilling events of our history."[12] Warren Burger faced similar problems during the Bicentennial in selling a planned gala in Washington, D.C. that was rejected by CBS, the same television network which broadcast the Philadelphia celebration, because it was unable to "solve the creative problems" and "develop an appropriate concept."[13]

This lack of interest was reflected in the few Bicentennial offerings, and the largely educational treatment of the document in America's most popular medium, television. Many of the television programs that brought constitutionalism into American living rooms during the Bicentennial were news specials,[14] in which television journalists explained various constitutional rights and features.[15] However, compared to the previous year's centennial celebration of the Statue of Liberty, network television news show gave the Constitution short shrift. From June 1986 to December 1991, the network news showed thirty-nine stories about, or related to, the Bicentennial in contrast to more than seventy stories about the Statue of Liberty celebration during the thirteen months from July 1985 through July 1986. Coverage of the Constitution's Bicentennial was mostly composed of "videogenic" events, such as the celebrations in Philadelphia and the recreation of Washington's inauguration, and the celebration lacked a period of concentrated coverage comparable to the media preoccupation with the celebration during the two-week period preceding and including Liberty Weekend.[16] While the telecasts of the Statue of Liberty Centennial ceremonies captured the attention of the majority of the television watching public, the nationally televised "gala" that was the centerpiece of the Constitution's bicentennial celebrations, was outshone in that ultimate measure of popular approval, the Nielsen ratings, by "NBC Investigates Bob Hope" (a parody of the recently concluded Iran-Contra hearings) and the movie *Mr. Mom.*[17]

The lack of attention paid to the Constitution is evident in the public's ignorance about the document. In 1986, the Hearst Corporation sponsored a national survey which tested the American people's familiarity with the Constitution. By most standards, the public flunked. Sixty-four percent of those surveyed believed that the Constitution made English the national language, and sixty-eight percent believed that the Constitution did not permit states to legalize marijuana within their own borders. Fifty-nine percent of those surveyed could not correctly identify the Bill of Rights, and sixty-six percent did not know the approximate number of amendments. Many people confused the Constitution with the Declaration of Independence; eighty and seventy-seven percent respectively believed that the phrases "all men are created equal" and "life, liberty and the pursuit of happiness" were in the Constitution, and twenty-five percent believed that the purpose of the Constitution was to declare independence from England. On the positive side, fifty-four percent knew that the Constitution was written "to create a federal government and define its powers," and substantial majorities knew that only a person born in the United States could be elected President, and that the President is not directly elected through the popular vote.[18]

In his history of the Constitution's importance in American culture, *A Machine That Would Go of Itself,* Michael Kammen proposes three areas of inquiry for explaining public ignorance about the Constitution: how the schools have taught the Constitution to students, "how information about the Constitution filters down to laymen," and the associated problem of relations "between the Constitution, the Supreme Court, and the media."[19] Kammen is undoubtedly correct in attributing much of the public's unfamiliarity with the Constitution to poor public education, inadequate and careless media accounts of the constitutional tradition, and a lack of communication between the judiciary and the public. However, public ignorance of the Constitution can also be traced to problems inherent in the Constitution's role as a symbol of popular sovereignty.

The Obscurity of a Constitution and the Necessity of a King

The most difficult problem with the Constitution's role as a symbol of the political system can be traced back to its roots in the Latin word *constitutio*. As far back as Cicero, *constitutio* has served as "a descriptive term for the political community 'as it actually is.'"[20] Such a complex reference is neither specific nor stable, nor is it easily compressed into a single symbol. The nebulous nature of a constitution was noted by Walter Bagehot, who declared that the concept of the British Constitution, consisting of the interaction of institutions, parties, and public opinion, involves "complex facts, difficult to know and easy to mistake." Bagehot compared the obscurity of the British Constitution with the concrete and tangible institution of the monarchy, observing:

> When you put before the mass of mankind the question, 'Will you be governed by a king, or will you be governed by a constitution?' the inquiry comes out thus—'Will you be governed in a way you understand, or will you be governed in a way you do not understand?'[21]

Bagehot's reflections are not restricted to Britain, but help to explain the American preoccupation with the native institution closest to the monarchy, the presidency. American political culture does not lack for representations of presidents, and has endowed the presidency with many of the charismatic qualities traditionally associated with sovereign monarchs.[22]

While British currency bears the portrait of the sovereign, American currency carries likenesses of former presidents and other dead statesmen, but not a single phrase from the Preamble nor any representation of popular sovereignty. And, while Constitution Day has become Citizenship

Day, and has never had the status of a full-blown national holiday, Lincoln's and Washington's birthdays have long been celebrated as such, although they were recently combined into the generic Presidents Day. The relatively powerful image of the presidency undoubtedly contributed to the belief of that forty-nine percent of the public who agreed with a pollster's statement that "the President can suspend the Constitution in time of war or national emergency."[23]

The relative paucity of representations of the Constitution in American culture results from a distinctive problem in democratic theory, the difficulty of embodying popular sovereignty. As the popularly enacted charter for the American state, the Constitution symbolizes the formal political relationships between individual citizens and the state based on the theory of popular sovereignty. Unlike primitive societies, which lack the idea of a distinct political sphere, "[i]n modern states, written constitutions and other such documents are used as symbols of organizational distinctiveness."[24] Understanding the American constitutional system as a distinctive entity requires that citizens are able to conceive of both an identifiable popular sovereign and a political state which is separate from, but dependent on, that popular sovereign. However, because Americans have never conceived of the state as fully autonomous from society, the Constitution is a weak symbol, lost in the mist that surrounds the American state. One early observer of the emerging American state, Alexis de Tocqueville, found it particularly difficult to conceive of the state within American political culture because "although everything moves regularly, the mover can nowhere be discovered. The hand that directs the social machine is invisible."[25] Contemporary observers have agreed with Tocqueville that "an American sociopolitical self-examination simply leaves no room for any valid notion of state."[26]

If the American state is poorly defined, the popular sovereign is even more problematic. Rather than identifying any single instrument of government as sovereign, Tocqueville described popular sovereignty as an almost mystical form of government:

> The people reign in the American political world as the Deity does in the universe. They are the cause and the aim of all things; everything comes from them, and everything is absorbed in them.[27]

The phrase "We the People," which often appears as a symbol of constitutionalism, evokes just this sense of popular omnipresence. "We the People" serves as a symbol of a national identity while remaining inherently ambiguous in its reference to an unspecified first person plural. While the term "people" may be used for an aggregate of individuals, to speak of 'the people' is to announce a collectivity that differs from the sum of its individual parts. " 'The people,' " notes Edmund Morgan, "are a fiction dreamed up by an advocate and infused with an artificial, rhetorical, reality by the agreement of an audience to participate in a collective fantasy."[28] Defining a people is a rhetorical act that binds together those who agree with it and those who fall within its limits. Taking American constitutionalism seriously requires one to assume that the "people" is an important and identifiable entity. Yet, the phrase "We the People" does little to define the popular sovereign which it identifies.

The essential problem with popular sovereignty, and a central problem of American constitutionalism, is that the popular sovereign is difficult to understand and virtually impossible to depict. As Edmund Morgan observes, "[t]he sovereignty of the people is a much more complicated . . . fiction than the divine right of kings. A king, however dubious his divinity might seem, did not have to be imagined."[29] With a sovereign that has to be imagined, the state must be embodied before it becomes real. "The state is invisible," Michael Walzer has written, "it must be personified before it can be seen, symbolized before it can be loved, imagined before it can be conceived."[30] A well-defined, visible sovereign is so important to the process of representing social relations that a thinker as capable of dealing with abstractions as Hegel could believe that:

> opposed to the sovereignty of the monarch, the sovereignty of the people is one of the confused notions based on the wild idea of the 'people.' Taken without its monarch . . . the people is a formless mass and no longer a state.[31]

Monarchs are necessary, according to Hegel, primarily for their value as symbols of popular sovereignty; they provide the polity with a center that embodies all of its members.[32] Even politically powerless monarchs, such as the British sovereign, perform this important cultural role.[33]

The importance of monarchy for imagining political relations derives from the three central characteristics of a political symbol: condensation, multivocality, and ambiguity. Condensation refers to a symbol's ability to "unify a rich diversity of meanings;" multivocality involves symbols' potential to "be understood by different people in different ways;" ambiguity denotes a symbol's capacity to express ideas that cannot be expressed precisely or definitively.[34] Although the level of debate over constitutional issues and interpretation is enthusiastic testimony for the document's multivocality and ambiguity, the Constitution does not perform the function of condensation well. Because the Constitution involves a multitude of different actors and rules, it does not present a well-unified picture. People can more easily understand government as a single, unified figure than as a group or as a set of rules or as an organization. That Martin Luther King's birthday has become an occasion to celebrate the civil rights and equality of all Americans demonstrates the way in which individuals can effectively function as symbols for abstract political ideals. The ability to understand abstract political concepts is learned. Studies have shown that schoolchildren first associate government with individuals, such as the current president or George Washington, or with icons, such as the flag or bald eagle, and are only later able to associate it with social processes and institutions, such as voting or Congress.[35]

Unlike justifications for the constitutional monarchy, or even the American presidency, which focus on the capacity for unity,[36] explanations of the Constitution almost inevitably lead to descriptions of its capacity for differentiation. The most familiar doctrines of American constitutionalism all testify to this emphasis on multiplicity; the trinity of the legislative, executive, and judicial branches, the doctrine of separation of powers, the idea of checks and balances, and the theory of federalism are all means of dividing government into smaller and more precise elements. Except for the Preamble, which describes the ideals and purposes of the Framers, the document is structured by its internal divisions, which reflect the separation of governmental powers; with the exception of the Preamble's first three words, "We the People," the idea of a unitary actor is foreign to the constitutional framework. Indeed, identifying "the people" as a sovereign body precludes identifying any single governmental institution as sovereign.[37] Rather than unifying the complex social relations which make up American government, the Constitution replaces them with a new set of complicated relationships.

The division of functions among several institutions makes good sense as a mechanism for limiting governmental power, but it also makes the representation of society that much more difficult. Walter Bagehot observed that "[t]he best reason why Monarchy is a strong government is, that it is an intelligible government."[38] A. V. Dicey, another Victorian analyst of the British constitution, also claimed that the monarchy was the only institution that could be "representative of imperial unity."[39] The problem of representing popular sovereignty has required the invention of new national symbols to substitute for the feudal symbols of the monarch. Eric Hobsbawm has noted that, while modern forms of art and technology may have lost much of their symbolic and ritualistic elements,

> most of the occasions when people become conscious of citizenship as such remain associated with symbols and

semi-ritual practices (for instance, elections), most of which are historically novel and largely invented: flags, images, ceremonies and music.[40]

Such symbols help to structure the consciousness of belonging to a visible state, a sovereign body, rather than a society, making one a citizen. Symbols of sovereignty are, in the terms of Durkheimian sociology, "collective representations" through which a collectivity represents itself to itself.[41]

Collective representations provide citizens with a symbolic vocabulary to use when referring to themselves as a single body. In this respect, the Constitution, and particularly the phrase "We the People," signifies American union and social solidarity. Yet, within American political culture, the ideals of social union and solidarity come into conflict with an individualistic culture characterized by ambivalence about social categories and collective identities. This ambivalence, which Richard Merelman calls "loose-boundedness," results from a lack of consensus on the values and principles that constitute American identity, and makes the process of collective representation problematic in American culture.[42] The popular sovereign is a creature of historical and social dimensions which can be only partially realized through political forms. Its representation through cultural symbols is no less difficult.

Constructing the Popular Sovereign

In his *Philosophy of Right,* Hegel noted that a "constitution is essentially a system of mediation,"[43] a system, in other words, composed of institutions that lie between citizens, and supersede direct social relationships. The political myths animating American constitutionalism both describe contemporary society and tell the story of how Americans transferred part of their sovereignty to the state in a way that created a single if divided identity. The Constitution represents the abstractions of both state and society because America lacks a visible, singular sovereign.

However, because the boundaries of the American state and American society are indefinite and uncharted, the document representing the relationship between society and state is left adrift and becomes, in the terms of modern semiotics, a floating signifier.

A government based on popular sovereignty condenses the social relations of a nation into a single symbol and slights many of the complex system of affiliations that comprise it. Social relations and political relations require distinct forms of representation. As a contract between individual and state, the American Constitution bypasses other forms of association, following those theories of social contract that diminish the importance of intermediate groups because of the emphasis which they place on the individual. As the medievalist Otto Gierke observed, with the advent of liberal political theories the "Sovereignty of the State and the Sovereignty of the Individual were steadily on their way towards becoming the two central axioms from which all theories of social structure would proceed."[44] However, the connection between the sovereignty of individuals and the sovereignty of the state is often difficult to understand.

Citizens' distinctive identities are difficult to symbolize within a national polity of the size and diversity of the United States. The relationship between citizen and nation is difficult to symbolize in a concrete fashion, and the size and heterogeneity of the national union embodied in the Constitution often leads to portrayals of national identity that are composites of more parochial forms of identity. Images of the Constitution may blend local and national identities to symbolize the document's role in the creation of the Union. One example, currently in the Smithsonian Institution's collection, is an arrangement by artist Mike Wilkins of personalized license plates from all fifty states and the District of Columbia that sounds out the words of the Preamble. Wilkins' piece places the familiar words of the social contract in a contemporary medium accessible to ordinary citizens who might use it for their own forms of self-expression.[45] An example from the Bicentennial, the

Festival of the States held in Philadelphia in 1987 as part of We the People 200's national celebration there, featured marching bands from each state, and a plan to construct a bicentennial fountain out of rocks from each state in an effort called "Rocks Across America."

Yet American national identity is often unmediated, with individuals claiming their place within the national polity without the intercession of any other intermediate associations. The idea of individuals asserting their membership in the Union through their personal signatures is quintessentially American, resulting from the manner in which American constitutionalism is founded on rhetorical acts of social union. Fundamentally, the Constitution was a "bootstrap" operation in which the people, through both the delegates to the Constitutional Convention and the ratification conventions, renamed themselves, "we the people," as a sovereign that was mythologically coextensive with the national state.[46] As Jacques Derrida phrases it, "this people does not exist *before* this declaration, not *as such* . . . The signature invents the signatory. The latter can only authorize to sign once it has arrived at the goal, so to speak, of its signature."[47] Not only are the signatures at the bottom essential defining elements of both the Declaration of Independence and the Constitution, but other forms of civil culture have incorporated the simple listing of citizens names as a way of establishing authorship or membership in a particular class; the Vietnam Veterans Memorial in Washington, D.C. is the best known example of this. During the Constitution's Bicentennial, several programs using names and signatures to signify individuals' direct connection to the document and personal ratification were proposed, but never materialized. A company named Cornerstone Marketing presented the federal Commission with the idea of soliciting signatures for the Constitution that would then be permanently displayed in either an outdoor walk (the "Path of Awareness"), bound volumes, or microfilm; this program was promoted as a way for citizens to "immortalize" themselves.[48] Similarly, Britten Banners, a company that manufactured large banners for events, proposed to collect citizen signatures on a banner that would be hung on a Philadelphia office tower behind Independence Hall during the We the People 200 celebrations.[49]

These plans did not come to fruition, but they illustrate the difficulty of portraying American social and political relations. While the representation of citizens according to the identity of the states in which they reside retains the language of the political in describing the composition of the Union, the representation of American citizenship as a social or cultural condition is complicated by the history of the United States as an association of "masterless men."[50] European democracies evolved out of feudal societies in which each citizen's political status was determined by his or her position in the feudal order; citizenship in America evolved without the aid of corporate associations. In portraying the American nation, commemorators used the states to serve as both mediating political entities and as constituent elements of the larger popular sovereign. To be an American is primarily a matter of political affiliation, while political and national identity in other countries is largely cultural, highly dependent on class, language and folkways.

The creation of a new national entity composed of individual citizens also allowed the delegates to the Constitutional Convention to circumvent the existing intermediate political bodies, the states. Madison argued that the state legislatures would be unlikely to ratify a constitution that transferred many of their powers to a federal government, while a direct appeal to the citizenry might prevail: "The people were in fact, the fountain of all power, and by resorting to them, all difficulties were got over. They could alter constitutions as they pleased."[51] The symbolic link between the Constitution and the people can exist without the aid of other mediating institutions, including the states. During the ratification debates in North Carolina, for example, one Antifederalist even conceded that "[t]he expression, 'We the People of the United States' shows that this government is intended for the individuals."[52] The "We" who authorized the

Constitution did so without explaining who it was, why it was empowered to do so, or its continuity with past sovereigns.[53]

By constructing a universal "we," the Constitution's Framers represented popular sovereignty without resort to such medieval forms as "corporations" or "estates" which might represent class interests.[54] This lack of feudal institutions has produced a uniquely democratic tradition, as Louis Hartz, and Alexis de Tocqueville before him, has argued.[55] The American republic did not tie representation by political institutions to membership within a clearly defined social classes unlike the ancient republics and Britain.[56] Gordon Wood concludes that the constitutional system was not a republic at all, but "a mixed or balanced democracy." While governmental power was separated in the three branches of government like the ancient republics, the Framers had

> eliminated the substance, thus divesting the various parts of the government of their social constituents. Political power was thus disembodied and became essentially homogeneous. The division of this political power now became (in Jefferson's words), "the first principle of a good government."[57]

The Constitution unified the populace through the creation of a new national state and divided that state internally, mirroring the checks and balances of feudal society in a manner compatible with a democratic American society lacking clear social divisions. Without such formal mechanisms as corporations or estates, the relationships and interests that structured early American civil society were less easily defined than are those in European corporatist states. Mistaking the absence of formal "corporations" for a lack of community cohesion, Hegel considered America to be only a form of "civil society," where social relationships remain primarily private, making democratic Americans incapable of true citizenship.[58]

Democratic citizenship means that an individual is both a private person, living under the rule of law, and a public person, actively engaged in the creation of that law.[59]

Citizens' membership in the sovereign body is coequal with their legal personality, as was made clear in the Supreme Court's most infamous case, *Dred Scott v. Sandford,* where Scott's ability to sue for his freedom, his legal "personality," was denied because he was not a citizen. As Chief Justice Taney wrote,

> The words "people of the United States" and citizens are synonymous terms and mean the same thing . . . They are what we familiarly call the "sovereign people," and every citizen is one of this people, and a constituent member of this sovereignty.[60]

Within the American constitutional tradition, legal personhood and citizenship coincide. To be a member of the sovereign body is to be capable of self-rule, both as an individual and as the member of a polity. The idea of autonomy underlies the connection among citizenship, sovereignty, and personhood. In the liberal, democratic tradition, the figure of the citizen is characterized by autonomy; she obeys only those commands she authorizes. The popular sovereign is the democratic citizen writ large, and capable of legislating for all who are part of the body politic, an artificial person incorporated through social union.[61]

In the United States, the creation of a national identity was simultaneous with the creation of a popular sovereign. As Will Harris notes, "the people as a whole" act as the Constitution's authors in an act of collective self-representation; this unity "is a major premise in an argument for the Constitution" as the paramount authority.[62] The act of "incorporation," which signifies the union of individuals into a single body, is an important part of the process of representing the solidarity of a people who transform themselves into a nation-state. Such an understanding is compatible with social contract theory. If the democratic state depends upon popular sovereignty for its legitimacy, a citizen does not have a contract with the sovereign, but may only contract with fellow citizens as to how they might together rule themselves.[63]

The creation of sovereignty and the radical revision of a society's political structure are extraordinary events. Bruce

Ackerman describes such moments as "constitutional politics" which differ from "normal politics"—those everyday decisions made by the government which do not require approval by "the people." Instead, constitutional politics involve qualitatively different acts of law-making that embody the popular will in permanent and fundamental ways.[64] Ackerman's distinction between normal and constitutional politics reflects the Lockean tradition, adopted by the Founding Fathers, that sovereignty is only partially transferred to the national state. Locke argued that there was a fundamental form of popular sovereignty, which Locke called "constituent" sovereignty, which required that the people could consent to the government that would rule them.[65] In this vein, Thomas Paine wrote, "A constitution is not the act of a government, but of a people constituting a government."[66] A second type of sovereignty, "ordinary" sovereignty in Locke's theory, was the government's capacity to make and enforce laws.[67] This form of sovereignty is reserved to officials of the state, and cannot be exercised by the people as a whole.[68] The distinction between constituent and ordinary sovereignty is necessary because "[s]overeignty cannot be represented, and government is distinct from sovereignty."[69] Constituent sovereignty in the Lockean tradition is inalienable and indivisible.[70] The distinction between constituent and ordinary sovereignty gives the Constitution a split personality as a political symbol. As the instrument by which the people expressed their identity and their authority to establish a system of self-governance, the Constitution remains a symbol of popular sovereignty. However, the Constitution also symbolizes citizens' alienation of ordinary sovereignty to institutions composed of elected officials.[71]

Alienation and the Constitution

The Constitution represents all Americans, not as an aggregation of individuals, by incorporating them as individuals into a single artificial person—the American body politic. As a symbol of the political relationships among a group of individuals, the Constitution becomes confused with the abstract relationships that it embodies. Bertell Ollman expresses this thought succinctly:

> As creations of men created to serve them in their communal relations, all forms of the state, like other intermediaries . . . take on the very powers they were meant to mediate.[72]

The act of incorporation requires that individuals forming a corporation alienate some of their own powers to this artificial person. In the process of incorporation, an entity's powers are placed in trust. Thus the entity's will is alienated so that the entity, and its wishes, become immortal. Corporations have a particular similarity to the body politic. Historically, the degeneration of monarchies, where sovereignty is clearly invested in a single person, was prevented through the legal fiction of a second corporate entity, the king's second body.[73]

The medieval doctrine of the king's two bodies distinguished between the human king and the national "body politic" of which the king was head. While the monarchy was inherited through family bloodlines, the sovereign power was associated with the king's fictional body, which was only his as the representative of the people.[74] The immortality of the sovereign, illustrated in the cry "The king is dead, Long live the king," belongs to the entire nation. The body politic also mirrors corporations in its ability to unite the resources and wills of the many into a single (figurative) actor that will outlive the loss of its mortal members.

The process of incorporation is compatible with constitutionalism; Chief Justice John Marshall's definition of a corporation is not far from a definition of a constitutional system:

> an artificial being, invisible, intangible, and existing only in contemplation of law. Being the mere creature of law, it possesses only those properties which the charter of its

creation confers upon it . . . Among the most important are immortality, and if the expression may be allowed, individuality; properties by which a perpetual succession of many persons are considered as the same, and may act as a single individual.[75]

Both corporations and constitutional democracies are forms of alienated sovereignty which allow for an entity and its powers to survive beyond the life span of any individual and to combine the powers of many individuals while also restraining the ability of those individuals to exercise their powers.[76] Both corporations and the state are "permanently organized groups of men" to whom "we seem to attribute acts and intents, rights and wrongs."[77] And, both corporations and the state draw their legitimacy from the alienation of the personal wills of their members.

This act of alienation has two distinct dimensions. The first is the act whereby one entity transfers certain powers or rights to another; this may involve such acts of agency as a power of attorney as well as formal acts of delegation. The second is the increasing separation and distance between entities that were once in a close relation, which may appear as a split within a single entity. In modern political thought, this second meaning of alienation refers to situations where citizens no longer believe in the ideals embodied in their political institutions, or when citizens do not believe that institutions embody the ideals that legitimate them.[78] Citizens may be described as alienated when they are no longer emotionally attached to, or participating in, public institutions or processes for collective decision-making.

Citizen alienation from social institutions involves a key tension within democratic theory. Without citizen participation, institutions for collective decision-making lose much of their legitimacy. Yet the term "alienation" also describes the essential process by which a society creates representative institutions. Citizens no longer need to participate, as many of their decision-making functions are assumed by the representatives to whom they alienate their sovereignty. Moreover, alienation also refers to the process by which a society symbolizes itself through the form of a fetish. As defined in the anthropological literature, a fetish is the product of the alienation of a person or group's properties to another entity, which then acts in place of, or symbolically represents, the first entity.[79] Although the term has come to mean specifically psychological or religious substitutes for unmet desires or anxieties, the term fetish properly designates entities that embody a wide variety of social relations; a fetish, like a constitution, is always a form of mediation. In all cultures, fetishism properly defined has four characteristics: fetishes concretely represent abstractions; fetishes are given human qualities; the fetish is conflated with what it represents; and it is unclear whether people control the fetish or the fetish controls people.[80]

The Constitution functions as a fetish in all of these ways. The document's image is often used as a symbol of popular sovereignty and the political system. As an artificial person, the Constitution is often perceived to have a capacity for action; individuals may claim that "the Constitution protects" this or that activity.[81] The fetishization of popular sovereignty in the form of the Constitution can be expressed in a number of ways. In the 1920s and 30s, Edward Corwin criticized the "cult of the Constitution" that had turned the document into a way of securing the established order that "harks back to primitive man's terror of a chaotic universe, and his struggle toward security and significance behind a slowly erected barrier of custom, magic, fetish, tabu."[82] Similarly, Max Lerner identified Americans' need to feel "some link with the invariant" as the basis for "the fetishism of the Constitution."[83] More recently, Sanford Levinson's argument that Americans possess a "constitutional faith" has also evinced this fascination with the Constitution as a stable source of national identity, and Michael Kammen has argued that the Constitution has been conceived of as "a machine that would go of itself," without, it seems, human energy or direction, providing an external basis for American political beliefs.[84]

An empirical study by Larry Baas of individuals' attitudes towards the Constitution provides additional evidence that the Constitution functions as a fetish in American political culture.[85] Baas found three basic attitudes towards the document among the individuals he studied. The largest group clearly manifested fetishistic tendencies, describing the Constitution "in protective and benevolent terms [which] apparently gives them assurances against an uncertain destiny and a belief that someone is in control and will take care of them."[86] A second group had a negative view of the Constitution and viewed it as failing to protect people against others with more power; the terms of their disappointment suggest that they expected the Constitution to serve the role of protector. The final group viewed the Constitution as a normative framework for interpretation and political action; this view is essentially free of political fetishism, and Baas found it to be disproportionately held among intellectuals.

Similarly, the importance of legalism in American political culture is partially attributable to the fetishization of law. The notions of a nation under law, and the "rule of law, not men" are meant as criticisms of monarchy and arbitrary rule, but they also imply the displacement of popular sovereignty. A radical democrat, Thomas Paine both associated the law with the sovereign and depicted that sovereign in abstract terms when he declared that "so far as we approve of monarchy . . . in America the law is king."[87] As J. P. Nettl has argued,

> In the United States the intellectual tradition of coping with sovereignty has been to deny its existence altogether; in practice only law is sovereign and probably the "function" of sovereignty can indeed best be taken as being fulfilled and institutionalized as law.[88]

Through the process of fetishizing sovereignty in the general form of law, and the particular instance of the Constitution, Americans have come to understand the Constitution as "the people's second body."[89] This fetishization has allowed the Constitution to function as a symbol of permanence set against the transitory nature of regimes and the mortality of its constituent members. The state, as Edmund Burke declared, is a "partnership not only between those who are living, but between those who are living, those who are dead, and those who are to be born."[90] As a written social contract which has survived many generations, the Constitution preserves the values of the dead, and is thus understood as a "living" totem from the past by each generation, which, in turn, hands it down to "those who are to be born."[91]

Representing Constitutional Fetishism

Cultural symbols are not created in a vacuum. The Constitution's capacity to serve as a symbol of the alienation of popular sovereignty depends on its public portrayal in such fora as education, the press, and entertainment. Civic commemorations provide a particularly dynamic forum for the dramatization of national identities. How such commemorations symbolically condense historical and social relations could be seen in the nationally televised "We the People 200 Gala" broadcast from Philadelphia on September 17, 1987. Although it should have been the highlight of the Bicentennial celebration, the Gala was frustrated by the message of unity and inclusion which had been sounded throughout the day.[92] The multiple demands of teaching the public about the development of constitutional doctrine, recounting the debates of the Constitutional Convention, promoting tourism to Philadelphia, and celebrating the cultural diversity of America all combined to make the gala a thematic mess. The two messages which most clearly shone through the gala's surface performances were that the Constitution "speaks" to Americans and that it "includes" all Americans.

The Gala's treatment of both of these themes began after an introductory fanfare, when actor Gregory Peck introduced the birthday document itself from its shrine in the National Archives. Peck had earlier in the year engaged in contemporary constitutional politics by opposing the nomination of Robert Bork to the Supreme Court because, as he stated in a television advertisement, Bork "doesn't believe the Constitution protects your right to privacy."[93] In more ceremonial surroundings, Peck proclaimed that:

> The Constitution spoke to the former slave, who finally broke the chains of bondage and vowed never to be bound again. It spoke to the woman who demanded and received representation at the ballot box . . . It speaks to the President of the United States, who places his hand on the Bible and swears to uphold the Constitution, just as it speaks to the immigrant, taking the oath of citizenship. It speaks to the radical firebrand, shouting unpopular slogans to a small group of skeptics in a public park, just as it speaks to the broadcaster on national television, informing viewers of the possible dangers threatening their constitutional rights, and it speaks to the newborn infant, whose rights begin at birth.

Accompanying each of these descriptions of the Constitution's function was a photograph of a hand and forearm. The "slave's" arm was still shackled, a "woman's" hand placed a ballot in a box, the "President's" hand was placed on a Bible, the "immigrant's" was raised for an oath, the "firebrand" held a rolled up manifesto, and the "broadcaster" held a microphone. All of this "speaking" by the Constitution was equated with popular action, thus both presenting the Constitution as a fetish invested with the voice and history of the American people. As a fetish, the Constitution was external to the historical actors or social groups *to* which "it spoke," but in Peck's narration the process of historical struggle by which subordinated social groups were included in American political life and through which political practices emerged was transformed into a process of textual revelation whereby the Constitution's meaning was made clear.

In Peck's narrative, constitutionalism was both inclusive and a process of speaking for another. Peck's comments posited a dialectical relationship between public and text. In this narrative of constitutionalism, the process of the alienation of constitutive sovereignty from people to document was reversed. Rather than animating this document with the power of popular sovereignty, the people were themselves given energy and power by the document itself. And, in a second development of this dialectic, the performers featured in the Gala substituted for the Constitution in speaking and singing to America about its beliefs and experiences.[94] The variety of performers reflected American diversity, and the sheer numbers of performers on stage dwarfed the live audience at times, providing the television audience with the image of two nations facing one another.

The "We the People 200 Gala" was thus a textbook example of Emile Durkheim's theory of collective representation, whereby the representation symbolizes the collectivity, and the symbol is re-presented to the collectivity.[95] Collective representations provide citizens with a symbolic vocabulary to use when referring to themselves as a single body. In this respect, the Constitution, and particularly the phrase "We the People," signifies American union and social solidarity. The very title of the program, "We the People," identified both its subject matter and its audience, and after saluting "We the People" as "the people who make America work," master of ceremonies Walter Cronkite announced that "tonight, this celebration is for us." Cronkite's statement implied that the citizenry, and not institutions, were responsible for making the Constitution function; the Gala carried this theme forth through numerous and vivid depictions of the American citizenry that overshadowed its explicitly political representations.

During the Gala, it became more difficult to establish exactly what was celebrated. During the singing of the national anthem, a Boy Scout troop from Colorado carried the flag from the space shuttle *Challenger*. The Philadelphia Pops Orchestra, with several rows of horn players decked

out in colonial garb, and the Mormon Tabernacle Choir provided a full-scale musical assault as Sandi Patti, who spe-
cializes in patriotic performances at such events as Liberty
Weekend, hit all the high notes. The television cameras
panned through the audience, highlighting former Chief
Justice Burger and the Rev. Jesse Jackson, then a candidate
for the Democratic nomination for President. The multipli-
cation of symbols allowed by the occasion placed the Gala
within the cultural form of postmodernism, with its fusing
of cultural traditions.[96] Anything American seemed to be
cause for celebration.

The Gala's theme was summarized in the two songs
specially written for the occasion. Pop singer Barry Manilow
concluded the performance with his own special composition, "Let Freedom Ring." After beginning with two verses of
"My Country 'Tis of Thee," Manilow's anthem enumerated
the ways in which freedom was a musical being that could
proclaim itself to the people:

> Let Freedom ring
> Let its music resound throughout the nation
> Let it celebrate sweet liberty . . .
>
> Let the promise not be satisfied
> Until no one is denied its song . . .
>
> Let Freedom ring
> It brought us this far
> It proclaims who we are
> Let Freedom sing."[97]

Manilow was backed up in this endeavor by the full weight
of the Mormon Tabernacle Choir, and while it was an impressive performance, the song did not deliver any message
more specific than that freedom was important and pervasive in America.

The Gala's theme song, appropriately entitled "We the
People," crystallized the Bicentennial message in a single

performance. The song's refrain made the document corporeal once again, a virtual singing body politic:

> We the People, I was written by great men
> We the People, You must read me once again
> We the People, I'm the Law by which we live
> We the People, Your Constitution, My words speak for everyone.[98]

The document was once again reduced to its Preamble; its identity was coequal with the public that both authorized it ("my words speak for everyone") and accepts its authority ("the law by which we live"). A chorus "of citizens who truly are 'We the People'," according to Cronkite, flanked the professional vocalists.[99] Peter MacDonald, president of the Navajo Nation, Julius Erving, the former basketball player, and "Famous Amos," the cookie salesman, joined others dressed as nurses, police officers, and construction workers in representing democracy American-style.

The incoherence that characterized the Gala reflected the inability of commemorators to decide on any particular theme. Performers' words or lyrics had to praise both people and state, and to condense, within a popular form, the contradictions of constitutionalism. Country singer Lee Greenwood, crooning the evening's theme song, summed up the traditional understanding of the document as a vessel for civic virtue:

> I live now in the heart of all America,
> in the minds of those who would be free.
> I am the voice of countless millions,
> I am you and you are me.
> I will be there for the children of our children,
> to shoulder the burdens they must bear.
> But even great defenders need defending,
> You must stand guard, you've got to care.[100]

The attempt to condense all of the populace and its tradition into a single entity, an *I* if not a *We,* resulted in an unusually high degree of fetishization of the Constitution within the Gala, yet there was little sense of what was distinctively American or even constitutional because of its symbolic overload. As Donald Horne writes, *"There is not room in a public culture for all of a society's 'realities.'* If they were all 'there,' then there would not be a public culture. A public culture is a form of limiting and organizing 'realities.'"[101] The Constitution, speaking for and including so many realities, is too varied to be represented even by a variety show.

Ultimately, the attempt to overcome the absences in our social and political relationships was best captured by three mass market newsweeklies. During the Bicentennial, *Time, Newsweek,* and *U.S. News and World Report* all published cover stories celebrating the Constitution's two-hundredth anniversary. *Time* portrayed the Constitution as a document that represented all Americans through a cover graphic composed of Americans of various races, occupations, and historical periods, obliterating distinctions of social class and time. Under the headline, "We the People," *Time* gathered an elderly black woman, a Confederate soldier, a Cub Scout and a flower child, who all took their place beside a coal miner, a mountain man, a telephone operator, and a gentleman in a tricornered hat.[102] *U.S. News and World Report* celebrated with a cover graphic that portrayed Benjamin Franklin and George Washington announcing the Constitution's signing in front of Independence Hall into microphones; the headline announced "We Did It!" An inside story detailed how, as the actors portraying Washington and Franklin posed for the photograph, autograph seekers descended on the two-hundred-year-old celebrities.[103] *Newsweek*'s cover promoted the Constitution as "The Genius of the People"; the cover photograph depicted a group of young boys reaching to touch the Liberty Bell. The photograph conveyed a sense of continuity between past and present which could be communicated through such rituals as touching the relics of the Founders.[104] These newsweeklies' covers typified the impulse within modern constitutionalism to portray the Constitution as the product of a collective "we" which endured over time. While the magazines lacked the theatrical elements of parades or televised galas, they conveyed the same sense of collective participation in remembering the roots of national identity in a more common and material form.

CHAPTER TWO

The Conscious Creation of Constitutional Culture

The national celebration of the Constitution's Bicentennial began in earnest on October 2, 1986 in Orlando, Florida, or, to be more precise, at Walt Disney World. The occasion was the celebration of another anniversary, Walt Disney World's own 15th birthday party. The federal Commission on the Bicentennial participated in this notable event by providing Walt Disney World with a "theme" for the weekend, by attending celebration functions and, by supplying, in the person of Chief Justice Burger, a keynote speaker.[1] Disney also assembled ten thousand journalists for the event, many of them travel and feature writers,[2] and both Disney and the Commission tailored their message for the media audience. As a surprise, journalist Nicholas Daniloff, who had been held by Soviet authorities as a hostage in a diplomatic dispute, made his first public appearance since his release. Burger introduced Daniloff as someone "who has recently . . . had occasion to experience firsthand the difference between our kind of a free system and another kind which is widely prevalent," and Daniloff spoke forcefully of his time in a Soviet prison, and what the Constitution and freedom had meant to him while in captivity.[3] However, on his way to the speaker's podium, Daniloff had to avoid a hug from Mickey Mouse.[4]

Mickey's offer of a hug threatened to trivialize Mr. Daniloff's experience in the Soviet Union—a threat which, however amusing, had to be taken seriously.[5] The same could be said of the Bicentennial itself, The programs in Orlando combined politics and popular culture in a way that blurred the boundaries between the constitutional principles and the imperatives of marketing. Warren Burger saluted his hosts at the end "for blending patriotic tradition, teaching and entertainment all in one."[6] Burger's mission was no less one of combining patriotism with entertainment, and he was as dedicated to furthering the celebration of the Constitution through association with Main Street USA, as Disney was interested in associating its own vision of Main Street USA with the Constitution. While Burger provided Disney with an opportunity to communicate its dedication to the American political tradition in concrete terms Disney offered Burger its ability to broadcast that message to the entire nation in a manner which associated the document as a symbol of popular sovereignty with a popular culture that was predominantly commercial in nature and organized by private entities like Disney.

The production, reproduction, and transmission of America's public philosophy, including the constitutional tradition, largely occurs through privately controlled media. The privatization of our shared culture has important implications for understanding the presentation of public institutions and political values in American popular culture. In 1986, the reconstruction of the Statue of Liberty and Liberty Weekend, which celebrated the Statue's rededication, were acclaimed as successful because of the involvement of private corporations and citizens, and, just as importantly, the lack of involvement by the federal government.[7] Similarly, corporate and private donations were a major element in the American Revolution Bicentennial of 1976, where they were also depicted as a measure of civic involvement and demonstration of patriotic feeling.[8] Such ideas have great appeal. Citizen organization and financing of celebrations provides the public with an opportunity for a direct relationship with their past, unmediated by governmental action. During the Constitution's Bicentennial, Warren Burger argued that small private contributions should be used to restore the homes of James Madison and John Marshall just as such funds had been raised for the Statue of Liberty's restoration, because "the value of the programs . . . was not just in the money they raised. The value was in the involvement of all these people."[9] Less glamorous than Lady Liberty, Madison's and Marshall's homes were eventually restored with federal funding, after private funding failed to materialize.[10] To the extent that few Americans can identify, much less fully appreciate, the achievements of James Madison and John Marshall, citizen involvement in the restoration of their homes was unlikely. Indeed, the Constitution's Bicentennial failed to attract the spontaneous popular support envisioned by its planners, who simultaneously decried public ignorance of the document. Yet, it would be ironic to expect citizens to actively contribute to a celebration of an event or institution to which they are not already committed and of which they are largely ignorant.

Commemorations of historic events and political ideas are typically required to undertake two very different tasks. The first, celebration, involves public declarations of praise and increased visibility for the event or idea commemorated; this is easily accomplished through the type of mass media that typifies a modern, commercial culture. The second, education, is a far more ambitious undertaking, requiring greater depth of presentation and greater commitment by consumers, and is unlikely to be well-served by the private media, entertainment venues, or advertising. While he often referred to the Bicentennial celebration as "a history and civics lesson," Burger also described "a really disturbing lack of understanding about our system throughout the country"[11] as the justification for what he termed "essentially a marketing job."[12] Indeed, public indifference toward the Constitution was largely understood by the federal Commission on the Bicentennial as a marketing problem to be solved by providing the document with greater name recognition. Rather than emulating the Constitutional Convention by working in secrecy or emulating the complex and subtle arguments of the Federalists, the task for marketers is "to gain . . . a differential advantage in distribution" for their product.[13] The Commission's task was to sell the Constitution back to the American people, in whose name the document was written. At the same time, organizers of the celebration hoped to illustrate to the American people how they already had a connection to the Constitution.

Modern celebrations of the Constitution can no more be understood apart from that commercial and material culture than the original meaning of the Constitution can be understood without reference to the state of the nation in 1787. Yet modern practices, such as private-public partnerships and licensing of commemorative souvenirs, may not only be incorporated into a celebration of the Constitution as practical means of disseminating information about the document, but may be justified by reference to the values of the Constitution. Corporate contributions, private media, advertising, and souvenirs may be elevated from necessary evils to evidence of the continued vitality of constitutionalism because of their capacity to involve citizens, however superficially, in the public sphere. The techniques which the planners of the Constitution's Bicentennial used to represent the Constitution to the public reflected many of the values which compose American constitutionalism.

The Governmental Role in a Constitutional Culture

The ambiguous nature of the federal government's role in the celebration of the Constitution's birth and ratification results in a series of paradoxes. The federal government's ability to reach its citizens directly is a result of the transformation of the national state's administrative capacities. In 1788, the greatest single reason for resistance to the Constitution's passage was the fear that the new federal state would use its national powers to enslave the people and rob them of their natural sovereignty. The new Constitution's proponents wished to represent it as the will of the people and took pains to demonstrate how popular support for its ratification had been. In a particularly illustrative example, the "Grand Federal Procession" that welcomed the ratification of the Constitution in Philadelphia in 1788 was organized and funded by the city's guilds and merchants, as were similar processions in New York and other cities. The organizers of the Philadelphia celebration were proud of the extent of public participation—half of the city's population either marched in the parade or attended the festive meal that followed—and the civic-mindedness that prevailed among the participants.[14] However, the procession's organizers were most proud of the fact that

> [t]his extraordinary exhibition was not undertaken in consequence of any order or recommendation of government, nor was any part of the expense borne by the public treasury. The *voluntary* exertions and contributions of the citizens furnished the whole.[15]

That, two hundred years later, the organizers of the Constitution's Bicentennial would attempt to attain the same level of citizen support with a minimum of governmental involvement demonstrates how much constant this distrust of national power has been within American political thought. Yet the federal government is today far more present in the ceremonial life of the country.

When Tocqueville detailed the features of the American system of governance that saved the people from tyranny, the lack of centralized, national administration was first on his list.[16] While visiting America in the 1830s, Tocqueville noted:

> Nothing is more striking to a European traveler in the United States than the absence of what we term the government, or the administration. Written laws exist in America, and one sees the daily execution of them; but

although everything moves regularly, the mover can nowhere be discovered. The hand that directs the social machine is invisible.[17]

Today, however, the national government has become so evident that "the most striking aspect of the modern state is its overwhelming size."[18] Theodore Lowi has written that a constitution describing the modern American state would begin "[t]here ought to be a national presence in every aspect of the lives of American citizens."[19]

Yet the national government is not the only modern institution present in the life of every American. The national media have also united American public culture through vast networks of television stations, magazines, wire services, and newspaper syndicates.[20] Huge commercial enterprises such as chain stores, franchises, mail order catalogues, and globally distributed brand name consumer products have blurred many of the sources of local distinctiveness, blending regional differences into a single national, commercial identity. The growth of national media and an international marketplace has created organizations capable of communicating with citizens and coordinating action across the nation through media which are supplemental to that of the state. Unlike citizens, who as individuals are limited in their ability to wield political power, corporations' capacity for political power grows with their size. By the middle of the twentieth century, the growth of corporate power led one observer to label corporate America as itself a state within a state, an "*imperium in imperio,*" and a second sovereign comparable to the states under the compact theory of the Constitution.[21]

The distribution of power between the state and private sector within the United States means that any attempt to unify the nation in a celebration of its own Constitution would include efforts by extensive media networks and large corporate organizations. Efforts by such organizations could help to obscure the face of the federal government and better communicate the idea that private society was celebrating the Constitution. The federal coordinators of the Constitution's Bicentennial endeavored to portray the document and the celebration as symbols of popular control over the machinery of government and of the government's rootedness in the people, their economic prosperity, and their local communities. Yet, the participation of large, powerful, omnipresent corporations in civic celebrations may be no less corrosive of citizens' capacity for self-representation than the participation of a large, powerful, and omnipresent government. The federal Commission on the Bicentennial's commitment to working with national corporations, national volunteer organizations and national media, as well as with local or state-based grass-roots organizations, resulted in a federal agency acting as the celebration's manager.

The organization of the Constitution's Bicentennial manifested the desire for a return to an idealized past without centralized authority. The limited privatization of a civic celebration under federal direction reflected two theories of the proper relationship between government and private citizens. In the first, private corporations were portrayed as public-spirited institutions, part of whose purpose was to represent the public, while the federal government was depicted as primarily coordinating and encouraging private activities, belying the Commission's legal responsibility for regulating and organizing the celebration. In the second, cooperation among the media, government agencies and private corporations provided planners with another opportunity to dramatize an imagined public consensus through popular participation.

Such attempts to portray a diffuse and decentralized political system can even be found in the self-portrayal of government agencies. The creation of the federal Commission on the Bicentennial of the U.S. Constitution was itself an attempt to bypass the normal mechanisms of the government and downplay large bureaucracies, such as the Department of Education, which might themselves symbolize the alienation of political power away from the democratic process. By establishing a temporary, independent commission, Congress separated the Commission from the electoral process and all other forms of citizen oversight.[22] Moreover, the Commission's organization both symbolically mirrored the constitutional separation of powers and violated that separation by dividing the appointive powers among the three branches. The statute establishing the Commission required that the Speaker of the House, President *pro tempore* of the Senate, and the Chief Justice (or their designees) all sit on the Commission, and then divided the remaining twenty seats among the Judiciary, House, Senate (four seats each), and the Executive (eight seats).[23] Such an arrangement would have been unconstitutional in a federal agency charged with interpreting and enforcing federal law, where all members must be nominated by the president. However, a federal district court approved the arrangement because "the duties of the Commission are primarily ceremonial."[24]

What was originally envisioned as a coordinating role expanded as the lack of interest by private organizations meant that the Commission would take on more responsibilities and require more staff and resources. In the original plan, the Commission would operate with only six staff paid from public funds, twenty other staff members drawn from other federal agencies and paid through their budgets, and up to forty staff whose positions would be funded by private donations.[25] By 1986, the limits on the number of staff the Commission could hire or detail from other federal agencies were gone.[26] By 1987, the Commission had one hundred staff positions, ninety-two of them filled with "permanent" employees.[27] At its peak in 1988, the Commission had one hundred and thirty staff.[28] Although early plans for the Commission had foreseen federal expenditures of less than $2.5 million,[29] the total amount obligated by the Commission from fiscal years 1985 to 1991 was over $83 million.[30] Excluding the almost $39 million in grants that were passed through the Commission, its operating costs still ran to $29 million, or ten times the original estimate.[31] Nor was the

Commission quite as temporary as originally planned. Its life was extended twice; first through the end of 1991, so that it could coordinate the celebration of the Bill of Rights Bicentennial,[32] and then until June 30, 1992, so that it could close its books and produce an official history of the celebration.[33]

The ideal of popular celebration was maintained at least rhetorically during the Bicentennial. However, the divergence between the ideals of a popular celebration and the actual celebration grew larger as the federal Commission found itself doing more of the work with less support from the private sector. The Commission's growth and longevity were not unknown phenomena for federal agencies and reflected the impulses for bureaucratic expansion that are partially responsible for Americans' jaded view of government agencies. What should have been equally problematic was the support it did receive from the private sector. That support came largely from major corporations, which were portrayed as private citizens contributing to a public celebration out of charitable impulses although such private citizens were as bureaucratic and powerful as the government agencies to which they served as ideological counterpoints.

The Corporate Contribution to the Bicentennial

In receiving Dwayne Andreas, chairman of the Foundation for the Commemoration of the United States Constitution, President Reagan described Mr. Andreas, the Chairman and CEO of the Archer Daniels Midland Corporation, as "a private citizen who has . . . decided to take an active personal role in assisting the Bicentennial Commission" and described the Foundation as "a fundamental link between the Commission and the private sector." In his two paragraph statement, the president used the word "private" five times, as well as such words as "personal" and "nongovernmental" to stress that Mr. Andreas' role was not public and that he had "volunteered." At no point did the president mention Mr. Andreas' corporate office, or that the Foundation's fund-raising efforts were concentrated on corporate donors, or that the Foundation's board was composed entirely of corporate executives, attorneys with ties to both business and government, and former government officials or their widows[34] The formation of the Foundation seemed to equate participation of private citizens with a private sector dominated by corporations.

In the United States, corporations are depicted as private entities, more akin to individuals than to the government bureaucracies which are their closest organizational relations. Irving Kristol has noted that corporations were historically accepted so long as they conformed to the notion of private enterprise in which individuals compete on an equal playing field. In Kristol's version of American history, populist revolts against corporate power have taken place when corporations no longer resembled "the flesh and blood entrepreneurs who founded them."[35] Although they are primarily large organizations structured to efficiently maximize their own commercial interests, corporations often portray themselves as private citizens concerned about the public good. As Paul Starr notes, liberals think about the public and private spheres in dualistic terms; the state is public, individuals are private, and "[i]ntermediate entities, such as corporations, typically have been divided between the two categories."[36] In contemporary political culture, corporate activities have been seen as less threatening to personal freedom, because, as private action, they are free from the taint of coercion associated with state involvement.[37] The definition of corporations as private was part of how planners of the Bicentennial portrayed the celebration as popular event organized and funded by "the people."

Corporate philanthropy reflects a preference for "private action," even when undertaken by corporations, to "public action" undertaken by the government. This ideological preference for private voluntary action was reinforced during the Reagan and Bush administrations by tightened government budgets.[38] The establishment of the Commission on the Bicentennial was justified by former President Ford because, although the government could not afford the cost of the Bicentennial, "you could justifiably rely upon private contributions to finance much of the work of the Commission."[39] The federal government's promotion of private sector funding for commemorative projects was crucial to the American Revolution Bicentennial of 1976,[40] and the Statue of Liberty Centennial of 1986 was so generously underwritten by corporate America and was featured in so much corporate advertising, that observers could quip that "one might have thought [the Statue] a monument to American business."[41] In contrast, many earlier commemorative agencies, such as the federal commission in charge of the bicentennial of George Washington's birth in 1933, had refused any commercial ties or corporate money.[42]

Americans' attitudes toward corporations have changed dramatically over the last two hundred years. In early America, commercial enterprises were not organized as corporations, instead corporations were private organizations which served the public good and were granted special status because of their charitable purposes.[43] Although commercial corporations are more prominent than such charitable organizations today, Edwin M. Epstein has noted, in the twentieth century, "the notion of the corporation as 'a creature of the state' has now come full circle from the early nineteenth century."[44] Government has again come to rely on corporations to provide essential social services that might otherwise be seen as requiring government action. In particular, both local and federal government have relied on corporate contributions to support civic celebrations. The fund-raising success of the Los Angeles Olympics in 1984 and the Statue of Liberty-Ellis Island rededication in 1986 led the federal Commission on the Bicentennial of the Constitution to hope the corporate sector would fund many of its efforts. The Commission's fund-raising goals were certainly impressive. In 1986, Commissioner Herbert Brownell compiled a list of projects that should receive private funding totaling almost $57 million[45] and Congress raised the limits on both individual and corporate contributions by ten-fold over the original legislation, bringing the amount corporations could contribute directly to the Commission to $1 million.[46] This change allowed corporations even more influence over the Commission and its programs.

None of the changes were particularly necessary. A "private" Foundation for the Commemoration of the United States Constitution[47] was created without any of the restrictions placed on the federal agencies. The Foundation was closely connected to the Commission but outside of its control,[48] and was organized to recruit corporate sponsors for the Commission's projects. Instead, the Foundation proposed projects of its own worth almost $79 million.[49] The Commission's experience with corporate sponsorships generally, and the Foundation specifically, was disappointing. Although an incomplete list included forty-seven different companies involved in bicentennial activities, almost all involved the distribution of Constitution-related materials or advertisements as part of the companies' own product promotions.[50] The Foundation received most of the corporate money, a sum totalling less than $5 million,[51] and the Commission itself received virtually no corporate contributions.[52] Those corporations that did contribute were either particularly interested in communicating with other elites or had problems with their public image.[53] When Edward Corwin and Max Lerner analyzed "the cult of the Constitution" in the 1930s, they interpreted the Constitution's symbolic power as a result of its capacity to signify political stability and safeguard the polity against disorder.[54] This function of the Constitution as a shield against chaos may have made it a particularly attractive symbol for the financial services firms, such as Citibank and Merrill Lynch, and business services firms, such as IBM and Xerox, which were disproportionately involved in the Bicentennial. The two most prominent consumer goods companies involved were tobacco and food conglomerates RJR Nabisco and Philip Morris, who, attempting to improve their corporate image, sponsored more accessible national events demonstrating good citizenship.[55]

The corporate community was most supportive of the Commission's work in advertising and promotion. Both the

Commission and its corporate patrons were oriented towards the public, and they formed a partnership which provided the Commission with access to corporate advertising and marketing programs, whereby the Commission might disseminate short messages concerning the Constitution on cereal boxes and milk cartons. By focusing on marketing rather than corporate philanthropy, the Commission was able to gain access to a larger portion of the corporate pie. As the Commission's director noted, "the best way to obtain corporate funding is from corporate advertising and marketing budgets which in some instances may be 100 times larger than the philanthropy budget."[56]

However, the abstract nature of the document made it a more difficult commodity to sell in exchange for corporate support than such readily recognizable icons as the Statue of Liberty. The executive director of Philadelphia's We the People 200 celebration expressed this sentiment in the clearest possible way: "[t]he Constitution as a celebration topic is just not sexy . . . It doesn't sell soap. It doesn't sell any product or service because it's not tangible."[57] The most important problem Bicentennial planners had to solve in soliciting corporate sponsorship was creating tangible events which would provide the visual appeal that the document itself lacked. This was the approach used by We the People 200, which produced the nationally broadcast parade and entertainment gala on Constitution Day in Philadelphia. We The People 200's strategy revolved around packaging their events as "the National Celebration in Philadelphia," and courted major corporate sponsors who were each expected to give $2–3 million and offered such premiums as the opportunity to use Independence Hall for board of directors meetings.[58] We the People 200 created a one-day event designed to turn a civic celebration into entertainment, following the promising precedent of "Liberty Weekend,"[59] while CBS purchased the one day package including the We The People 200 parade and gala for $2 million.[60] We the People 200 hoped television coverage of the parade would make both the parade and gala attractive to corporate sponsors. Indeed, We the People 200 expected to raise the almost $4 million cost of the parade through corporate sponsorships,[61] but received pledges of less than $1 million despite a visit by President Reagan to promote its efforts[62]

This emphasis on big events also caused problems in fund raising for the federal Commission and its associated Foundation. While heavy fund-raising for the Statue of Liberty Centennial competed with early fund-raising efforts,[63] they had even less success with corporate contributions after the big public events of 1987 had concluded, leaving them without a promotional product to sell.[64] The few events which did receive corporate funding were planned by the Commission, but then coordinated through the Foundation, allowing sponsors to retain a high degree of control over the projects' content[65] As Warren Burger testified, "we now develop a project and say, 'Here is a program' as we did with American Express on the Freedom Trailer and with Al Neuharth [Chairman of Gannett, publisher of *USA Today*] on the High School Essay Contest. Then they pay all the bills."[66] With payment of the bills also went much of the credit and control over content. In the interest of presenting the celebration as sponsored by the public, Burger and the Commission were glad to see that credit go to others.

Marketing the Constitution

While corporate funding for events and programs failed to meet expectations, the federal Commission had other methods of achieving its goal of involving commercial and media organizations in the marketing of the Constitution. The most important of these was the inclusion of messages about, and images of, the Constitution in the advertising and packaging that make up a large portion of the semiotic life of the nation. Modern promotional techniques have transformed the packaging of consumer goods into message boards that circulate throughout society as the products to which they are attached circulate through the economy and into the homes of citizen/consumers. "Piggybacking" messages about the Constitution on such promotional materials furthered three purposes at once. First, such curious marketing combinations of consumption and constitutionalism as blurbs about the Constitution's signers and ratification on school lunch milk cartons (courtesy of Champion International, Inc. and the International Paper Company)[67] were self-financing forms of promotion. Second, reading a cereal box blurb about the Constitution (courtesy of General Mills) transformed ordinary activities into a participatory experience in civic education, albeit at a low level of involvement. Finally, such promotional materials provided the federal Commission's corporate partners with opportunities to depict themselves as concerned citizens deeply committed to the nation's core values. More interesting for those analyzing the place of the Constitution in American culture were the assumptions which the advertising campaigns made regarding the Constitution's role in American life and the kinds of relationships which Americans had with the document.

Making the Constitution come alive to contemporary Americans challenged even modern advertising and marketing professionals. The federal Commission on the Bicentennial worked with the Ad Council and the New York advertising firm of Scali, McCabe, Sloves to create a series of public service announcements for newspapers, magazines, radio, and television. Any campaign had to confront the problem of representing the spectrum of abstract social relations which comprise American constitutionalism. In marketing, abstractions that potential consumers cannot see, taste, or otherwise experience before purchase are called "intangibles."[68] Intangible commodities have to be made real through representations which convey specific messages but which, because of the product's intangible nature, cannot be simple illustrations. The less tangible the product, the more its various qualities must be represented through surrogates.[69] Because of the abstract nature of its product, the Commission's marketing campaign had to use a number of surrogates to present its message to the public. The Commission's strategy included providing the celebration with a more concrete identity through the creation and licensing of a logo.[70] The logo enmeshed the Constitution within a web of patriotic symbols; the Commission on the Bicentennial's name and the years of the bicentennial encircled the red, white, and blue logo.[71] In the center of the logo, a scroll emblazoned with the first three words of the Preamble, "We the People," emphasized the Constitution's textual nature and function as a symbol of popular sovereignty. An unfurled American flag topped with a bald eagle silhouetted the scroll, further associating both the document and celebration with more concrete symbols of American sovereignty.[72] Interpreting the Constitution required such iconographic references because of the absence of a historic tradition of visual portrayals of the document.[73] Ralph Henry Gabriel has argued that the flag served the early republic in lieu of a monarch, replacing a personalistic embodiment of sovereignty with a (literally) material one, yet neglecting the Constitution as a possible replacement.[74]

The Commission's logo associated the Constitution with both the diffuse source of sovereignty—the people—and two more concrete symbols of the national state—the flag and the bald eagle. The lack of a well-defined national culture that is defined in other than political terms thus means that "Americanism" is best represented through political icons, such as the Liberty Bell, flag, or bald eagle. The difficulty of symbolizing the Constitution requires that these surrogates serve as representations of the nation, while the document itself represents the abstract relationship between the popular sovereignty and the state. The Commission's advertising campaign cleverly avoided the problem presented by the lack of a symbolic vocabulary for constitutionalism. Its slogan, "The Constitution: The Words We Live By," announced that most citizens already had a significant relationship with the Constitution, but were simply unaware of it. In ads, the campaign slogan was accompanied by video or other print intended to demonstrate the ways in which Americans took the Constitution for granted, and, in particular, to compare the Constitution with other national symbols. Readers discovered that "After the Declaration of Independence Our Founding Fathers Wrote Something Even More Important," and that "The President Doesn't Take an Oath to Defend the American Flag or the Statue of Liberty." The American Legion reiterated the theme with billboards that proclaimed "It's not just a piece of history."[75] The ads not only emphasized the Constitution's central role in defining American national identity, but also accomplished one of the key aims of any marketing strategy, "positioning," by situating the Constitution in a relationship to other, better known, political symbols.[76] In "positioning" the Constitution against the Declaration, the Flag, and the Statue of Liberty, the Commission's advertising agency used identifiable political symbols to demonstrate the Constitution's centrality to the American political tradition. However, the advertisements had a defensive tone, assuming that the reader did not believe that the Constitution was as important as the symbol to which it was being compared.

Other ads illustrated the importance of the Constitution to the creation of government institutions and offices by portraying the document's role in transforming ordinary citizens into officials with the power to act on behalf of the citizenry. One ad depicted young military inductees swearing allegiance to the Constitution, while another ad, shown in both 1987 and 1989, used inaugural footage of presidents from Kennedy to Reagan (and later Bush) swearing to uphold the Constitution and breaking up the presidential oath into clauses repeated by successive presidents. The ads symbolized the Constitution's function in remaking individuals as officials, soldiers, and citizens and depicted continuity in repetition of the Constitution by new generations. Each television ad ended with a still picture of the "Shrine" in the National Archives, suggesting that the order and permanence of the Constitution lay behind these images of continuity and stability. Similarly, the print ads for the Bicentennial of the Bill of Rights contrasted images of American normalcy with scenes of political oppression abroad and used the motto, "Before You Take Your Rights for Granted Consider There Are Others Dying to Have Them."[77] Associating the Bill of Rights with American order, the advertising campaign "positioned" the Constitution as a favorable alternative to foreign disorder and violence.

The federal Commission's advertising campaign to celebrate the bicentennial of the Bill of Rights in 1991 used another slogan which depicted the Constitution as underlying common experience. A television spot assured Americans that "Every day Americans use the rights guaranteed by the Bill of Rights, and they don't even know it." This message followed idealized images of American life: freedom of religion was illustrated by an Amish buggy; a middle-aged man assembled his fishing tackle on the porch of a Victorian house to demonstrate the Fourth Amendment right against unreasonable search and seizure; a couple shook hands with their lawyer to symbolize the right to counsel; and two African-American women entered a gymnasium to exercise their right to vote.[78] The advertisements depicted ideal American lives in a perfect example of Michael Schudson's comparison of American advertising with socialist realist art; both offer the public idealized depictions of their own lives, and encourage the public to emulate these images in their own lives.[79] Just as importantly, portrayals of individuals acting in ways protected by the Constitution or participating in constitutional government provided viewers and readers with explicit visual referents for the abstract idea of constitutionalism.[80]

The Commission's television advertisements also focused on such principles of consumerism as choice and transformation. After portraying a number of different religious communities at worship, one advertisement explained religious freedom with the statement, "In America, you can talk to God any way you want or not at all," presenting the First Amendment as a guarantee of the "best selection." Similarly, in an advertisement which had much the same structure as any "before and after" ad for a diet or exercise program, actor Charleton Heston intoned that "there was a time when an eighteen-year-old could not vote, a time when there was no meaningful way for young adults to express their opinions."[81] The ad presented the extension of suffrage to eighteen-year-old adults as largely the work of the Constitution itself, rather than the intervention of a political movement. However, the ads which most clearly conflated constitutionalism with commercial culture pointed to the relationship between the Constitution, and particularly the First Amendment, and the print and broadcast media in which the ads appeared. Print advertisements presented the Constitution as underlying the daily text of the nation by reminding readers that "the Uncensored Content of this Newspaper is Made Possible by the Constitution of the United States," and television spots featured Uncle Sam reminding viewers that the Constitution was responsible for "the freedom of this station to broadcast the show you're watching."[82]

The common theme of the Commission's advertisements, that Americans were enjoying benefits bestowed by the Constitution, had a goal of "remind[ing] the customers of what they're regularly getting," a crucial goal when advertising something as abstract as the Constitution.[83] The advertisements served what might be identified as a "cognitive, low-involvement" strategy. Advertising campaigns are often classified along two dimensions. The first dimension characterizes a consumer's attitude towards the product as one of "thinking" or "feeling" depending on whether the inclinations are primarily cognitive or primarily emotional. The other dimension in this scheme measures the level of "involvement" between a consumer and the product.[84] While a sports car might be advertised through a "high-involvement" strategy with an emotional orientation, the ads for the Constitution associated the document with images of American political icons and individuals going through daily routines, and appealed primarily to thought by reminding viewers to think about their own lives in terms of constitutional rights and responsibilities. Unlike "high-involvement" advertisements, which point out some great unfulfilled need in one's life and promise that purchasing that product will fill that need, the ads for the Constitution told Americans that the Constitution was already filling needs which they did not even know that they had, regardless of their investment in it. The advertising campaign thus assumed that, as a product, the Constitution required little involvement by its consumers.

The sole exception to this "low-involvement" strategy was education. Many of the Commission's advertisements instructed readers that "there is no better way for you as an American to reaffirm the principles for which our country stands than to learn more about the Constitution"; none of the advertisements mentioned political activity as an appropriate way to reaffirm democratic principles.[85] The Commission's advertising campaign also provided its audience with easy ways to become involved, and all of the ads provided viewers or readers with an address to write for more information. The Commission was given a special zip code to which people could send inquiries addressed simply as "Constitution,"[86] and both the Safeway and Winn-Dixie supermarket chains printed coupons good for a copy of the Constitution (from the federal Commission) on their paper grocery bags.[87] The focus on citizens' daily activities in the Commission's ads was congruent with the themes of most public service ads, which advocate individual responsibility as a mechanism for change without criticizing institutions, officials, or governmental policies.[88] In advertising the Constitution, the Commission informed people that supporting the Constitution did not require them to do anything that they had not done before.

The Constitution and the Politics of Taste

During the Constitution's Bicentennial, the federal Commission's advertising campaign and solicitation of corporate sponsorships was largely free from criticism. Yet, one particular advertising gimmick led to an exchange of public letters as comic in their style as they were serious in their critique of contemporary forms of political communication. After General Mills printed side panels for its Cheerios cereal with bicentennial messages including the Commission logo, Gara LaMarche, executive director of the Texas Civil Liberties Union, expressed dismay in a *Washington Post* opinion piece entitled "The Constitution in a Cereal Box?"[89] LaMarche criticized Warren Burger's plans to place the Constitution "on the checkout counter of every supermarket in the U.S.," and called instead for a celebration of "the persistent strain of individual courage that translates words on a piece of parchment into advances for human liberty."[90]

LaMarche's criticism had several aftereffects. National Endowment for the Humanities Chairwoman Lynne Cheney defended Burger, and criticized LaMarche as an elitist, arguing that "underlying what went on in Philadelphia in 1787 was the notion that this document would belong to the general population."[91] More typical was cartoonist Garry Trudeau's critique of the Constitution's commercialization in his *Doonesbury* comic strip. Including a complete copy of the document, without amendments, in his strip, one of Trudeau's characters urged readers to clip out the strip, attach it to a cereal box, and enjoy "mighty fine breakfast reading and whole-grain goodness to boot."[92] For Trudeau, the Constitution's association with such commodities gave it the quality of a commodity as well, while others, following LaMarche, worried that "the whole process tames and sentimentalizes the Constitution."[93] Indeed, General Mills ran its bicentennial messages concurrent with a contest that promised its winner "Breakfast in the Capitol," marketing civic virtue as a game and further equating the Constitution and the morning meal.[94]

Such considerations did not deter the Commission. In response to the criticism over the Cheerios boxes, Burger claimed that he had jokingly spoken to a cereal executive about putting the Constitution in cereal boxes at a dinner party and only later discovered that the executive had taken him seriously.[95] But Burger defended McDonald's place mats that featured the Preamble and images of the Founding Fathers by noting their wide distribution: "Ten million place mats a day. Someone may belittle that . . . but it's in the very best of taste."[96] The McDonald's campaign was not unique; Roy Rogers restaurants and members of the American Hotel and Motel Association (AHMA) also distributed place mats with constitutional themes, and the AHMA promotion even suggested distributing "pocket constitutions" with a personalized inscription to guests as a replacement for such other forms of advertising as matchbooks.[97]

The use of the Constitution as a form of advertising similar to matchbooks illustrates how superficial such mass distribution may become, yet the incorporation of constitution-alism into modern commercial culture served a second, important function. As Grant McCracken observes, "[w]hen culture appears in objects, it seeks to make itself appear inevitable, as the only sensible terms in which anyone can constitute their world. Culture uses objects to convince."[98] If the Commission's advertisements sought to persuade people that the Constitution was an important part of their lives, then grocery bags, place mats, and milk cartons bearing constitutional themes were the proof, bringing the document and its authors into the realm of daily life. In one Roy Rogers place mat, this theme was particularly evident in the place mat's text as it described various constitutional rights and alerted readers/diners to "the Constitution's immense influence in our everyday lives. So it's easy to see, hear, and realize how lucky 'We the People' are."[99] However, while such promotions brought the Constitution closer to "We the People," it also brought the document closer to the banality of mass culture. And, almost all of these objects were themselves transitory and disposable, seemingly contrary to their message of an enduring Constitution.

Bringing the Constitution out of the rarified atmosphere of the National Archives and associating it with such profane entities as breakfast cereals threatened its value as a symbol of social and political order. La Marche's criticism of the Commission and Trudeau's parody of the cereal box panel decried both the Constitution's commercialization and the loss of its stature through its association with ordinary life. Such a loss of stature occurs as commodities circulate throughout the economy; commemorative objects lose their meaning as they move from context to context.[100] The process of exchange disrupts the meaning of objects by regarding them as exchangeable for everything else.[101] Preserving the meaning of commemorative commodities requires severe restrictions that run counter to the ideology of the free market.

Concern over commercialization even before the Constitution's bicentennial led to the congressional requirement that the federal Commission "prevent the emblem from being displayed on some types of tasteless and vulgar memorabilia."[102] The Commission's own regulations further codified veneration of the Constitution, requiring that licensed products, goods, or services "in no way reflect negatively upon the Government, the bicentennial commemoration, the Constitution, or the Commission's activities," and maintaining strict control over the items that it authorized.[103] The logo also preserved the seriousness of the commemoration by surrounding the Constitution with the images of the bald eagle, flag, and the motto "We the People," thus placing the celebration's logo within a patriotic, noncommercial context. The function of the federal logo in preserving the patriotic meaning of the celebration may be better appreciated when contrasted with Bisontennial Ben, a bison character wearing federal period costume and carrying quill and parchment. Bisontennial Ben was created by the Disney Company and adopted by the California Bicentennial Foundation on its own line of merchandise after the federal Commission rejected Disney's offer of the buffalo mascot.[104]

Such commercialized forms of civic virtue were not without their defenders. William J. Bennett, then Chairman of the National Endowment for the Humanities and later

Secretary of Education, argued against the denigration of souvenir objects:

> No one wishes to salute low-minded activities, but commerce itself is not a low thing and has no small place here. It was not undignified and certainly not unnatural that the '76 celebration had a commercial element. There was nothing wrong, I would say, in the Declaration of Independence ashtrays and portraits of Abigail Adams on sea shells. Such souvenirs were neither a heresy nor a civic sin.[105]

While Bennett argued that "commerce itself is not a low thing," in his own argument he uses only the worst sort of kitsch as examples of commercialization. Bennett's use of religious language to defend such objects against criticism only heightens the contrast between the tackiness of the souvenirs and the importance of the event celebrated.

Bennett's analysis misconstrues what is problematic in popular material representations of the Founding Fathers or sacred texts. Such objects are not viewed as sacrilege because of their association with commerce, but because a representation is transferred across the cultural categories that define it as sacred or special. "Dirt," Mary Douglas has written, is "matter out of place."[106] When the Declaration of Independence becomes an ashtray, rather than a piece of parchment, it enters the realm of the profane. The disposal of cigarettes into the form of the Declaration symbolically dirties the document itself.[107] Such commercial items cross the boundaries of good taste by throwing together the sacred and the profane in a way that shocks or dismays those who would preserve the sacred order.[108] While Americans may have a more flexible sense of boundaries between sacred and profane than other cultures,[109] they may still be uncomfortable with the intrusion of commercialism into patriotic occasions.[110]

Constitutional commemorators had looked to merchandising as a way to increase involvement in the activities that they had planned for the Bicentennial, but they also hoped that product sales would help pay for the celebrations. During the bicentennial of the American Revolution, licensing fees brought in over \$1.5 million.[111] We The People 200, Inc. viewed merchandising as a potential source of funding for their celebration of the Constitution's Bicentennial in Philadelphia, and projected \$250,000 in income from merchandising;[112] instead, proceeds amounted to less than \$95,000.[113] Similarly, the federal Commission hoped that the licensing program would generate revenues of greater than \$1 million,[114] however, its net income from sales, royalties, and donations amounted to less than \$350,000.[115] Either citizens did not find the Bicentennial offerings very attractive, or the Constitution simply did not create much excitement among citizens. More important than the lost revenue, the dismal sales of such merchandise demonstrated that consumerism and education are two fundamentally different activities.

Conclusion: Representing Private Society

According to Michel Foucault, one essential difference between modern states and feudal Europe lies in the grand displays of power that were often orchestrated to demonstrate the authority of feudal lords and monarchs and to educate their subjects about their proper place in the social and political order; such displays included great royal pageants, tournaments featuring martial arts, and public executions. The modern state has done away with such periodic grand spectacles in favor of smaller scale, but more systematic, demonstrations of its power through mostly invisible institutions, such as public schools and prisons.[116] While the prison warden has replaced the executioner in the modern state, the court pageant master, whose job was to communicate royal power to the public, has been replaced by practitioners of the modern arts of public relations, marketing, and advertising, who have displaced royal pageants with more modest displays which extend into daily life through the mass media, commercial products, and even the packaging for those products.

Representative democracy and marketing are highly compatible because of their common assumption that the public is sovereign. If marketing is "the bureaucratic form of Sophism,"[117] it must persuade the public to its point of view, and, like the royal pageant masters of the Middle Ages, must flatter the sovereign. In modern democracies, the public is sovereign, and the job of marketing is not to demonstrate sovereigns' power over their subjects, but to re-present collectively-held norms back to the public, and convince the public that its views coincide with those of the sponsor.[118] Advertising must not only create a message for the client, but must also deliver an audience for the client's message.[119] Using public relations to deliver an audience for constitutionalism may also require a message which describes how the Constitution was fundamental to the political order without referring to any specific doctrines which might be controversial or too detailed to sustain general public interest.

At the same time, marketing, as the special province of business, significantly changes the meaning of private participation in civic events. Corporations' media, organizational and financial resources make them important partners for government in organizing civic commemorations. In the nineteenth century, civic observers might worry that governmental power could overwhelm private power,[120] a result of "a social situation where it was exceptional to find substantial private power based on concentrated assets and disciplined continuity of organization."[121] In modern times, when corporations have developed resources which are superior to government in areas such as the media, the specter of private power overwhelming public institutions is similarly a cause for concern. As Stephen Skowronek has argued, the administrative state has grown to replace the political parties of nineteenth century, which both expressed the popular will in an organized form and often provided social services to their constituents.[122] Modern American corporations also provide a large number of public services that are supplemental to government services, contracted for by the government, or, in the case of corporate charity, replace governmental action as organized expressions of private civic spirit.[123]

Cooperative relationships between corporations and government bureaucracies allow the American state to portray itself as representative of civil society. Characterizing corporate undertakings as private activities sustains the distinction between civil society and the state and obscures the concentration of power in each. In *The Liberal Tradition in America,* Louis Hartz observed that the American liberal suspicion of power was joined with an acceptance of corporate wealth in a form he labelled "democratic capitalism" and that concentrated power was suspicious only as "state action."[124] Hartz had argued in an earlier work that, in American economic and legal thought, large and powerful organizations were "clothe[d] . . . with a kind of personal individuality,"[125] and that the legal identification of corporations as individuals "mobilized democratic individualism in behalf of the corporation."[126] As private individuals, corporations are able to present themselves as bulwarks against governmental oppression, and proponents of a more public corporate role have argued that "through corporation philanthropy or otherwise, the "corporate citizen" has a responsibility to guard and to strengthen the structural and procedural devices of constitutionalism"[127] by preventing governmental monopoly of power.[128]

When corporations work together with government bureaucracies acting as "coordinators" or "clearinghouses," the result is the equation of such corporations with the larger citizenry and the presentation of federal agencies as part of civil society. During the Constitution's Bicentennial, contributions by the corporate sector and the use of constitutional themes on commercial products and as part of marketing promotions provided elites with ways to dramatize private support for the American system of government. Emphasizing the level of corporate involvement in the Constitution's Bicentennial while actively demoting the Commission's role to that of "clearinghouse" and "catalyst," allowed federal Commission and other interested elites to depict the celebration itself as a triumph of representative democracy, in which a weak central government followed the lead of civil society, while providing the advantages of centralized administration.[129] In the postmodern commemorations which celebrated the Constitution's Bicentennial, corporations played the part of civil society, providing the idea that the Constitution was celebrated by the larger public rather than a government bureaucracy. It was an ironic illusion, in which the public became private, the private became public, and the political was equated with the social.

CHAPTER THREE

The Constitution in Public History

On September 16, 1987, a group of thirty-nine Americans whose surnames were identical with the signatures on the bottom of the Constitution gathered at Independence Hall to sign the copies of Constitution and celebrate its bicentennial. However, because this was 1987, instead of 1787, Independence Hall did not remain in Philadelphia, Pennsylvania. It had instead taken up residence in Knott's Berry Farm in southern California. Moreover, the signatories to the modern document were not statesmen, but schoolchildren selected because their surnames were the same as the Framers, and therefore chosen to participate in a "teach-in" on the Constitution. The production was less of a reenactment of the original ceremony than a simulation. The building and the signers were both substitutes for the "real thing," chosen more for some external similarity to the original than for any capacity to dramatize the meaning of the original event. Indeed, the staged teach-in was supposed to provide students with a greater appreciation for the text than if they had only studied it. There may have been some merit to the educational theories underlying the teach-in. Nevertheless, the use of a counterfeit Independence Hall surrounded by palm trees three thousand miles away from the birthplace of the Constitution raises curious questions about how Americans make sense of their past.[1]

The past is an important presence in American life and constitutionalism. While the Constitution itself has been preserved and transformed over the past two hundred years, American public history has been as much "re-created" as preserved. Independence Hall itself has been re-created in many American localities in the form of post office buildings and courthouses to represent the national government.[2] Henry Ford ordered a copy of Independence Hall built in Michigan after the City of Philadelphia refused to sell him the original so that he might move it to Greenfield Village.[3] Ford was not simply an idiosyncratic crank; he was representative of the impulses that have motivated other shapers of our public history to provide us with distortions of the historical record. As reproduced at Knott's Berry Farm and Greenfield Village, Independence Hall provides visitors with the sensation of authentic historicity.[4] The experience of the tourist or explorer, seeking out the authentic and the exotic, has been broadened in America by the creation of historical simulations, recently constructed sites that portray an "authentic" history.

That we possess a largely artificial past is all the more ironic because it is the result of an impulse towards authenticity. The city of Los Angeles surrounds Knott's Berry Farm with mansions that are re-creations of French chateaux and Italian villas, not to mention Chinese restaurants in the shape of pagodas, and Egyptian restaurants disguised as pyramids. Los Angeles provides visitors with a fine simulation of world culture and history, yet its cultural and architectural incoherence leaves visitors without a sense of human space or historic scale—compressing all of human diversity and history to a single city.[5] The presumed authenticity of the Chinese restaurant in the shape of a pagoda is, in part, a response to Americans' search for authenticity in material representations of other times and places.[6] The growth of such installations as Knott's Berry Farm, Greenfield Village in Michigan, and even Colonial Williamsburg in Virginia have become a way for Americans to bring themselves into a more direct and "authentic" relationship with their material past.

Conscious attention to history as a self-contained practice is largely a modern phenomenon, one which derives from the alienation of modern individuals from traditional forms of community. Many of the images and practices that we understand as historical are largely of recent invention, created to provide moderns with a sense of place and historical time. As Sheldon Wolin has observed, such commemorations of historic events "appear to be celebrating the past . . . [however] their most important function is to fix the collective identity in the present."[7] Historic preservation and the re-creation of historic events are ways for citizens to present the ideals and aspirations of contemporary society in a narrative that carries the authority of tradition; historic commemoration serves as a mirror for modern Americans searching for their ancestors in themselves. Lacking a well-developed consciousness of history or place, many Americans interpret their history as a single mission of destiny from Puritans through the Founding Fathers and the Civil War to the present. As Daniel Boorstin declares, "We Americans are reared with a feeling for the unity of our history and an unprecedented belief in the normality of our kind of life to our place on earth."[8] This sense of "manifest destiny" and unbroken progress has been compiled from a dizzying and often incoherent set of sources, and has been celebrated in "authentic reproductions" that attempt to still the progression of time and oppose the frenetic pace of historical change in the United States through a history stopped dead in its tracks.

The history of preservationism manifests its ironic and contradictory heritage. The two great patrons of historic preservationism were also the two men who did the most to destroy the old America. Henry Ford, whose popularization of the automobile transformed American society, re-created nineteenth century America on a grand scale through his construction of Greenfield Village in Dearborn, Michigan. John D. Rockefeller, whose Standard Oil company fueled

Ford's automobiles, rebuilt Williamsburg, Virginia as a colonial village.[9] Umberto Eco has noted that preservation of historic treasures by American industrialists "is the bad conscience of . . . imperialistic efficiency, just as cultural anthropology is the bad conscience of the white man who thus pays his debt to the destroyed primitive cultures."[10] The materialism that characterizes contemporary American capitalism is the fundamental basis for historical preservation—which focuses on maintaining the material past, while discounting our ability to reach the past through such media as the written language or humanistic imagination.

The equation of historical consciousness with material reality rather than informed reflection lay behind the attempts by Ford and Rockefeller to rebuild entire communities at any price. Such attempts do great violence to history. (Re)building historical recreations necessarily tears artifacts out of their acquired setting to discard the "impurities" that have accumulated around them during the intervening years, and eliminates the temporal distance that lies between the present and the past. The most egregious example of an artificial Independence Hall is not in Greenfield, Michigan or Orange County, California, but the "original" Independence Hall in Philadelphia. Independence Hall became its own simulation when the National Park Service consciously re-made it as the "authentic" site of eighteenth century history through extensive renovations and by demolishing the modern office buildings that surrounded it, thereby creating the Federal Period oasis that is Independence National Historic Park.[11] Through paintbrushes and wrecking balls, Americans have consciously attempted to eliminate the distance between their historical origins and their contemporary circumstances, unintentionally creating a false division of past and present, and erasing the dirt, debris, and wrong turns that comprise a living tradition.

Historical re-creation is highly problematic for the way in which it compresses the process of representation. Like liberal democracy, historical observances and community celebrations are forms of self-representation. As Hanna Pitkin has noted, "representation means . . . *re-presentation,* a making present again."[12] Making something present *again* implies that it has been lost or separated, and when the distance between the representative and the represented becomes too great, one begins to speak of "alienation." Rituals of representation are occasions to reduce the historical and social distance between citizens and their history and to reconnect citizens to what is "real" and "authentic" in the national culture. Yet, re-presentation generally relies upon the use of narratives that tell the story of how the society came to be. Historical re-creations erase much of the social and temporal distance between moderns and their historical predecessors, thus reducing the importance of historical change and social struggle and making the present seem a natural result of the events of the distant past.

In the case of the Constitution, the differences between the distant past and the immediate present have real political consequences. The theory of constitutional interpretation known as "original intent" directs judges and justices to derive their decisions from the intentions and words of the Framers of the Constitution.[13] This position, generally associated with political conservatism, greatly troubles many liberals, who view the changes of the past two hundred years as generally positive, and who have no desire to return to the Constitution of 1787. Bruce Ackerman, a critic of original intent, speaks of a "bicentennial myth" through which "modern Americans tell themselves stories that assert the deep continuity of two centuries of constitutional practice, narratives that thoroughly enmesh today's events in a web of constitutional reference stretching back two hundred years to the Founding."[14] Instead, Ackerman argues that the history of American constitutionalism is marked by several important divisions, and ranks the post-Civil War Amendments and the reevaluation of the Commerce Clause in 1937 as moments of the same importance as the Constitutional Convention of 1787.[15]

Ackerman's delineation of several radical disjunctions in our constitutional history follows the comments of Justice

Thurgood Marshall, who argued that the Constitution currently understood was fundamentally different from, and
superior to, the original Constitution. Marshall warned that
a Bicentennial which commemorated the original document
would not recognize "the Constitution's inherent defects,
and its promising evolution through 200 years of history,"
but would constitute only "a blind pilgrimage to the shrine
of the original document."[16] According to Marshall, "[w]hile
the Union survived the Civil War, the Constitution did not.
In its place arose a new, more promising basis for justice and
equality."[17] Marshall feared that, in the rush to return to the
civic virtue embodied by the Framers, Americans would for-
get the struggles which were waged against injustices that
they endorsed and perpetuated, most notably the enslave-
ment of African-Americans. Both Marshall and Ackerman
were concerned that Americans "take the Bicentennial
Myth seriously"[18] and that the "Bicentennial Myth" continues to be promoted through legal opinions issued by the
courts, the writings of legal academics, and the institutions,
such as schools, that shape American political culture.

There was no better example of the institutionalization
of the "Bicentennial Myth" than the Bicentennial itself.
Many bicentennial celebrations re-created the myths of the
Constitution's origins in attempts to connect the public to
the civic virtue of the Federal period and to the textual im-
agery of the Constitution itself. Historic reenactments and
ritualized presentations were elements in the attempt to
"imagine" the Constitution. Seeking an audience for the
message of constitutionalism, and hoping to make the document and its message "real" for participants, commemorators in California, Philadelphia, and elsewhere produced
imaginary visions of America under the Constitution. Their
work was ideological in the sense of Louis Marin's definition
of ideology as "the representation of the imaginary relationship individuals maintain with their real conditions of existence."[19] Through the simulation of historical events, and
through public displays that attempted to delineate the
structure of modern society, bicentennial commemorations

provided participants with the opportunity to find themselves within representations of the past and present.

Two Theories of Civic Time

James Michener's novel *Legacy*, published in 1987 with the Constitution and amendments as an appendix, was one of the more modest recent efforts to publicly explain the meaning of the Constitution. Like Michener's other popular novels, which have used the plot device of successive generations who recount the history of some place or people, *Legacy* focused on seven generations of one family—the Starrs—who were implicated in many of the developments in American constitutional history. The modern protagonist, a military officer under investigation in the Iran-Contra scandal and apparently modelled on Lt. Colonel Oliver North, recounts the exploits of ancestors who include signers of both the Declaration of Independence and the Constitution, an ally of John Marshall on the Supreme Court, a Confederate officer under Lee (after first freeing his slaves), a leader of the women's suffrage movement (a maiden great-aunt), an opponent of the New Deal, and a supporting player in the fight for reapportionment.

While *Legacy* succeeds in telling large portions of American history within a single narrative, Michener has difficulty explaining what is distinctive about the Constitution *per se.* This is most apparent in the final scene, when the protagonist learns that he must act according to propriety and common sense to preserve the Constitution. Only then does the protagonist understand

> the Constitution which my ancestors had helped create, interpret and enlarge as a treasured legacy whose provisions bind the various regions and interests of our nation together. Philosophically as evanescent as a whispering wind, structurally more powerful than steel cables, that superb document will be effective only if each new generation believes in it—and keeps it renewed.[20]

As if to stress the unreality of Michener's narrative, the hero declines to assert his Fifth Amendment right against self-incrimination and takes responsibility for his actions. What the Constitution requires, beyond doing the right thing, is left unclear.

Michener's story describes the continuity of the constitutional tradition through the framework of family reminiscence, suggesting that the Constitution is like a birthright that has become unique to a single family and fundamental to their identity through successive generations.[21] Michener's narrative also mirrors an integral element of tradition, that the stories which families tell about their ancestors change over time, and details are both lost and invented, becoming more true with each retelling. As Eric Hobsbawm has noted, the process by which nations create historical traditions "is essentially a process of formalization and ritualization, characterized by reference to the past, if only by imposing repetition."[22] When American history is told as the story of the Constitution, the historical evolution of constitutional norms is equated with the emergence of the American identity as presently understood.

In the hands of a storyteller like Michener, the Founding Fathers' Constitution appears to be of a piece with contemporary America, and contemporary America appears as the embodiment of the Constitution, its principles and its progenitors. Michener's tale ascribes the Constitution's longevity to the way that its norms have been internalized and transmitted between generations, and defines constitutionalism as a form of traditional authority. Michener's understanding of the Constitution's meaning thus entails a very particular understanding of political authority as well. As J.G.A. Pocock writes, different histories may legitimate different forms of authority. A historiography of continuity legitimates a form of traditional authority because it includes "society describing itself as perpetuating its usages and practices, transmitting its different forms of authority and, in these and other ways, maintaining its legitimacy." A historiography characterized by contingency is more sympathetic to a form of authority based on institutional rules and norms for it will celebrate "a continuous capacity for action rather than a continuous transmission of legitimacy."[23] Such a history would evaluate institutions according to how effective they were in contending with particular historical challenges to commonly accepted principles, justifying the institution through the effectiveness of its rules and further legitimating legal forms of authority. As Pocock argues, writing history of "in law-centered terms . . . is largely equivalent to writing it as the history of liberalism."[24]

The choice of a narrative for the constitutional tradition has important political implications. A historiography emphasizing customary beliefs and social norms for behavior provides a traditional form of authority, while a historiography stressing legal principles and institutional capacities to manage change is profoundly liberal. By specifying that the public celebration of the Constitution present "an understanding of the historical context of the Constitution, including an understanding of the values and mores of the period, the forces that shaped and affected the views and comprehension of the delegates to the Convention, and the events that produced the document and brought about its ratification within the states,"[25] Congress expressed a preference for a traditional history of the Constitution as a vehicle for values established in a distant past.

Such a history further suggests that the document's legitimacy derives from its origins, providing a larger role for both charismatic "Founders" and the original expression of consent through the ratifying conventions. One example of this tendency occurred in the legislation establishing the Commission on the Bicentennial, when Congress directed that the document's origins and creation, not the history of institutional conflict or constitutional interpretation through which the present Constitution has evolved, be the center of the celebration. Indeed, national elites may have little interest in portraying the Constitution through a liberal history of conflict over the limits of state power, especially when many of those conflicts, such as those regarding slavery and desegregation, were settled through the exercise of central governmental power, and may prefer to downplay the conflicts which shaped the Constitution by situating them in a remote past. The official indifference to continuing historical conflicts over the Constitution was intentional and Congress, through a Senate report, expressly declared the purpose of the celebration did not include "other significant historical events that might be reasonably related to the Constitution but not relevant to its drafting and ratification."[26]

The official exclusion of "other significant historical events" from the bicentennial celebrations favored the contemporary exponents of the "original intent" school of constitutional interpretation by focusing attention on the original intent of the Framers.[27] However, the Senate position ties into more than a single position on the way to interpret the Constitution in contemporary court cases. The Senate's preferred history was not politically correct, but it was anthropologically appropriate. Within anthropological theory, historical narratives such as the Federal period events commemorated during the Constitution's bicentennial, comprise "origin tales," stories "by means of which actual relations of command and obedience were explained and justified."[28] Origin tales are the most common subject of ritual. By isolating the events of the origin from profane history, ritual shows celebrants the proper structure of the polity and of the community, and links them with the origin itself.[29] Origin tales may also tell the story of how the community survived the deaths of its founders, and became a state through the transfer of that charismatic power from an individual to the ruling political institutions.[30] The ability to accept a process of political succession that is not based on inheritance distinguishes constitutional and traditional societies.[31] Indeed, many of the Framers placed themselves within a long line of charismatic "legislators" who laid down the laws on which entire societies were founded.[32] Part of the role of the legislator was to provide for the continuation of the nation.

The traditional emphasis on the Framers as charismatic leaders may provide elites with figures with whom they could implicitly associate themselves as a special class capable of political action.[33] One obvious attempt to partake in the charisma of the Framers was the meeting of both houses of Congress in Philadelphia on July 14, 1987 to commemorate the bicentennial of "the Great (Connecticut) Compromise" that established equal representation of states in the Senate and proportional representation by population in the House of Representatives. Fifty-five members of Congress, the same number as the original meeting of the Constitutional Convention, held a ceremonial session in Independence Hall to celebrate the birth of the legislature.[34] By occupying the same space as those whose accomplishments they celebrated, Congress was able to appropriate what Hans Gerth and C. Wright Mills labelled a "master symbol." Such symbols may be used by persons in official roles to "justify their role by linking it, as if it were a necessary consequence, with moral symbols, sacred emblems, or legal formulae which are widely believed and deeply internalized," and help to legitimate government by "lending meaning to the enactment of given roles."[35] By returning to the site of the original legislative compromise, Congress dramatized the extent to which it is, even today, the realization of the Founders' visions and the result of the Framers' deliberations.

The idea that the Constitution is a unique document embodying important insights into human nature, political power, and institutional dynamics is intimately connected with the worship of the Framers. In the traditional history, the Constitution functions as "the document into which the Founding Fathers had poured their wisdom as into a vessel."[36] As cultural and political heroes, the Framers of the Constitution serve an important function by embodying those virtues that are essential to the success of the nation. National mythologies, Anthony Smith notes, generally involve a cycle of birth, golden age, decline, and a promised rebirth. While the national identity "sets the pattern and direction . . . humans and heroes alone can 'realize' it. That is why the legends are personalized, and why the golden age is also the age of 'heroes.'"[37]

Heroes are most often chosen because their historical roles are seen to embody important ideals.[38] For example, one survey has shown that Americans who see Abraham Lincoln as a "greater" historical figure than Thomas Jefferson are more likely to favor values of nationalism and "order" to "freedom."[39] Representing the survival of the Union as the result of Lincoln's effort, rather than as, for example, the superiority of Northern techniques of armaments manufacture, exemplifies how traditional history emphasizes human agency. Traditional histories are thus a vehicle for promoting the idea that national success is a matter of individual character and leadership, not the reform of institutions, laws, or social practices, and those who would rebuild nations must first learn to emulate those who built them. The civic republican notion of "Representative Men" was most succinctly expressed by Ralph Waldo Emerson when he declared that "There is properly no history, only biography."[40] During the Constitution's Bicentennial, Warren Burger campaigned for restoring the homes of James Madison and John Marshall as concrete vehicles for conveying the ideals of these heroes of constitutionalism.[41] Preserving the qualities of the eighteenth century proceeded from the desire to honor the Framers. Insofar as commemoration is a way to honor the famous dead, it "seeks to *preserve* and *stabilize* the memory of the honoree, and to do so in a time-binding, invariant manner."[42] This impulse is often manifested in statues made of stone that will resist change and make the hero immortal. In constitutional discourse, such an impulse is expressed through an interpretation of the Constitution as carved in stone and acting as if its authors are still with us in a material way.

Traditional Narratives and Liberal Institutions in Constitutional Theory

It is a paradox that America, often rebuked for its lack of historical consciousness, pays so much deference to its past in interpreting its Constitution. As Michael Schudson asks, "Why should historicity be so compelling a rhetorical trump in American culture of all cultures?"[43] American civic rituals are dominated by the past; two-thirds of the events of the American Revolution Bicentennial were oriented to the past, with most others oriented to the present and only a small fraction oriented toward the future.[44] The emphasis on popular sovereignty within American political culture makes this emphasis on the past even more paradoxical. Americans have often looked to the heroic statesmen of the past who announced political ideals and wrought great deeds to express the ideology of the American state. Yet, many commemorations have celebrated the "common people," "fighting men" or "working men and women" of the nation in historical form, providing citizens with representations that are heroic without being narcissistic.[45] Such representations can only portray those historical changes which are easily embodied. The task of representing the whole of American history and society contained within the constitutional tradition is a far more difficult, and perhaps impossible, task.

The distinction between traditional and liberal history reveals itself in the two competing myths of the Constitution's transmission from its Framers to the legislators and ordinary citizens of today. The traditional myth focuses on the Framers and depicts the Constitution as a set of norms internalized by successive generations which steers each generation toward the virtues embodied by the Framers. In contrast, the liberal myth focuses on the institutions established in the Constitution as responsible for the nation's stability through the mechanisms for separating, checking, and balancing power within the government.[46] The traditional myth, by emphasizing the actions of individuals and the transfer of values between generations, situates authority in the people. The liberal myth, by focusing on institutions which mediate the conflicts that arise over the course of history, is suspicious of democracy as embodied in the people. In their most abridged form, the two histories conflict over where the emphasis should be placed in James Madison's statement that "[a] dependence on the people is, no doubt, the primary control on the government, but experience has taught the necessity of auxiliary controls."[47]

The traditional myth asks citizens to be virtuous in their emulation of the Framers, and a historiography based upon the traditional myth will largely portray the nation's past as a history of constancy and infidelity to the original charter. In contrast, the liberal myth emphasizes how institutions overcame the flaws of the Framers' Constitution, and mitigated the excess of democracy. In the liberal history, the Framers were concerned that their successors would be profligate, and therefore insulated the workings of government from popular control. Having constructed a vital public space, they hoped that future generations would lose themselves in the private pursuits of commerce, rather than follow in the revolutionary example of the forebears.[48] This liberal view of the Constitution also implies that the principles underlying the document are more important than the Framers or the original document. In this view, the Constitution only partially embodies the spirit of liberty that must be fully realized through improved institutions and practices. Alexander Bickel labeled this understanding of the Constitution as a prophecy to be realized through institutional reform as "the idea of progress," and claimed that it animated many of the progressive decisions of the Warren Court.[49]

The liberal interpretation of constitutional history has much in common with what Herbert Butterfield has termed the "whig interpretation of history," in which

> the whig historian can draw lines through certain events, some such line as that which leads through Martin Luther and a long succession of whigs to modern liberty; and if he is not careful he begins to forget that this line is merely a mental trick of his; he comes to imagine that it represents something like a line of causation.[50]

Within the liberal historical narrative, American history has been a march toward greater freedom, without setback or undue difficulty, as Americans uncover the hidden potential of the Constitution. One does not need to be a cultural conservative to worship the powers of the Constitution. For liberals, the Constitution symbolizes an underlying legal order that is perfected through the unfolding of history. During the Bicentennial, this view of the Constitution was presented through such events as "Roads to Liberty," an exhibition co-sponsored by the federal Commission and the American Express Company, that displayed an original copy of the Magna Carta, along with copies of the Northwest Ordinances, the Constitution, the Bill of Rights, the Emancipation Proclamation, and the Civil Rights Act of 1964.[51] The display placed the Constitution within the organic tradition of English common law as well as the political struggles of the American Revolution, Civil War, and civil rights movement. Such a view of the Constitution was also espoused by liberal Justice William Brennan in a speech when he referred to an "amended Constitution" that included not only the various amendments adopted after the original document, but "the bedrock principles of another great text, the Magna Carta."[52]

Traditional and liberal historiographies are quite compatible at times. While liberal historiography focuses on historical evolution as recorded in texts and legal innovations, and traditional histories emphasize continuity and spotlights individuals and actions, a focus on the Constitutional Convention and the subsequent ratification debates may combine traditional and liberal histories. The creation and adoption of the Constitution included examples of political innovation intended to make institutions durable, effective, and appropriately limited in their authority and functions, providing ample justification for the liberal account of the Constitution's longevity. Even the liberal account of the Constitution as a set of institutions and legal rules capable of accommodating social contradictions and conflicts is compatible with the traditionalist idea that the values and ideas of the Framers continue to shape the nation's history.

The liberal account of the development of constitutional norms also serves as an important counterweight to romantic views of the Founding. Arguments on behalf of original intent jurisprudence often resemble nineteenth century British accounts of a primitive Saxon democracy which had become corrupted through years of legalistic tinkering. One critic of such history, A. V. Dicey, responded with great contempt to the idea that "that the cunning of lawyers has by the invention of legal fictions corrupted the fair simplicity of our original constitution, underrates the statesmanship of lawyers as much as it overrates the merits of early society."[53] For Dicey, locating the ideal form of governance in the past was "at bottom a delusion of the legal imagination. The idea of retrogressive progress is merely one form of the appeal to precedent." Such appeals are, moreover, "a useful fiction by which judicial decision conceals its transformation into judicial legislation."[54]

The question of whether the last two hundred years has improved upon visions of the original Constitution of 1787, or merely improved the implementation of that original vision, most sharply divides the traditional and liberal accounts of American constitutional history. The opposition between the two historiographies was also closely related to the description of the American public and who was represented through the Constitution. While the traditional account of the Constitution emphasizing the Federal Period may provide an effective way to represent civic virtue, it is also limited by the peculiar institutions of that time. Refusing to participate in a commemorative session in Philadelphia, Justice Thurgood Marshall pointedly noted how the Federal Period's inequalities were ignored: "[i]f you're gonna do what you did two hundred years ago, somebody's going to have to get me short pants and a tray so I can serve coffee."[55]

Marshall's remark served as a reminder that "the past that is shared . . . always stands in delicate relationship to the 'pasts' that are held dear by distinct groups today."[56] Indeed, the congressional focus on 1787 demonstrated the contradiction between understandings of representation prevailing in the eighteenth and late twentieth centuries. The eighteenth century idea of representation as agency that allowed the Framers to declare themselves "We the People"[57] has been replaced in contemporary America with an ethic of descriptive representation that requires representatives to reflect the diverse characteristics of the represented and which no longer assumes singular terms, such as "We the People," to be inclusive of all.[58] This contradiction was just as evident in the congressional mandate to the Commission on the Bicentennial of the Constitution which required the Commission to focus on the Constitutional Convention and the ratification of the document and omit references to subsequent developments, while also requiring that it emphasize "the contribution of diverse ethnic and racial groups."[59] The Congressional requirement that the Commission recognize diversity while celebrating the Framers to the exclusion of constitutional evolution had several comic results. A Senate committee report analyzed the mandate as requiring that programs describe how "America's Constitution benefitted from the diverse backgrounds of its drafters *and of those who influenced them.*"[60] In another episode, several staff members of the federal Commission criticized a play sponsored by the National Park Service, "Four Little Pages," because the play mentioned that there were "no poor men" at the Convention, although, as the Commission's staff director observed, there were "men who had been, were, or became poor."[61] And, in an incident which revealed their uncritical attitude toward the Framers, the Commission staff also criticized the Park Service's decision to retain a line in "Four Little Pages" which stated that the document of 1787 had "lots of flaws," referring to, among other things, its tolerance (if not embrace) of slavery.[62]

Such explicit attention to the problem of representation in the Constitution's Bicentennial followed the example of a number of other historical observances.[63] However, the Commission's attention to problems of minority representation came late in the celebration, when it appointed an "Ethnic/Minority advisory committee" while formulating themes for the Bicentennial of the Bill of Rights.[64] Representatives of a number of groups stressed that they thought that "those aspects of our history and imperfections of our laws or policies which have tended to exclude various ethnic groups from enjoying equal opportunity should not be ignored."[65] Such demands were impossible to reconcile with the narrow history favored by Congress. By excluding reference to events occurring since the adoption of the Bill of Rights, such as the formal declaration of racial equality, the abolition of slavery, and women's suffrage, the traditional historical narrative was a weaker justification for an inclusive Constitution than the liberal account, with its inevitable, progressive march through history towards the Civil Rights Movement and women's equality. But then, neither Madison or Hamilton would have been offended by being labeled as politically incorrect.

Ritual and Representation

In an important analysis of public ritual in republican Venice, Edward Muir observed that ceremonial processions publicly represent social and political relations in a visible form.[66] Venice, while a constitutional polity, did not possess a written constitution as the United States, and one might expect greater ceremony in an aristocratic republic than in a democratic republic. Michael Kammen has noted the difference between Muir's description of Venetian processions and the parades celebrating the ratification of the Constitution but ascribed that difference to more than simply the difference between democracies and aristocracies when he wrote that the "constitution and political culture of republican Venice were vastly different from those in republican America," because "[c]onstitutions that are written, succinct, and new cannot serve as 'mythical charters.'"[67] Two hundred years after those processions, the American Constitution is still a written document, essentially succinct, but no longer new. Its history has also provided the Constitution with many of the attributes of myth, and, while America has yet to develop any traditions which would rival Venice's ducal processions as a dramatization of its political order, the Constitution's Bicentennial included several parades in which the American political mythology was illustrated.

The complexity of the American constitutional tradition was particularly visible in the We the People 200 parade held in Philadelphia and broadcast nationally by CBS. Indeed, the parade was structured by its designers at Radio City Music Hall Productions to be three parades. The first section, a historical re-creation of the Grand Federal Procession of 1788, was a self-contained re-presentation of the Constitution's past. The parade's centerpiece, the "We the People 200" parade, was organized according to the clauses of the Preamble to represent the nation's achievements in the very form of the Constitution.[68] Finally, a participatory "Parade of America's People" provided an opportunity for Philadelphia organizations to demonstrate their support for the Constitution as well as demonstrating their particular identities. The overall theme of the parade was public support and acclamation for the Constitution, and it focused on illustrating features of the larger American identity instead of providing any detailed depiction of the Constitution or history.

The first segment of the parade re-created the Grand Federal Procession of 1788 that followed the Constitution's ratification, which was also an important part of Philadelphia's own historical mythology. As Susan Davis notes, "the procession moved into memory as a great success, to be recalled later as the time when the whole city (or so it was claimed) united in orderly performance."[69] The procession was an important symbol for the modern commemorators as the original demonstration of popular approval for the Constitution. The Grand Federal Procession of 1788 had involved the merchants and artisans of the city. Organized by Francis Hopkinson, a jurist and composer, and Charles Wilson Peale, a painter, the tradesmen created their own floats and marched beside them under banners proclaiming that the Constitution would benefit them in their occupations through more stable markets and tariffs against foreign producers. The parade began with several figures who represented such historic events and personages as the Treaty of Paris, George Washington, the Constitutional Convention, the document itself, and a group of foreign ambassadors. The marchers were then divided according to whether they were engaged in agriculture, shipbuilding and supply, or other trades. The dominant theme was federation, and the organizers prohibited displays which portrayed any individual state or in any way detracted from the nationalistic ideology of the Federalists.[70]

In 1887, Philadelphia hosted a commemoration of the Constitution's Centennial which itself included several references to the original Grand Federal Procession. The Grand Federal Procession of 1987 only confirmed that the celebration of the Constitution's ratification had itself become an independent tradition, the repetition of which served almost incidently as a gesture of approval for the document itself while primarily recalling the glorious tradition of celebration. The Grand Federal Procession of 1788 attempted to represent the social relations of the new nation to demonstrate the approval of all classes for the charter; the organizers of the centennial and bicentennial processions had, in addition, to represent the maintenance of citizen approval of the Constitution despite the passage of time.

The organizers of the Centennial celebration of 1887 used the theme of "Progress" to unite the "Civic and Industrial Display," which was particularly fitting for a parade largely composed of floats displaying the machinery of production, sponsored by the manufacturers and attended by the tradesmen who normally staffed the machines.[71] The procession portrayed civilization and civility as the products of the intervening century under the Constitution. As a particularly vivid example of this theme, Indian schoolchildren marched in the parade to represent the taming of the natural in industrial civilization.[72] The Constitution had created new forms of social and cultural progress and let loose an abundance of productive forces which had replaced the political and economic crisis of the Federal Period.[73] Such a message was particularly conducive to the interests of industrial elites, who viewed the Constitution as a charter for property rights and a framework for a national economy.[74]

The anticipation of future prosperity and continuous progress which characterized the Centennial celebrations were notably absent from the 1987 parade, which was also clearly less enthusiastic about the distance between the Federal Period and the present. The different approaches demonstrate how American society understood itself in relation to its past. In its concern with embodying the relationship between the present and the past, the Grand Federal Procession of 1987 went to great trouble to make the past "real" by re-creating it through portrayals of eighteenth century life and persons. Because historical periods are neither concrete nor easily imagined,[75] it had to be embodied in more material forms such as the technology and apparel of the day. The 1987 version of the Procession featured soldiers, fife and drum corps, clergy, victuallers, and bell ringers, all in eighteenth century dress. Like the original, this Grand Federal Procession featured floats representing the wheelwrights, blacksmiths, shipwrights, bakers, and merchants of the city. Unlike 1788, the floats and marchers were not organized by the sector of the economy which they represented, and while the 1788 Procession had been structured by hierarchy within the trades, with masters coming before journeymen and apprentices,[76] the 1987 version was considerably more democratic and therefore inaccurate in its portrayal of eighteenth century social structure.

The most elaborately staged portion of the 1987 celebration was not, however, the re-creation of the Grand Federal Procession. Instead, the centerpiece of the parade, entitled "We the People 200," was organized to demonstrate how the Constitution's Preamble represented all spheres of society. While the marchers in the Procession of 1788 were arranged to represent their social class and occupation, in 1987 marchers were arranged in a categorization of social activity which followed the Preamble's promises to further "domestic tranquility," "common defense," and "the general welfare."[77] As all of the other sections paid homage to the state, only "Promote the General Welfare" paralleled the original Grand Federal Procession's focus on civil society and economic activity.

However, unlike the Grand Federal Procession of two hundred years previous, or even the Civic and Industrial Display of 1787, the depiction of civil society in 1987 was disconnected from class or occupational affiliations. Floats depicted important American inventions, the arts, agriculture, sports, entertainment, education, a "Synchronized Briefcase Drill Team," and the construction industry (through a fifty-foot-high metal framework). While each of these portrayed one sector of the economy, they were not arranged in any discernible order. The theme of American prosperity was manifested in representations of material goods and technology. Instead of arranging symbols in a manner which would communicate the ideal of a Constitution as a set of relationships between citizens, the parade portrayed American constitutionalism through an incoherent succession of images first portraying the material past through the restoration of the Grand Federal Procession and material progress through the physical products of modern capitalism. Whereas the material served as a convenient cipher for the past and present, the social was largely absent from the public enactment of constitutionalism.

Making the Past Material

Re-creating the past as "heritage" is an ironic act in a country that values progress. Indeed, the value placed on the authenticity of historical reenactments and re-creations is a tribute to modern faith in technology and science, which allow for materially accurate re-presentations.[78] As Daniel Boorstin has observed, modern interest in heritage and preservation as ways of rebuilding entire past worlds was preceded by such modern media as the cinema that reproduce an entire world for their viewers.[79] Yet, despite their dependence on research and technical verisimilitude, historic preservation is ultimately the result of an American distrust of book learning; as Michael Kammen observes, "Heritage . . . involves an explicit element of anti-intellectualism—the presumption, for example, that history experienced through sites and material culture must be more memorable than history presented on the printed page."[80] Heritage, as opposed to history, presents itself as authentic, rather than true, and as a way of being that is distinctive from contemporary life.[81] And, unlike history, historical preservation and historical reenactments present the American past in a way that enables modern Americans to not only imagine life in that past, but to experience it.[82]

Since the beginning of the twentieth century, Americans have performed historical pageants which seek to reproduce preindustrial social relations.[83] Unlike traditional history, which emphasizes the Great Men to the exclusion of the "common people," heritage allows citizens to imagine themselves as virtuous citizens of the Federal Period without having to imagine themselves as heroic as George Washington or Thomas Jefferson. Heritage provides images of "the people" in a way that political history does not, and so promotes a notion of American history as a history of popular sovereignty. Such populist heritage events may include the re-creation of Federal Period military camp that illustrated the daily life and which was staged in Annapolis, Maryland in 1986 to celebrating the two hundredth anniversary of a call for the reform of the Articles of Confederation.[84] Heritage, and the movement for social history, attempts to make the relationship between past and present both material and popular by providing glimpses into the everyday experiences of the people.

The re-creation of the Grand Federal Procession during the We the People 200 parade was such an attempt to bridge the gap of time between the past and the present, demonstrating the twentieth century preoccupation with historical authenticity. The floats accurately reflected the technology and techniques of the Federal Period, and were built and staffed by professionals from such preservationist enterprises as Colonial Williamsburg and the Philadelphia Maritime Museum. The care, expense, and effort which went into the creation of the floats and the costuming of their crews illustrated that modern heritage attempts more than merely illustrating the past, but to provide us an avenue for "entering into" the past. This desire to return to the past was best seen in the case of the only organization that sponsored a float in all three parades, the Carpenters' Company of Philadelphia.

In 1788, the Carpenters' Company had celebrated the new union with a mobile structure that consisted of ten columns supporting a dome; three incomplete columns represented the states which had not yet ratified the Constitution. The 1887 float was accompanied by a second "Federal Edifice of 1887" which had thirty-eight columns representing the present number of states and several incomplete columns representing the territories awaiting statehood.[85] However, in 1987, the Company was back to its original structure, with three columns still uncompleted and thus frozen in time, although all of the states had ratified the document years before. The Carpenter's Company, a fraternal organization no longer consisting of carpenters, had to contract out for the building of its float. However, following the theme of authenticity, the Carpenters of 1987 dressed like those of 1787, whereas the Carpenters of 1887, lacking such a concern for authenticity, had worn contemporary Victorian dress.[86] Whereas the celebrants of the Constitution's Centennial had felt no need to go backwards in history, Bicentennial participants attempted to return as much as possible to the Federal Period. The reenactment dramatized the possibility of modern Americans returning to the past in a way which demonstrated both the possibility and the desirability of doing so.

The Constitution's capacity to connect us to our past goes beyond such stated public events, and may connect us to the general phenomenon of nostalgia. The modern form of nostalgia would be inconceivable without the temporal markers provided by material culture. "As time distances events beyond personal recall," David Lowenthal writes, "memory within any society gives way to history, and relics gain renewed significance."[87] Commemorative objects function as signs which citizens may use to furnish their own identities through contemporary practices of consumerism. Such practices may be encouraged during commemorative events, and the federal Commission on the Bicentennial of the U.S. Constitution created a program which marketed commemorative objects and Federal period reproductions. The Commission exploited the historicity of material culture by selling reproductions of the furniture in Independence Hall as a way for citizen-consumers to link themselves to the authors of the Constitution in a material fashion.[88] Such reproductions served the Bicentennial's function of "re-presentation, a making present again," of the past.[89]

Historic preservation and reenactments may also serve to tie together the discreet local events through which the greater historical narrative was constructed, thus tracing the presence of history across the geography of the nation. An important part of the nation's beginning, Washington's journey from Mount Vernon to New York, was reproduced in 1989, as it had been in 1889, when President Benjamin Harrison reenacted Washington's journey by train and steamship and was greeted in New York by a large and spirited celebration.[90] Unfortunately for the organizers of the Bicentennial, President George Bush could not be persuaded to reenact Washington's travels, and arrived in New York by jet for the finale without undertaking the journey. Instead, the actor who had played Washington for Philadelphia's We the People 200 and two historians, who played his travelling companions, undertook an authentic re-creation of the procession.[91] Unlike President Harrison's expedition, the focus of the bicentennial voyage was the social history of the original journey, rather than the political capacities of the office.

The emphasis on historical culture and sociality was continued in the other localities which held festivities celebrating the events of two hundred years prior. New Hampshire, proud of its role as the ninth, and thus decisive, state to ratify the Constitution, sponsored a series of community-based parades and fetes where residents wore Federal Period costumes. The state bicentennial commissions in Connecticut, Delaware, Massachusetts, New York, and Virginia also sponsored events on the anniversary of their state's ratification of the Constitution.[92] Other milestones, such as the Annapolis Convention, which called for improvements in the Articles of Confederation, the Bicentennial of the ratification of the Bill of Rights, and the Bicentennial of the first session of the Supreme Court, were also hailed with simple ceremonies.[93]

These smaller commemorations more closely resembled the incrementalist history of the early American republic than could any single, national event. However, like the national events, state and local commemorations drew upon an American tradition of historical pageantry to romanticize the past and reenact that past as one of simple virtue.[94] Both the national and the local celebrations used the material culture of the past to identify the Constitution as yet another relic of the Federal Period and to evoke the political deliberations of the period. That the historicity of the Federal Period was so evocative of the Constitution evidences how little we have made the Constitution our own and of our own time.

The Last Man and the End of (Public) History

During "We the People 200: The Constitutional Gala," the television special broadcast from Philadelphia on September 17, 1987, impressionist Rich Little personified various historical figures speaking lines which either directly derived from American constitutional discourse or included little lessons about constitutional history. Little's performance was eclectic in its portrayal of history and demonstrated the influence of popular culture on the representation of American political figures. At one point, Little impersonated Henry Fonda as Abraham Lincoln delivering the Gettysburg Address, at another he began his impression of Winston Churchill with the quote "Never have so many owed so much to so few," and then explained how this applied to the Framers of the Constitution. Along the way, Little inhabited the voices of Franklin Roosevelt, Robert and John Kennedy, and Martin Luther King, Jr. Little began his performance as Edward R. Murrow at the Constitutional Convention, and concluded his act with an impression of Walter Cronkite, the program's host, bringing the performance back into a journalistic mode and closing the historical distance over which he had traveled with a reassuring "and that's the way it is."

Little's tour through America's historical subconscious was an odd and facile form of historical reenactment which, framed by journalistic assurances, purported to be that which it was obviously not. The strangeness of being able to recall voices from the past, provided with new language, is, of course, a novelty act. Yet the restoration of historic sites and the reenactment of historical events is no less strange. An essay by Sigmund Freud on the "disturbance of memory" provides a useful starting point for understanding the distinctive nature of such contemporary practices. In this essay, Freud recollected his ambivalence upon seeing the Acropolis in Athens for the first time as a middle-aged tourist. While Freud contemplated the Acropolis, he noted two contradictory thoughts. His first thought was "'So all this *really* does exist, just as we learnt at school!'" Freud's second thought was that he "had been unaware that the real existence of Athens, the Acropolis, and the landscape around it had ever been objects of doubt."[95] Analyzing this paradox in his usual manner, Freud diagnosed this "feeling of derealization" as a repressive mechanism caused not by his ever having "doubted the real existence of Athens," but that he "only doubted whether I should ever see Athens."[96] The tension between his desire to see Athens and his belief that he would never actually see Athens led Freud to think that he might have doubted the existence of the Acropolis before he had ever seen it.

Freud's experience of "derealization" at the Acropolis has a particular resonance in modern America, where one may see "authentic" reproductions that are not real or which have been torn out of the historical or social contexts in which they originated. Indeed, imagine that Freud was able to view the Acropolis in original form, as it was in the time of Pericles or Plato, rather than as the ruin that it had become. Milton Singer notes in his application of Freud's experience at the Acropolis to the American phenomena of historical reenactments that those who reenact historical events or preserve historical artifacts are rarely those descended from the original actors or owners, but are newcomers who "are surprised to find that the things they had read about in their history books really do exist and that they have experienced 'the real thing.'" As Singer interprets this behavior, the reenactors and collectors of antiques "feel alienated from an authentically early American identity" and use such rituals and practices in an attempt "to overcome this alienation."[97] Historical ritual around the Constitution clearly falls into this tradition of Americans compensating for the repression of the past in their own lives.

The periodic commemoration of historical events thus does not celebrate traditions so much as it creates traditions that are seen as important components of national identity and provide symbols of stability in modern life. As Eric Hobsbawm notes, most national historical traditions have actually developed within the last few hundred years, and

> [i]t is the contrast between the constant change and innovation of the modern world and the attempt to structure at least some parts of social life within it as unchanging and invariant, that makes the 'invention of tradition' so interesting for historians of the past two centuries.[98]

Historical observances featuring the Constitution may remind citizens of the document's role as a symbol of political order and stability, and allowing citizens to situate themselves within a communal history. Only communal history goes beyond a personal narrative bounded by the horizons of what one can know within one's lifetime.[99] Traveling beyond the horizons of an individual's historical knowledge and competence may lead to a sense of disorientation and alienation from one's own identity. However, the history of a society can be internalized by individuals through communal experiences in which the individual learns to see time through the history of the collectivity. Only by accepting the experiences of the other members of the collectivity, whether past or present, can "the broad outlines of our description of the temporality of experience and action, and our account of the coherence of life . . . hold true for the community as lived 'from the inside' by its members who in reciprocal recognition constitute a *we.*"[100]

As ritual, historical reenactments and commemorations allow present-day citizens to "experience" such events as the Constitutional Convention or Washington's inauguration. In doing so, they pose a modest challenge to the western understanding of history as linear progress. Anniversaries, such as bicentennials, which provide occasions for retelling stories about a community's origins, only make sense within a cyclical calendar of weeks, years, and centuries that emphasizes continuity over change.[101] Against linear histories filled with contingency and conflict, "[h]istorical anniversaries impose circularity on longer periods of time, answering the need . . . for patterns that recur."[102] Historical re-creations and reenactments may symbolically disrupt the progressive linear understanding of time by suggesting that change is neither inevitable and irreversible.

The Constitution's perceived capacity for preserving civic virtue, and the perceived necessity for recreating that virtue, is also based on a cyclical conception of time. The Framers' fear of corruption and decay, inherited from the republican tradition and Puritan theology, arose from their understanding of history as revolving in cycles, in which nations rise and fall if their virtue is not restored periodically.[103] The Puritan tradition that shaped so much of American political culture defined itself through the idea of covenant, and gave birth to the Jeremiad, a literary form that bemoaned America's apostasy from the covenant.[104] Such an understanding was not limited to religious thought; celebrations recalling historic events became political rather than religious in the years leading up to the Revolution.[105]

The commemorative observances honoring the Constitution during its Bicentennial condensed the history of constitutionalism while making historic events more immediate. The galas and dramas represented contemporary American social relations as harmonious and without contradiction. These representations were not intended to overcome historical estrangement, but they did repress the tensions within American society by representing various racial occupational groups in balanced *tableaux* that presented their relationships as unmediated and consensual. Through such symbolic representation, social relations among racial and cultural groups that are often segregated could be visualized as part of a larger, integrated body politic. Such ritual events erase historical and social distance in ways that contradict daily experience. As Daniel Boorstin notes, "We have become so accustomed to our illusions, they have become so routine, that they seem no longer produced by any special magic."[106]

CHAPTER FOUR

The Constitution as a Written Document

Although it is over two hundred years old, the U.S. Constitution is often described as a "living Constitution."[1] And, as then-Associate Justice William Rehnquist quipped in 1976, "it seems certain that a *living* Constitution is better than what must be its counterpart, a *dead* Constitution."[2] Rehnquist's ambivalence towards the notion of a living constitution resulted from his concern that a living document might incorporate sources outside of the text itself, especially a judge's ideological preferences. The concept of a living constitution thus includes the possibility that the Constitution might be adapted to contemporary circumstances. Rehnquist's witticism aside, the converse of a living constitution is not a dead constitution, but a written constitution, which, frozen in its textual form, cannot change without amendment. As descriptions of the same document, a "living" constitution and a written constitution are incompatible.

Such incompatibility should not be surprising. The concept of the living constitution is an import from a nation without a written constitution. The British Constitution "lives" because it is an amalgam of piecemeal agreements and decisions about how to govern that are only described after their adoption as a "constitution."[3] The British Constitution includes all legislation and political customs that contribute to the functioning of the government—so that polity and constitution always conform, and referring back, quite properly, to the meaning of its Latin root, *constitutio,* signifying "the political community 'as it actually is.'"[4] Britain's unwritten constitution serves the commonwealth as an indescribable combination of legal requirements, traditions, customs, and habits which all change over time. In contrast, the British Crown serves an important role as a symbol of permanence and sovereignty despite the constant changing of "governments."[5] Yet, while American administrations are no more permanent than British governments, there is no more permanent or literal symbol for American popular sovereignty than the text of the Constitution itself. The practical significance of a living constitution is contrary to that of a written constitution. While a written constitution provides unchanging requirements that the actual government must strive to meet, a "living constitution" adapts the constitution to the government.

Will Harris notes that a written constitution changes the significance of constitutionalism itself: "To compose a polity in a certain way, by writing it down in a document, is to acknowledge that it could have been different in the absence of the writing."[6] Using a written constitution to denote some governmental functions as "constitutional" and others as "extraconstitutional" may serve an important purpose. The boundaries of a written constitution may more clearly demarcate the range of "constitutional law," making it easier to study and to distinguish from other forms of law, and thus providing the outlines of a "master science" within the general realm of law.[7] This is an important attribute not only for legal scholars and political scientists, but for the larger public to which it signifies which institutions and practices are closest to the polity's core values. Moreover, a written constitution may also serve an essential function for citizens beyond providing an essential legal framework for the political system. The written text may act as a symbol of the government which it establishes, providing the intangible with a material surrogate.

In a written constitution, Michael Warner writes, "[t]he text itself becomes . . . the only original embodiment of the people. In this act of literalization, the meaning of the charters' writtenness has been transformed."[8] The U.S. Constitution functions as a permanent and physical symbol of sovereignty in the same manner as a monarch. This capacity of the physical text may be explained through a concept common to both a popular sovereign and a monarch, the legal device of incorporation. Through incorporation, the individuals constituting the popular sovereign become a single individual, the body politic. Creating a body politic through a written constitution is different from doing so through an unwritten constitution because a written constitution provides the constituent elements of such a body politic, its "citizens" or "subjects," with an external referent to themselves. A written constitution necessarily involves the estrangement of the constitutional system from the citizenry that establishes it. As a physical text, the U.S. Constitution exists as a material object external to human subjectivity. Material objects, like custom or tradition, do not evolve gracefully and silently. Because writing preserves language in material form, a written agreement cannot be constantly renegotiated in the same way as an oral agreement.[9]

The Constitution's resistance to change is largely attributable to its written nature. Oral agreements are often renegotiated for very good reasons, such as encounters with novel situations or ambiguity in the original. Writing allows documents such as the Constitution and the Declaration of Independence to represent the origins and aims of the polity across time and untouched by the controversies of the moment, for "the written sign loosens the control of time," acting as a direct conduit of communication with the past and future.[10] As Freud wrote, "If I distrust my memory, . . . I am able to supplement and guarantee its workings by making a note in writing. I have only to bear in mind the place where this 'memory' has been deposited and I can then 'reproduce' it any time I like, with the certainty that it will have remained unaltered."[11] A written constitution creates an entity separate from the citizenry in whose name it is propagated and the state which it symbolizes. In a state with an unwritten constitution, constitution and polity are necessarily coequal. However, any polity founded upon a written constitution possesses an immutable reminder of the artificial creation of the state. Similarly, the form of a written constitution may symbolize the act by which citizens have alienated their wills to create a sovereign state. A written constitution is both a more external and a more permanent reminder of how citizens' wills have escaped them to become part of that greater will, the body politic, and a testament to the government's origins in the will of the people as a collective body. How citizens relate to the writtenness of the American Constitution as a symbol of the body politic, the state and their own history makes all the difference for our constitutional culture.

Written Constitutions as Cultural Entities

The process which created the Constitution as the authoritative statement about the distribution of legitimate power in the United States also removed it from easy renegotiation by subsequent generations. Successive generations have had to come to the Constitution as a text already invested with an authority of its own. Contemporary citizens confront the Constitution as a document whose text, although not meaning, is largely removed from the circumstances of ordinary politics. The relationship between the Constitution as a formal legal document and as the customs, habits, and principles of the people is described by Will Harris as the difference between printing and script. The Constitution as formal legal document influences us much as "the handwriting of the classical Romans was influenced by the chiseled letter forms on public monuments," while citizens themselves express their own understandings in a more dynamic script.[12] Yet, a typeface letter and the handwritten version of that same letter would be considered to possess similar meanings because both expressions are understood to refer to a common root. While there are important connections between our written and unwritten constitutions, there are also crucial differences.

There has been no lack of representations of the Constitution's written nature. The written form of the Constitution is a common element of our political culture, and has been represented in a variety of media, from its inclusion in the "Shrine" at the National Archives to high school civics texts to reprints provided by congressional representatives to their constituents. Over the course of American history, the text's age and stability have become increasingly important aspects of its visual reproduction, its flowing calligraphy appearing more antiquated with the replacement of script by not only block printing but electronic media. During the Constitution's recent bicentennial, this written form was presented in a wide variety of forms. Bicentennial coins issued by the U.S. Treasury depicted a federal eagle clutching a quill pen in its claw on one side and a quill with "We the People" inscribed across the other, connecting the document's textual nature with the concept popular sovereignty.[13] Print advertisements presented the Constitution as underlying the daily text of the newspaper and the published discourse of the nation by reminding readers "[T]hat the Uncensored Content of this [newspaper, magazine] is Made Possible by the Constitution of the United States."[14] Nor was any of this a particularly modern invention, the celebrations which accompanied the document's ratification in 1788 often included celebrations of the mechanism of printing.[15]

However, the consequences of the Constitution's textuality was best expressed by the slogan of the federal Commission on the Bicentennial's advertising campaign, "The Constitution: The Words by Which We Live." The slogan equated the document's framework for governance with the regulation of everyday life; an equation that was furthered through the slogan's dissemination on such items as bumper stickers, which materially incorporated it into the discourse of contemporary life.[16] Yet, the slogan could also refer to the written instruments that regulate activity within the modern administrative state. The slogan referred to "words" as sources of authority which provided material guidelines for those who would abide by the Constitution. Anne Norton notes the degree to which "[c]itizens increasingly rely on writing to represent themselves to the state and to one another."[17] From birth certificate to death certificate, citizens are subject to a regime of licensing, documenting, and certifying conducted through written media, all by a state established through a written form. Although many theorists have argued that the Constitution's form as a written document has important consequences for any theory of constitutional interpretation, there has been little written about the importance of the Constitution's form as a written document for the public's understanding of the political system and constitutional norms.

The multiplicity of print media today, and the ease of its production, makes our modern representations of the Constitution very different from the original. The hundreds of millions of copies of the Constitution printed in American civics, political science, and history texts or distributed through congressional offices and public literacy campaigns are treated in a fundamentally different way than the "original" Constitution, reverently ensconced in the National Archives. The "Shrine," which contains both the Constitution and the Declaration of Independence, protects the documents from the ravages of age, and even nuclear holocaust.[18] These precautions, taken because of the document's singularity and permanence, serve as visible reminders of its value. Needless to say, few such precautions surround other copies of the Constitution or the Declaration of Independence, even if those found in the appendices of civics and political science texts are just as unlikely to be disturbed by human touch.

The distinction between an original and a copy has important symbolic consequences for any theory of representation. The original Constitution represents the sacred moment in which the nation was created as a state and as a people, and symbolizes the nation's origins and values. Because of its unique history, the original Constitution possesses, and reproductions lack, what Walter Benjamin has labeled an "aura."[19] Briefly defined, an aura is that quality of an original which is missing from any reproduction. There are other ways of describing the attributes of an original's aura, such as "history" or "authenticity." Only an original has its unique history—and has weathered the indignities and difficulties of many years. The original Constitution, for example, was stored in the U.S. Treasury, the Washington Orphan Asylum, and in cellar storage at the State Department before President Harding transferred it into the custody of the Library of Congress.[20] An original develops character in the same way that the face of an elderly person develops a type of character unreproducible in the face of a younger person. A work's aura not only derives from its originality, but also from the history which has made it unique.[21]

The relation between an auratic original and the viewer is more complex than a simple question of age. As Walter Benjamin used the term to discuss original works of art, an "aura" denotes "the unique phenomena of a distance, however close it may be."[22] The key dimension of the original Constitution lacking from any reproduction is the original's association with its authors. The original Constitution's "aura" represents the distance that contemporary Americans perceive between themselves and the Constitution's authors. As a material messenger of its authors' plans for the nation, the auratic Constitution represents both our separation from the authors of our system of governance, and our connection to them.

A work's aura is also a product of the viewers' consciousness of their position in history and tradition. Benjamin associated auratic art with cultic worship in particular because of how both the work and the viewer became part of a tradition and community. According to Benjamin, the realm of thoroughly reproducible, profane art is politics.[23] Benjamin's distinction between the cultic and political is intimately connected with his theory that an aura is created by the distances between the work of art, its subject, and its viewer. Benjamin identifies a work's aura with a process that is analagous with fetishism: "to perceive the aura of a phenomenon means to invest it with the capacity to look at us in turn."[24] A work with an aura is rooted in the material world, for it is a concrete object, but its singularity and its capacity to express meaning require that we encounter it as a fellow participant in dialogue.[25] To identify a particular original piece of art as auratic is to signify that it is a unique and self-contained entity which may not be manipulated nor treated as a mere tool, but is an end in itself, with its own unique powers. Such an understanding of fetishistic powers is certainly compatible with an understanding of the Constitution's power as resting on the partial alienation of popular sovereign powers.

The power of an auratic artwork lies in its singularity, the lack of alternative uses for its image, and its place within history. Conversely, the profusion and juxtaposition of images in such postmodern media as music videos and virtual reality are the logical results of the death of the artistic aura, and the birth of a political art which respects none of the boundaries of the sacred, nor the intentions of its creators, and which allows for constant and unrestrained manipulation of image and text. Only with the original and unreproducible work does it make any sense to speak of a definable person or assembly as creators. With the invention of the printing press and the production of innumerable copies with fewer possibilities of mutation as well as reproduction, the capacity for authorship is diminished, authenticity becomes much more rare, and historical tradition itself less likely. As Benjamin described it,

> the authenticity of a thing is the essence of all that is transmissible from its beginning, ranging from its substantive duration to its testimony to the history which it has experienced. Since the historical testimony rests on the authenticity, the former, too, is jeopardized by reproduction.[26]

Benjamin's understanding of the dynamic of reproduction focuses on the way in which a reproduced object may escape the confines of historical tradition and "meet the beholder or listener in his own particular situation," and thereby results in "a tremendous shattering of tradition."[27]

Whereas auratic art had always presented its messages within the confines of traditions which privileged the image of the artwork over the viewer, Benjamin hoped that "the desire of the contemporary masses to bring things 'closer' spatially and humanly" was "the mark of a perception whose 'sense of the universal equality of things' has increased."[28] Technology thus "de-aestheticized" art by removing from it the traditions and distance which had characterized art in pre-modern times. Whereas art had previously represented that which did not exist in the present, such mechanical forms of artwork as photography and film were able to precisely simulate worldly images, replacing the magic of representation with the exactitude of reproduction and "transform[ing] the beguiled artworshipper of old into the critical viewer of today."[29]

Benjamin's reflections on the importance of mechanical reproduction for the popular reception of an image have a variety of consequences for American constitutionalism. The first is that all Americans may have easier access to the Constitution because it is readily reproducible through printing. However, a second consequence is more ironic. The concept of an original document, and the distinctive power of an original document of as great of antiquity and importance as the Constitution is, paradoxically, also the product of the printing press. Whereas hand-made copies also had their own uniqueness and imperfections, the aura of an original document is most apparent when such a document is compared with a mechanical reproduction.[30] The idea that an original document could have a special status only makes sense after the invention of processes of reproduction. The original Constitution symbolizes both our temporal distance from the Framers and the political distance that lies between the original delegation of popular sovereignty through the ratification of that document and our current political practices. But, its reproductions, mass produced and endlessly disseminated through school textbooks and congressional mailings, promise something different, a personal encounter with the words of the Framers in a form that makes those words, and their authors, immediate and present.

The Protestant Ethic and Constitutional Tradition

Writing may well bring citizens in contact with their nation's past, yet the process of interpretation depends on both the presence of the text and our distance from it. In interpreting texts, one may be neither too close nor too removed from its authorship. Yet, the terms of that distance, and who may have a more or less privileged "encounter" with the text, is very much at the center of theories of constitutional interpretation. Such theories of interpretation often revolve around their authors' own conceptions of how far this country has come from the model set forward in the Constitution. Interpretation of the Constitution often depends on one's perception of distance between 1787 and modern times, and of the possible routes for overcoming that distance.

Sanford Levinson has divided theories of constitutional interpretation into two camps defined by their affinities with Protestantism and Catholicism. According to Levinson, constitutional "protestantism" is the tendency to insist on "the legitimacy of individualized . . . interpretation" where the source of constitutional doctrine "is the text alone." As opposed to protestantism, a "catholic" reading of the Constitution would involve privileging the interpretations of the priests of American law and politics, the Supreme Court, and defining the legitimate source of constitutional doctrine as "the text of the Constitution plus unwritten tradition."[31]

Levinson's distinction between constitutional protestantism and catholicism depends on the existence of the distinction between an auratic Constitution and a mechanically reproducible Constitution. An auratic Constitution implies a catholic hierarchy of access to the proper procedures for reading, understanding, and authoritatively interpreting the Constitution, which can only be properly understood by those with a knowledge of its history and traditions. Conversely, constitutional protestantism requires equal access to a text that may be easily understood because it is in a comprehensible vernacular, with little need for recourse to outside sources. Yet, this analytical distinction is also useful for thinking about the importance of a written constitution for the creation of an interpretive community.[32] A prerequisite for any protestant theory of interpretation is that every reader must have a copy of the text so that he or she will be able to read and interpret it on an individual basis. Only after the invention of the printing press, when standard texts first became common and the citation of texts became possible, did text-based scholarship begin to evolve into its modern form.[33]

The way in which printing creates communities of interpretation shapes the significance of the act of constitutional interpretation itself. Within a protestant theory of constitutional interpretation, the Supreme Court's role is to persuade others to read the text in the same manner without appeal to authority. Joseph Goldstein's argument, that "the justices, as members of a collective body, have an obligation to maintain the Constitution . . . as something intelligible—something that We the People of the United States can understand," is archetypically protestant in its rejection of the mysteries of judicial decision-making.[34] Will Harris rejects constitutional catholicism for a different, but related, reason, arguing that, because the Constitution is, conceptually if not historically, the product of an agreement of the entire people over the terms of their collective political existence, any interpretation should be framed in such a way that it would be understood "by that audience as a debate over the terms of their collective form."[35]

While the protestant approach to the Constitution insists that the document be read in its plain language as a form of the theory of strict construction, the catholic approach to the Constitution asks the interpreter to account for a dynamic tradition that surrounds the document, reflecting the values behind it and serving as a source for new values that may or may not be compatible with the original Constitution. The protestant approach privileges the text as the object of interpretation, while the catholic approach places the text on an equal status with its context. The protestant approach is more compatible with both a reproducible constitution and an unmediated application of the text, the catholic approach is more cultic in viewing the document as a unique statement that is meaningful only within a particular tradition. While the Supreme Court might assume a teaching role in a catholic vision of a constitutional polity, the Court's frequent use of complex and extraconstitutional arguments in its jurisprudence makes its work an even more unlikely candidate for conversion in a form amenable to mass circulation.

The written text of the Constitution is itself a strange figure within this debate, seemingly favoring the protestant side. Unlike the text which signifies the beginnings of English of constitutionalism, the Magna Carta, the Constitution was written in the vernacular. The Magna Carta, written in Latin, was the province of jurists and priests, but was equally intelligible to such educated men, regardless of nationality. By the time of the Constitution's birth, legal texts were no longer commonly phrased in Latin. That the Constitution was written in the English vernacular of its day made it easily understandable within the polity to which it was addressed, and in whose name it was authored. This is an important, but often forgotten, difference between modern and pre-modern documents. Pre-moderns did not associate language with nationality. Vernacular language was most often a regional dialect, and elites communicated in Latin, with its international capacities.[36] The formation of a national identity coterminous with the use of a vernacular occurs with the creation of mass-produced copies which could be distributed by the political center.[37]

The reproducibility of the Constitution has important consequences for its meaning. Hand-written documents are restricted to circulation among small numbers of individuals, particularly elites with the means to reproduce even those small numbers. Moreover, such copies necessarily vary from copy to copy, providing its possessor with some distinction from his or her fellow. The printing press reduced such differences, both in the quality and content of copies and in access to documents. As Marshall McLuhan noted, "If print is uniform, it should create uniform rights for writer and reader, publisher and consumer."[38] The promise of the printing press to expand access to the media not only to readers, but also writers, led Walter Benjamin to proclaim that "[t]he distinction between author and public is about to lose its character . . . At any moment the reader is ready to turn into a writer."[39] In recent times, similar pronouncements have been made for the Internet.

The constellation of ideas that comprise constitutional protestantism assumes the possibility of common, democratic deliberation within a clearly defined community and a reproducible document written in vernacular language. To the extent that such deliberation resembles a conversation, it is often as much about the relative authority of the respective speakers as it is about the content of the document. Constitutional interpretation requires more than the capacity to read, it also requires the interpreter to communicate that interpretation to the larger public. For, while the protestant model of constitutional interpretation emphasizes the essential equality of all readers, there is a fundamental difference between reading and writing.

Writing allows an individual to distribute his or her interpretation to a larger public, reading is essentially a private matter with fewer political consequences. In colonial days, the distinction followed the division of private and public spheres among the sexes,[40] with reading taught by women to both boys and girls in "woman schools," while boys learned to write in "masters' schools."[41] Instruction in reading, which allows governments and other powerful institutions to distribute their own messages, was offered through mass literacy campaigns far earlier than similar instruction in writing, which might democratize the production of printed material, and empower the larger public.[42] To speak of a community of readers, or to describe large numbers of equal and unmediated encounters between a public and a single text is to fundamentally misunderstand the political implications of constitutional interpretation. The authority of the Supreme Court's interpretations derives not from the justices' particular insights into the document, but just as surely from their capacity to disseminate their interpretations. It is as much the capacity of modern institutions to distribute copies of the Constitution and their interpretations of the Constitution, as the ability for a modern, literate citizenry to read it, that is at the root of constitutional protestantism.

Have You Seen This Constitution?

During the week of August 2, 1989, residents of Tarboro, North Carolina opened their newspaper advertising inserts to discover that sirloin steak was selling for $2.49 a pound at the Piggly Wiggly supermarket. If they read the fine print beneath these prices, however, they found the text of Article One, Sections 5,6, and 7 of the United States Constitution underneath the prices of the weekly specials.[43] Having successfully competed with steak for the attention of patriotic Carolinians, the copy at the bottom of the Piggly Wiggly circular urged readers to write to the federal Commission on the Bicentennial of the U.S. Constitution for their own copy of the Constitution.

The mass production of constitutional discourse is rife with contradictory consequences for the creation of a community of constitutional interpretation. The choice of vernacular language for one's primary text makes interpretive protestantism appear to be more compatible with such marketing than catholicism. The protestant tendency to fit the scripture to the congregation has been a part of constitutional culture throughout American history. The Constitution's text, with its eighteenth century English, is less than perfect as contemporary advertising copy, and was certainly not written for consumption by the typical modern American.[44] In an exercise which would be humorous if it were not undertaken with great seriousness, several reading education experts examined the text of the Constitution and other important documents in American political history. They determined that, according to modern techniques of calculating the difficulty of texts, "both the Declaration of Independence and the Constitution are written on readability level usually found in texts for college students—an advanced level— and . . . above the level of all but about five percent of seventeen-year-olds."[45] The same experts also compared the Declaration and the Constitution with the Gettysburg Address and Ronald Reagan's 1987 State of the Union address, and found the speeches easier to read, yet still required a high school education.[46] As one way in which public understanding of these texts can be improved, they suggest that even historic documents be "rewritten" or "simplified."[47]

The lengths to which contemporary Americans will go in order to provide their fellow citizens with a link to their own fundamental principles is quite instructive. A number of measures designed to increase the document's "accessibility" were attempted during the Constitution's Bicentennial. In an attempt to make the document more easily grasped, the National Endowment for the Humanities (NEH) designated a grant for braille constitutions.[48] Many organizations translated the Constitution into languages other than English, presumably for use by non-English speaking immigrants. Government agencies engaged in propaganda efforts overseas provided additional translations of the document for consumption abroad. The Constitution, several Federalist papers, and several other documents relating to American constitutional history were placed on the Internet, to be read and copied by all those who were computer, if not politically, literate.[49] And, in the most problematic technique for overcoming the inherent difficulty with a two-hundred-year-old product, the California Bicentennial Foundation rewrote the document in contemporary colloquial language.[50] Behind such efforts lies the theory that, even if text of the Constitution is not easily understood, the document contains truths simple enough to be appreciated by everyone.[51]

While such alternative constitutions have proliferated, the most widespread symbol of this protestant view of the Constitution has been the "pocket Constitution." The concept has a long history. Thomas Paine wrote in the *Rights of Man* that "[e]very member of the [Pennsylvania] Government had a copy; and nothing was more common when any debate arose . . . than for the members to take the printed Constitution out of their pocket, and read the chapter with which such matter in debate was connected."[52] Justice Hugo Black, an arch-protestant in his approach to constitutional interpretation, carried such a booklet in his jacket every day, insisting that "[w]hen I say something about [the Constitution], I want to quote it precisely."[53] Black more often used the booklet as a prop than as a reference because he had memorized the document, but made it such a fundamental part of his persona that he was buried with a copy in his suit pocket and copies were distributed to mourners at the funeral.[54]

Placing the Constitution in the hands of every citizen in a way that would allow that citizen to forever refer to it on a regular basis is the most literal way to make the Constitution present again. During the Constitution's Bicentennial, the distribution of pocket Constitutions was at the center of the federal Commission's program to create greater knowledge of the document. Chairman Warren Burger proposed the distribution of 50 million copies of the document, one for almost every household in the U.S.[55] Burger's ambitions were ultimately accomplished; in its final report, the Commission asserted that government agencies, private corporations, scouting organizations, and the military distributed a total of 55 million pocket Constitutions during the Bicentennial.[56]

The capacity to disseminate information on a universal scale is unique to late capitalism. The mass production and repetitious circulation of messages through the media of advertising and promotion is an important attribute of both capitalist economics and culture.[57] Citizens may find their political concerns influenced by their immersion in this flow of messages and meaning. Indeed, technologies of reproduction and distribution have not simply amplified already existing forms of political communication, but have created entirely new forms of public discourse. The federal Commission on the Bicentennial's focus on mass production of Constitutions as a cure to constitutional illiteracy, and presumably civic disinterest, was not unique to the Bicentennial. Over the years, Congress has authorized the printing of copies of the Constitution at the public expense so that its members might distribute them to constituents.

The distribution of large numbers of pocket Constitutions with the purpose of encouraging citizens to engage in a direct, personal, and unmediated encounter with the document is itself predicated on a specific model of learning. Within such a model of learning, the encounter with the text is assumed to be capable of resulting in changed behavior. This model of civic learning itself evolves during the early Republic out of the Puritan tradition of teaching reading through the Bible. Such a theory of pedagogy suggested that the encounter between the learner and an uplifting text might change the learner's character and behavior.[58] Such a transformative encounter with a superior, and uplifting, text was at the heart of a different form of constitutional culture, one involving the original, auratic Constitution.

The Display of the Text

In his later years, Thomas Jefferson foresaw the eventual enshrinement of the original copy of the Declaration of Independence, writing to a friend of his hope that "[s]mall things may, perhaps, like the relics of saints, help to nourish our devotion to this holy bond of our Union."[59] The ability to travel across space and time provides documents with the capacity to symbolize the accomplishments of their historical authors in a manner that is most comparable to the physical remains of medieval saints. Objects created before the development of industrial techniques of reproduction, such as manuscripts, possess a singularity that derives from the impossibility of their reproduction. Unlike mechanical reproductions, an original is defined by "its presence in space and time, its unique existence at the place where it happens to be."[60] The documents' unique association with sacred institutions and persons provides them with an ability to instill respect and awe, and to order the world around them.

The power to define a set of orientations for a polity is an essential attribute of any sovereign. Such power is demonstrated in many different ways. Clifford Geertz has noted how monarchs in many different cultures would travel throughout their realms to demonstrate the monarch's omnipresence, strength, and ability to maintain the peace, and impressing their subjects with the vigor and power of their entourages.[61] The sovereigns' entourages set the monarch apart and made him sacred, for the sacred is "that which is *set apart,* that which is *separated*" from the profane.[62] An entourage not only transported the sovereign, but displayed the sovereign as a specially protected center of power even as he moved throughout his realm. Monarchs' entourages were a way to reconnect the center of the political order with the subjects who constituted the periphery, symbolically integrate the collectivity into a single entity, and remind those in the periphery that the sovereign, although absent, could become present in awesome ways.

In the United States, such grand spectacles have tended to be both stationary and democratic, such as in the forms of the Great Expositions of nineteenth century Philadelphia and Chicago, or the twentieth century's World Fairs. Although the United States lacks a monarch, we have also had royal entourages. From time to time, historically significant and therefore auratic copies, of the Declaration, Constitution, and Bill of Rights have traveled forth as symbols of the American political order—visiting among the people, rather than insisting that the people come to them.[63] Exhibitions of such documents as the Declaration, Constitution, Bill of Rights, and even the Magna Carta are an integral part of American civic commemorations. Perhaps the largest tour of traveling historical documents was the Freedom Train of 1947, which contained among other paper treasures, Washington's copy of the Constitution and the Bill of Rights.[64] A similar exhibit, including an early Magna Carta, also toured the country during the American Revolution Bicentennial.[65] The Constitution's Bicentennial generated several such tours. While the entourages assumed various shapes, "Roads to Liberty," sponsored by American Express, was typical. Along with one of the oldest copies of the Magna Carta, antiquated copies of the Emancipation Proclamation, the Northwest Ordinances, and other milestones in American constitutional development toured the countryside in a customized semi-trailer truck.[66]

While Roads to Liberty was the first such tour during the Bicentennial, others followed. The H.M.S. *Rose,* a reconstructed sailing frigate, carried Rhode Island's copy of the Bill of Rights and copies of such documents as the English Bill of Rights and the Virginia Declaration of Rights to cities along the eastern seaboard.[67] An even more impressive display was mounted by the Philip Morris Companies to commemorate the Bicentennial of the Bill of Rights. The tobacco and food conglomerate sponsored a $60 million advertising campaign and multi-media tour that traveled to every state of the Union, and featured Virginia's copy of the Bill of Rights in a state-of-the-art mechanical display.[68]

Roads to Liberty and its siblings have typically received the "royal treatment" which their function as symbols of sovereignty would appear to demand. In the 1940s, the Freedom Train's arrival in each community had been marked with "Rededication Week" ceremonies, and visitors signed a "Freedom Scroll."[69] These ceremonies were largely imitated in the festivities welcoming the "Freedom Trailer," as Burger referred to the Roads to Liberty tour.[70] Organizations that could not afford the millions of dollars that it cost to tour with an original document could make do with

"The Blessings of Liberty," an exhibit assembled by Project '87. Rather than presenting original or facsimile documents, the Project '87 exhibits used narrative and illustrations to provide an instant museum exhibit for local sponsors.[71] These displays also had venerable predecessors; in 1937, as part of the sesquicentennial celebrations of the Constitution, the federal Commission organized the manufacture and distribution of facsimile "Shrines" containing reproductions of the Declaration and Constitution to public schools and libraries.[72]

Democratizing and multiplying such displays necessarily undermines presentation of the sovereign as a single and unified entity. Thus, while royal entourages gained their power from their singularity, the profusion of patriotic symbols during the Bicentennial actually undermined the attempt to create a symbolic center. After Roads to Liberty did not include Philadelphia on its schedule, the City of Philadelphia staged an exhibit of the Magna Carta owned by private citizen, H. Ross Perot; loath to pass up the opportunity to display the document in the city that was hosting the most extensive celebrations of the Constitution's Bicentennial, the Commission then brought the Freedom Trailer to the City of Brotherly Love.[73] But, the Freedom Trailer's tour was ended unceremoniously when the Magna Carta and other documents were removed from its possession by Tennessee police carrying a court order and transported to a Nashville museum which had a previous agreement to exhibit it.[74]

American political culture lacks the sort of symbolic center that provides monarchs with their ability to represent all of society. As a symbol of political legitimacy, the Constitution must compete with predecessor documents, like the Magna Carta and the Declaration, or successor documents, such as the Emancipation Proclamation and the Gettysburg Address, as well as such other icons of democracy as the Liberty Bell, the bald eagle, and the flag. The Constitution even had to compete with the Bible, as was demonstrated in a prize-winning essay by a Filipino student who wrote that "All these written laws embodied in the Bill of Rights, I believe, are rooted in the Golden Rule: 'Do unto others what you would like them to do unto you,' or simply put, Do good to others."[75] As Geertz notes in his essay on monarchial power, the power of the sovereign requires the ability to command all around it; sovereigns rarely survive rough treatment or competition.[76]

American political culture has a history of competition among political symbols. Daniel Boorstin argues, "The image has reached out from commerce to the worlds of education and politics, and into every corner of our daily lives . . . Our national politics has become a competition for images or between images, rather than between ideals."[77] The creation of so many images has its consequences. Much of the eighteenth century reverence for print was founded on the scarcity of books and other reading material; each encounter with a text was to be treasured.[78] The multiplicity of images in contemporary society has cheapened the value of print. The explosion of texts has meant that collective ideals and representations must compete with each other, and may become confused for each other. During the Constitution's Bicentennial, the images of the American institutions and practices which were utilized as ways to bring the Constitution to the people were confused with the Constitution itself. When the sovereign is separate from the people, such as a monarch accompanied by her entourage, the relationship is easily understood. When the sovereign and the people are the same, it is only logical that the sanctity of the sovereign will fade, its image will relinquish its resonance, and the meaning of sovereignty itself will be lost. In the case of the popular sovereign, the symbol of sovereignty and the sovereign begin to coincide when textual representation ends, and the people begin to represent themselves.

Inscribing Popular Sovereignty

Anne Norton has observed that the Constitution's Preamble remade the people into the image of the word. In

Norton's political theology, "[t]he citizens of an inscribed nation, the authors of written constitutions, take upon themselves a written identity . . . those who are constituted in politics and language give their ideal and political constitution primacy over their natural constitution."[79] Similarly, Will Harris argues that the act of the constitution writing is not only about self-representation and self-creation, but about recognizing the collective self as the author of the political community:

> a purposefully composed text creates its own normative author. It constructs the popular sovereign it needs to be authoritative, and it nurtures the political life of a People whose citizenship provides it with the only reality it can have or need. What they have modeled is themselves, in public and realizable form.[80]

The texts which stand at the center of the American consciousness, the Declaration of Independence, the Constitution, the Gettysburg Address, and the more memorable presidential inaugural addresses, provide Americans with pictures of themselves and representations of their larger national identity, and demonstrate the importance of authorship in the construction of political authority.

The success of the Fourth of July issues from the fact that it celebrates, in the Declaration of Independence, the document that justifies the nation's existence. Beginning early in the nineteenth century, Independence Day became an important national institution because of its capacity to unite the citizenry in a collective ritual where the words of the Declaration were recited and elaborated upon as the core of the American identity.[81] No such treatment has been accorded the Constitution, nor have fireworks become associated with it. That American ritual has embraced the Declaration more than the Constitution should not surprise anyone; the Declaration itself was meant to be publically proclaimed and given "a voice," in a way that the Constitution, as a legal document, was not.[82] As late as 1882, the

Constitution was stored in a tin box in a closet at the State Department, while the Declaration was mounted in a place of honor.[83]

The social relations embodied in such texts as the Declaration and the Constitution may be given more dramatic form through public ceremonies and parades.[84] In such public performances of political texts, the people may be remade in the image of the word. Such a transformation occurred during a nationally televised "We the People 200" parade on September 17, 1987, which served as a dramatic climax for the bicentennial celebrations in Philadelphia. During the parade, the text of the Constitution served as a representation of American society. The constitutional order was symbolically inscribed onto the citizenry through the division of marchers into sections according to the clauses of the Preamble. The We the People 200 Parade was actually only one portion of a larger parade; it followed a recreation of the Grand Federal Procession of 1788, and preceded a "Parade of America's People" in which local citizens paraded in units of their own choice and design.[85] The images of the nation contained in this human Preamble thus symbolically linked the historical act of the alienation of popular sovereignty and the self-representation of the people themselves.

The Preamble served as an appropriate center for the bicentennial parade because it provided a poetic justification for the relationship between American society and the state that governs that society. The decision to represent the nation through the Preamble to the Constitution was made by a creative team from Radio City Music Hall Productions which structured the parade so that its themes would be familiar to everyone, represent the demographic and geographic diversity of the nation, and present the nation as unified.[86] Those who marched as "We the People" embodied the text before the nation it had created, depicting both its internal divisions and external boundaries through the various categories of the text that had established the new order, and thus placing the language of the Constitution in a fetishistic relation to the people themselves.[87] Where the people had been represented by the text two hundred years before, the text was now represented through the people.

The parade contained numerous allusions to the Constitution's textuality. The first section of the parade, entitled "We the People, of the United States," brought together two different representations of the process of authorship. The first float depicted the Constitution's authors through a gigantic inkwell hung with giant portraits of five of the Founding Fathers, and followed by a descendant of each of the Constitution's thirty-nine signers. In contrast, the source of the Constitution's authority, the people, were represented through the parade's three Grand Marshals. Walter Cronkite, a white news anchor who seemingly personified authority, rode in an antique automobile with Coretta Scott King, widow of black civil rights leader Martin Luther King, and Peter MacDonald, president of the Navajo Nation. Absent Hispanic and Asian-American representation, the trio symbolized American racial diversity at the time of the Constitution's adoption. The combination of the two displays betrayed a desire to fuse popular authority with the legitimacy of long dead patriarchs. However, the ideological impulse which allowed the Founding Fathers to conflate their authorship of the Constitution with popular authority through the phrase, "We the People," was more problematic in contemporary America and required a more explicit acknowledgment of diversity.[88]

The following sections were less tied to the Constitution's textual nature. Three floats representing the states and symbols of the westward expansion constituted the second section, "In Order to Form a More Perfect Union."[89] The third section, "Establish Justice, Insure Domestic Tranquility" represented the work of civil governance through portraits of the forty presidents, local members of Congress who rode in antique automobiles, and floats bearing the seals of both houses of Congress and the President.[90] The separation of powers was portrayed through a set of scales that held models of the Capitol and the White House, thus dissolving the judiciary into a metaphor for the constitutional system, rather than a branch with its own interests and powers.[91] Sections of the parade also celebrated the contributions of the military and economic prosperity.

The final section of the parade, "Secure the Blessings of Liberty to Ourselves and Our Posterity" continued the celebration of civil society begun in "Promote the General Welfare," and added the theme of an active public conversation. The only float incorporated three elements of the First Amendment: speech, embodied in a lecturer on a podium; religion personified by a gospel choir; and the press, illustrated by a working eighteenth century printing press. The "Blessings of Liberty" float thus depicted those rights that allow individuals to express themselves in public ways. Liberty was further equated with the public use of language by the "printer's devils" who distributed copies of the Constitution to spectators as the float passed by. Other civil rights, economic rights, and the rights of defendants were not celebrated in any part of the parade.

The We the People 200 Parade was a less than satisfactory explication of the importance of the Constitution in American life. However, its purpose was to illustrate, not to explain, constitutionalism, and, taken as a whole, the Radio City Music Hall Production's representation of the nation through the clauses of the Preamble revealed a sophisticated understanding of the relationship between state and society. The image of citizens marching in the shape of the words of the Constitution was a particularly fetishistic interpretation of the idea of a "government of laws, not men," one which made the viewer understand the power of words to reshape a nation and that nation's image of itself.

The Cultural Significance of a Written Constitution

A written, reproducible constitution can be a profoundly populist document. The law has long served as a form of mysterious and sacred knowledge in American life, unknowable to the majority of the population; Alexis de Tocqueville compared American lawyers to Egyptian priests, and the common law to undecipherable hieroglyphics.[92] When the Constitution is disentangled from the case law which has grown from and around it over the past two hundred years, it becomes a far more approachable and democratic text. Yet the possibility of a direct and unmediated relationship between text and citizen is still remote. Even those who would encourage citizens to pursue an unmediated relationship with the Constitution must do so through highly mediated programs of civic education, entertainment, or public service advertisements. The distribution during the Bicentennial of 55 million pocket Constitutions by the federal Commission and others was a testament to the ability of modern mediating institutions to build a direct and unmediated relationship between citizens and the literary representation of their own sovereignty.[93] It also illuminated the basic structural problems of representing community within a mass society.

In attempting to make the Constitution more real and less abstract, planners of the recent Bicentennial celebrated this textual representation of popular sovereignty through visual representations of the Constitution's literary qualities as much as its political dimensions. During the Bicentennial, the Constitution's textual form was interpreted through a number of images. A giant quill and ink bottle began the We the People 200 parade in Philadelphia,[94] a quill was emblazoned on Bicentennial coins,[95] and the archaic cursive of the first three words of the original document was reproduced on virtually every commemorative object or school lesson plan. Words and other literary images are important symbols of the recorded history that replaces memory as a social activity binding a group together.[96] Yet, because the words themselves represent abstract concepts, they require embodiment in more easily understood forms.

A political system that is defined by writing is representational at its very foundations. Written words do not represent social relations directly, but point to the spoken word and language. Neil Postman argues:

> Because the phonetic symbol always refers to things that are not present and most often to things we do not know about, it permits us to go (to quote Harold Innis) "beyond the world of concrete experience into the world of conceptual relations."[97]

Yet, both the Declaration of Independence and the Constitution speak to us in the names of, respectively, the states and the people, without acknowledging that their authors were themselves representatives of these social institutions or abstract principles.[98] These texts speak to us directly, mediating our social relations with both the opacity and transparency of language, and promising that our social and political relationships may be as easily understood as words on a page.

CHAPTER FIVE

The Constitution as a Symbol of Democracy

For a symbol of popular sovereignty, the Constitution gains much of its importance because of a fundamentally undemocratic process—judicial review. As critics often observe, judicial review allows the views of unelected judges to prevail over the wishes of the citizenry as expressed through their representatives. Many of these same critics also suggest that the only way to justify judicial review as a democratic process is to use a jurisprudence of "original intent."[1] Such a jurisprudence constrains the range of proper judicial interpretations to those understandings which were current at the time when the Constitution was written and ratified because "[i]f the Constitution is law, then presumably, like all other law, the meaning the lawmakers intended is as binding upon judges as it is upon legislatures and executives."[2]

Yet, if the Constitution's authority depends on the fiction that the people are indeed its authors, we are faced with the problem that not a single current member of the modern American body politic can claim authorship of its most important provisions. As Bruce Ackerman writes, "The good news about the [Supreme] Court is that it is interpreting the constitutional principles affirmed by the American people at times when their political attention and energy was most focused on such matters; the bad news is that the Americans who made these considered constitutional judgments are dead."[3] In a single sentence, Ackerman describes one of the most troubling dimensions of American constitutionalism, that while judicial review of democratically enacted statutes is inherently undemocratic, the Constitution is no more a product of democratic deliberation by *this* American public. The document's longevity allows contemporary Americans to avoid making many difficult and complex political decisions, and to concentrate instead on their own private pursuits. The essential question which faces any theorist of modern constitutionalism is whether modern Americans are free to choose whether or not to belong to the national covenant established through the Constitution. The answer must be no, for any other answer leads to anarchy. Yet, it is hardly a satisfying conclusion.

　　The incompatibility between democracy and a constitution founded on the alienation of sovereign powers may manifest itself in several ways, as is illustrated by the experience of two Connecticut towns, Cornwall and Woodbridge, during the Constitution's Bicentennial. In 1988, each town reconsidered their votes against the Constitution's ratification during Connecticut's original ratification convention in 1788. Cornwall repudiated its vote against ratification (with only the town Libertarian in opposition), while Woodbridge reaffirmed its opposition to ratification. The two towns did not differ in their support for the Constitution; they simply disagreed about what the process of ratification meant. In Cornwall, the vote was seen as "a chance to vote for the Constitution of the United States," while, in Woodbridge, a resident justified the vote against ratification as "preserv[ing] the fact that people have the right to vote 'nay.'"[4]

　　While Cornwall voters saw themselves as possessing a unique opportunity to enunciate their personal approval of the document, Woodbridge residents used their town meeting to demonstrate that they did not accept the alienation of their sovereignty and wished to keep their ability to express dissatisfaction with government close at hand. In ratifying the Constitution, the proud patriots of Cornwall personally validated the ancient transfer of ordinary sovereign powers from the people to the government, while, of course, retaining their powers of constituent sovereignty. The staunch antifederalists of Woodbridge, on the other hand, who wished to "preserve the fact that people have the right to vote 'nay,'" symbolically kept their ordinary sovereign powers and their power of constituent sovereignty close at hand. Yet, the stubborn Yankees of Woodbridge, Connecticut are no less governed through the Constitution than any other residents of the United States.

Today, authentic town meetings are as rare as committed antifederalists. Direct democracy by town meeting is difficult to practice in a large or extended polity, and the more the United States has grown, the more difficult it has been for citizens to exercise their powers of self-government in person. Cornwall, Connecticut had a smaller population in 1988 than in 1788, but there are few communities left of its size, and many of those have been incorporated into larger metropolitan areas.[5] Yet, no matter how few examples remain, participatory self-government remains an important theme within American democratic thought, coexisting uneasily with a constitutional tradition that relies on the capacity of representation to mitigate the excesses of local interests.[6] Small group decision-making serves an important symbolic function by associating democratic authority with the social sphere, rather than the state and political officials.[7] In many of its forms, small-scale participatory democracy provides participants with both the opportunity for collective control over decision-making and with ritualized opportunities to demonstrate their commitment to self-government. Outside of elections, such opportunities to affirm one's consent to the laws passed by the democratic majority are rare in the larger context of American politics.

While ritualistic opportunities for symbolic reaffirmation of the regime's legitimacy rarely occur within the national political system, they are often provided in more limited and local ways. Elites often affirm the idea of an active public that cares about, and participates in, political decisions, albeit by describing civic activities in particularly formal and circumscribed manner. Thus, a Senate report recommending the celebration of the Constitution's Bicentennial declared:

> The Republic depends on citizens to vote responsibly, to give testimony at public hearings, to participate in juries, to engage in discussions of public affairs, to offer voluntary service in community settings, and to raise the responsible citizens of the future in family settings. Without a working knowledge of our charter of freedoms and voluntary activities in conjunction with such understanding, our *participatory* government would soon perish.[8]

This description of citizens' duties notably omits such political activities as public protest, petition, and participation in political organizations (or voting "irresponsibly"), but portrays such otherwise private activities as raising children as supportive of the state. Citizenship is described as a package of activities in which citizens participate in a sporadic or periodic fashion; citizenship is a limited element in such an identity—largely akin to a part-time job.

Even more striking in this excerpt is how it depicts citizens' responsibilities as voluntary. As Gary Peller has argued, one of the structuring dichotomies underlying American constitutional discourse is the association between the private sphere and voluntariness, on one hand, and the state and coercion on the other.[9] In the Senate's description, civic obligations seemingly occur in a zone between the public and private spheres; even in their most public roles, citizens still act according to the private sphere's norm of voluntariness. The ideal citizen might volunteer for many of these activities, but a sense of duty, much less the compulsion required in jury duty, is absent from this description of participatory self-government. And, perhaps what is most interesting is the way in which this vision of voluntary civic action avoids the very principle of sovereignty—the capacity to make an ultimate decision and to enforce it through coercion.

This description of a consensual, voluntaristic state is closer to a vision of society than of polity, and closely akin to the smaller, voluntary associations which provide many individuals with a sense of solidarity and fulfillment that they do not receive from large-scale political institutions. Communities and voluntary associations provide forms of social control and cohesion both supplemental, and occasionally opposed, to the state.[10] The growth of the state in modern times has stimulated what Robert Nisbet termed the "quest for community" as an antidote to the state's omnipresence in citizens' lives.[11] Yet, the role of such organizations in the modern administrative state is not so clearly oppositional, but instead provides a vehicle for typifying governmental actions as social as well as political in nature. When federal or state programs are administered through community-based organizations, the state assumes (at least partially) the form of voluntary associations, socializing the political and politicizing the social.

Assemblies and community meetings have long provided a social context for the popular validation of political decisions. The Constitution's authors included the provision that it should be ratified by state conventions, rather than the state legislatures, to circumvent the existing political structure. This was partially good politics, as the legislatures could not be expected to hand over part of their power very readily. However, ratification by popular assemblies, rather than the state legislatures, also presented the Constitution as the system of governance embraced by people themselves.[12] The form of assembly embodied by the state ratification conventions of 1788 was labeled a "constituent assembly" by Tocqueville to distinguish it from a "legislative assembly" which makes ordinary laws.[13] While the British Constitution provides for a combined form of constituent and legislative assembly, the U.S. Constitution separates these two forms of representation. And, while the Constitution specifies that the states may form representative assemblies as one mechanism by which the public might ratify amendments to the original document, the only such conventions convened in the past two hundred years repealed Prohibition in 1932.[14]

The power of primarily social forms of community and association to represent popular consent to a form of governance is magnified because the United States lacks any single political body which might serve as a constituent, rather than legislative, assembly. Parliament's capacity to represent the British people in modifying their Constitution is denied to the only assembly within the American national state, the Congress, which must rely on the consent of other assemblies to amend the United States Constitution. Though the Constitution's provision for constitutional conventions recognized that popular consent to a form of governance may be best symbolized by a representative assembly of the governed, such assemblies have not occurred in over two hundred years.

That citizen assemblies ratified the original vision of the Constitution reminds us that social contracts, like the Constitution, are based on collective consent, and not individual consent. Popular consent to the Constitution was of paramount importance; the Constitution's authority is based wholly on the popular approval specified in its sections concerning ratification, and is silent about principles other than consent that might grant it legitimacy.[15] Modern forms of liberalism and communitarianism provide very different grounds for understanding the characteristics of both collective and individual forms of consent toward the Constitution within the context of American identity and citizenship.[16] Liberalism implies a weak theory of community in which the citizen is a largely independent actor who may consent to the legitimacy of the nation of which she is a member, but who is formed prior to such consent. Communitarianism insists that the state and its institutions are an essential part of the citizen's formation, and that the citizen can do little other than to consent to that which is familiar and most real to her. For liberals, citizenship is a contract which is freely entered into; for communitarians, citizenship is a set of relationships and entanglements which one cannot easily enter. And the terms "community" and "voluntary association," which both refer to small groups with participatory decision-making processes, indicate very different social phenomena corresponding to communitarianism and liberalism, respectively.

Traditionally, communities are properly tightly bounded and require conditions that are not easily found in a mass society "(1) a territorial base . . . (2) primary relationships (face-to-face encounters); (3) stability; (4) some conception of a principled commitment to a collectivity."[17] In traditional forms of community, the community fashions its members as much as it is formed by them, so that community values become an integral element in individual identity.[18] In this account, individuality develops from community, community does not develop from individuals. Thus, communitarians define true community as "a shared way of life that partly defines the identity of the participants."[19] Communitarianism and liberal voluntarism coexist uneasily in American political culture and thought. Theories which view the community as a formative and permanent element of individual identity are not compatible with the norms of elective membership which underlie the liberal idea of voluntary association.[20]

Voluntary association differs from traditional community because such associations do not aim to create consensus about a diverse set of issues within a stable group, but endeavor to attract participants who cooperate to further particular, and possibly temporary, interests. Participants may enter and exit voluntary associations in a manner more similar to the figure of the entrepreneur than to that of the citizen.[21] This understanding of community is ultimately liberal, for it allows people to choose and create new communities which are secondary to their already established individual identities, and does not require that the individual accept and respect communal norms with which they disagree. Many such voluntaristic "communities" have formed and prospered because they provide participants with a sense of comradery even if limited to particular and discrete interests. As Philip Abbott has argued, technological and social change has led Americans to invent new forms of "instant community" over the years.[22] Within a mass society, such forms of instant community may reduce "both the anomic precariousness of individual existence in isolation from society and the threat of alienation to the public order."[23] The instant communities invented by users of computer bulletin boards or the electronic church allow individuals to participate with what Abbott calls "intimate anonymity," which results from participants' ability to easily join and leave exit the association in a way that members of a small town cannot.[24]

The differences between the forms of community and voluntary association lie at the center of the problem of consent in a constitutional culture. Having been made Americans under this Constitution, our consent is not as free as our modern versions of voluntary association would tell us. However, the model of free consent prevails largely because the membership of American communities, both local and invented, has become fluid and diverse in a way that precludes consensus on many norms and mores. Communitarianism remains strongly rooted in the ceremonies and rituals that are part of American civil life. Yet, the transience of modern American life, where many families enter and leave neighborhoods, cities, and regions on a frequent basis, strongly favors the liberal account of citizenship as an elective status. Whether Americans truly have the capacity to choose the Constitution is another question entirely.

Constitutionalism and the Rituals of Consent

Ritual acts of consent towards the Constitution comprise an important part of American political tradition. The most visible acts of consent occur when individuals assume new responsibilities. When government officials assume their office, they repeat versions of an oath to uphold the Constitution that is found within that same document. When new citizens recite an oath to support the Constitution, their status changes with their affirmation of the principles of the polity which they join. When new soldiers are inducted into the armed forces, they promise to abide by the decisions of civilian institutions and, through them, the larger public. The function of such oaths in these transformative rituals illustrates how loyalty to the Constitution is constitutive of many of citizens' public roles and how strongly communitarian elements survive in the American. Yet, the oath to support the Constitution has also been overshadowed by the Pledge of Allegiance "to the flag . . . and the republic for which it stands." Even the Celebration of Citizenship, the central event planned by the federal Commission on the Bicentennial of the Constitution, was originally titled the "Universal Pledge of Allegiance," and concluded with President Reagan leading a nationwide audience in the Pledge of Allegiance, which does not even mention the Constitution, rather than an oath to support the Constitution.[25]

The language of American citizenship is largely communitarian. The very term "alien" demonstrates the extent to which citizenship is associated with integration into a political order. Those outside that order are "alien," and must be "naturalized" to attain the status of citizen. The medieval doctrine of naturalization required that the new citizen was "reborn" as a subject of the monarch, marking a dramatic break from his or her previous status. Such a total transformation is difficult to reconcile with liberal theories of social contract, which assume that any individual may join a community by accepting the authority of its governing institutions without necessarily internalizing its culture and traditions.[26] In a communitarian vein, Sheldon Wolin argues that citizenship is a birthright because an individual who has been born into a polity has a genealogy that reflects the "unique collective identity" that is the sum of his or her ancestors. Wolin argues that for citizenship to be simply a matter of contract or consent, our identities would have to be essentially interchangeable, with little to define each of us as unique or individual.[27] Socialization is an important element in the process of becoming a citizen, and studies have shown that immigrants who are better integrated into the community are more likely to become citizens than immigrants who are not.[28]

The ritual aspects of naturalization imply the existence of a covenant, not a contract. While individuals enter into contracts for instrumental reasons that leave the identity of the self untouched, the language of covenant is filled with expressions of status, duty, and commitment.[29] While contracts may be signed between equals, and may be invalid when the disparity in power or information is too great,[30] covenants establish hierarchies. Within the context of a naturalization ceremony, the oath signifies the individual's submissive relationship to the larger political community, by whose laws the individual agrees to be bound. Such oaths not only express an individual's commitment to specific principles or practices, but to "strengthen resolve" to fulfill his or her new duties.[31] In the liberal tradition, however, such acts merely signify the consent of the governed. With little regard for the ritualistic aspects of consent, liberal democratic theorists have used consent primarily as an analytical tool, arguing that the proper measure of legitimacy in the liberal state is whether people should consent to a government or policy. The lack of a historical example for the social contract which has been "mocked by every schoolboy who knows he didn't sign a contract,"[32] has not deterred liberal theorists from isolating consent as an ideal purified of coercion, personal interest, or political context.[33] Such theorists are similarly indifferent to the communitarian dimensions of ceremonial consent.

The process by which aliens become naturalized citizens is more compatible with communitarianism than liberalism, but it is a strangely voluntaristic form of community. As then-Speaker of the House Jim Wright declared during the nationally broadcast Celebration of Citizenship, "America is a set of ideas and ideals. We are a family bound together not by blood, but by belief."[34] The following day, President Reagan defined American citizenship in political rather than cultural or historical terms when he noted in his speech at the We the People 200 parade in Philadelphia, that "people from every corner of the world can come to this country and become an American [sic]," noting in contrast that one would not become Japanese if one moved to Japan nor French if one moved to France.[35] In the United States, citizenship involves the bonds of community, but the boundaries of the political community are permeable, allowing one to escape his or her previous history and assume a new, altered identity. National ritual events, such as the "Liberty Weekend" celebration of 1986, have used the personal journey of immigrants from repression and scarcity in foreign lands to the liberty and prosperity of America as a way of symbolizing the transformation of immigrants' diverse history and culture into a single political identity free of the historically and culturally bounded identities of the past.[36]

However, the immigrant experience of taking an oath to the Constitution only partially addresses the problem of consent in modern American constitutionalism, for most Americans obtain their citizenship status as a matter of birth. When a nation-state dependent for its legitimacy on the consent of the governed outlives its founding generation, the question arises whether succeeding generations must consent explicitly or are presumed to do so tacitly. In the late twentieth century, the document's longevity posed the question of whether modern citizens are bound by the consent given by the founding generation or by immigrant ancestors who had taken an oath to the Constitution upon their naturalization. Echoing the skeptics' complaint that *they* never signed a social contract, liberals, such as Stephen Macedo, may quip, "That much of the founding generation actually consented no more binds the present population to the Constitution than Washington's marriage oath binds them to Martha."[37] This view of the Constitution as a contract without transformative implications for citizens' identity disregards the Constitution's influence on American culture.

These diverse views of the Constitution as contract and covenant underscore a debate over the role of the document as the source of a stable agreement over time about the fundamental principles of the American polity. Transgenerational theories of political obligation do not satisfy those, such as Thomas Paine and Thomas Jefferson, who viewed the Constitution as a contract to which one generation had consented, but which could not bind the next generation without its consent. Such a conception of generational equity lay behind Jefferson's proposal that every generation be allowed to choose its own form of government and to vote on the Constitution. Jefferson's scheme was opposed by many, including James Madison, who saw periodic reconsideration of the Constitution as a source of instability and political intrigue.[38] Madison's concerns were likely warranted. Constitutional conflicts over slavery, desegregation, abortion, and many other issues have led to violent confrontations and division over vital issues of identity and the nature of the American polity.

Sanford Levinson has argued that Americans cannot choose whether they would live under the Constitution because the choice is no longer theirs. The American political tradition is largely defined by the terms and language of the Constitution, so that American identity itself does not make sense without the Constitution. As Levinson notes, entering into an association by taking an oath or consenting to an agreement often leads to the formation of communities from which we gain our identities.[39] This dimension is also acknowledged by Bruce Ackerman, who writes that if Americans

> did not try to discover meaning in our constitutional history, we would be cutting ourselves off from each other in a way that could not be readily replaced . . . To discover the Constitution is to discover an import of oneself—insofar as one recognizes oneself as an American.[40]

Such claims attest to the importance of the Constitution in describing the shared culture that typifies American identity and underlies American political culture. This definition of citizenship is shared by the general public as much as by elites. Several very different studies have shown that Americans are more likely to describe their national identity in political terms, while citizens of other nations are more likely to associate citizenship with cultural background.[41]

The Constitution may serve as a symbol of popular consent. Yet, an oath to uphold the Constitution is not a rational choice taken by a free actor because of the document's importance in the formation of the national character. American citizens do not take such an oath purely as a way of signaling their consent to the political order. Rather, they may affirm a constituent element of their identity and signify an emotional connection to the nation as a political and social organism. What cannot be assumed is that citizens will agree on the content of that identity. Thus, while formally signaling the acceptance of the Constitution as a source of political legitimacy, political ceremonies do not provide any guidance as to which Constitution is accepted. Public affirmation of the Constitution is more problematic when one considers the content of that consensus.

The Constitution as a Symbol in a Pluralistic Society

On September 17, 1987, the two hundredth anniversary of the signing of the Constitution, at a ceremony held at four o'clock in the afternoon, the time when the Constitutional Convention had signed the final draft of the document, Jacqueline Wexler of the National Conference of Christians and Jews (NCCJ) handed Warren Burger a list of names symbolizing the six million signatures to the Constitution that the group had solicited from schoolchildren.[42] The NCCJ signature campaign promoted the Constitution's role as a guarantor of tolerance and civil liberties in a diverse society, and those who signed NCCJ's forms signaled their approval of a liberal, pluralistic society—a conception of American society quite different from that ratified in 1788.[43]

In addition to the NCCJ, the Christian Church (Disciples of Christ)[44] also organized a campaign to "sign-on" to or "reaffirm" the Constitution, and a group called the Williamsburg Charter Foundation organized citizen ratification of its own "reaffirmation" of the values invoked in the First Amendment.[45] B'nai B'rith International, a Jewish group, sponsored a Bicentennial Sabbath featuring activities through which members could display loyalty to Constitution as well as its congruence with their religious tradition.[46] Signature drives and other ritual demonstrations of approval for constitutional principles were a way in which religious organizations could apply to the Constitution their traditional practice of communal affirmation of beliefs.

The need to affirm one's membership is a feature of covenanted communities, whether religious or political. In contemporary society, with diverse religious views and political ideals, maintaining a covenanted community is a particularly complicated task. The idea of the United States as a community of believers, who share a common affirmation of the Constitution, democratic values, and a commonly held civil religion, involves a great degree of imagination in postmodern America. But the idea of a national community of believers is made more powerful by its connections to religious community.[47] Religious community has always been a central element of American life, and the rhetoric of religious community has been a central part of American political language going back to the John Winthrop's exhortation to the Puritans that they build a "city on a hill" and continuing through President Bill Clinton's "New Covenant."[48] Within this view of American political culture, the Constitution serves American politics much as a sacred text serves a religious community. Its acceptance defines the scope of the community to which only believers are admitted, its content dictates how the community shall be organized, and its structure mirrors that of the community.[49] The Constitution that was so celebrated was the social covenant, not the political.

The Constitution may well serve as an important symbol of religious freedom in the United States. Religious organizations that wished to join the celebration of the Constitution's bicentennial added few specifically religious elements to the commemorative activities. Among activities listed in the federal Commission on the Bicentennial's *Resource Guide for Religious Communities,* only participation in "The Year of Thanksgiving for the Blessings of Liberty" proclaimed by Congress had an even vaguely religious tone.[50] In other programs, religious communities were treated primarily as venues for political education, and religious leaders were provided with excerpts from the Founders' public declarations concerning and a "Bicentennial Sermon File" to encourage discussions of constitutionalism within congregations.[51] Other programs and services promoted for use by religious organizations, such as publications, commemorative souvenirs, and convention exhibits, were as appropriate for secular groups as for religious groups.

Religious groups faced the question of how best to combine their particular religious beliefs with the political ideals expressed through the Constitution's religious liberty and anti-establishment clauses. The ideals which some found in the First Amendment far exceeded a shield between church and state, but found a larger ethic of civility and tolerance in the document. This ethic of civility was particularly prominent in the "charter" composed by the Williamsburg Charter Foundation. The Williamsburg Charter was signed at the site of, and on the two hundredth anniversary of, the Virginia legislature's call for the addition of a Bill of Rights to the Constitution. However, the Charter was not as much a celebration of the First Amendment as an attempt to negotiate a consensus about its meaning. The organizers of the Williamsburg Charter believed that American politics had been too long afflicted by religious conflict. There are few areas of life in contemporary America where there is less agreement on values than religion and religious issues.[52] The Williamsburg Charter aspired to justify a religiously pluralistic society, while also avoiding "the respective weaknesses of relativism, interest-group liberalism, or any form of mere 'process' and 'proceduralism.'" Such a solution eluded the group. Ultimately, the Charter's chief author, Os Guinness, revealingly described its approach to pluralism as "an agreement within disagreements over deep differences that make a difference."[53]

Agreeing to disagree may suspend conflict, but it does not provide much substantive ground for agreement. In modern America, the Charter bemoaned, there was no longer a sense of community, and "citizens of a republic based on democratic accommodation have succumbed to a habit of relentless confrontation."[54] Indeed, the very problem of religious conflict is largely unresolvable because of the existence of community. Such conflicts are more likely to occur between religious communities than between unaffiliated individuals. The Charter's authors hoped that such confrontation would end when combatants would appreciate that the First Amendment's "Religious Liberty provisions are not 'articles of faith' concerned with the substance of particular doctrines or of policy issues," but were rather seen as "'articles of peace' concerned with the constitutional constraints and the shared prior understanding within which the American people can engage their differences in a civil manner."[55] By so interpreting the First Amendment, the Charter's authors began their journey towards a distinctly procedural vision of constitutionalism.

Having agreed that people disagree, the Williamsburg Charter revealed two very different and contradictory theories of community describing, respectively, religious and political community.[56] In religious community, belief was prescribed as the primary ethic. However, in political community, the primary ethic was "civility." Sociologist John Murray Cuddihy argues that the American emphasis on civility within religious pluralism has evolved out of a history of maintaining multiple religious communities as separate entities within a larger, secular society. While other societies have become more secular as they have modernized, Americans have instead become more fastidious about separating the premodern world of religion from the modern world of science, occupation, and politics.[57] Cuddihy labels this form of civility, which tolerates religious differences because it does not recognize them as relevant in the public sphere, a "solidarity of the surface."[58]

The "solidarity of the surface" defines the grudging respect among contending religious communities which are themselves characterized by more substantive common values and closer personal ties. The attempt to differentiate between religious and political community reveals religionists' discomfort with the world of politics. Political debate must be revived, the Charter's authors proclaimed, but "[w]ords such as *public, secular* and *religious* should be free from discriminatory bias. 'Secular purpose,' for example, should not mean 'non-religious purpose' but general public purpose."[59] Yet, politics is largely about language and the ability to define the meaning of words. As Cuddihy notes, the idea of civility in American public religion has been transformed into "the show of 'trust' we call 'good faith.'"[60] The Williamsburg Charter was filled with anxiety over the possibility that different communities might offend each other, as is the case when people try to make the best of a bad situation. This is hardly a satisfactory description of community.

Predictably, the Charter's organizers were most successful in attracting the endorsements of leaders and groups who were already satisfied with a limited yet still significant role for religion in the public sphere. Among those who signed the Charter were former Presidents Ford and Carter, Chief Justice William Rehnquist, and political figures ranging from Robert Dole to Ted Kennedy, and from Coretta Scott King to Phyllis Schlafly.[61] Representing a compromise position as it did, those furthest from the center did not participate; neither such figures of religious orthodoxy as Jerry Falwell or Pat Robertson, nor such bastions of secularism as the American Civil Liberties Union or American Humanists Association were in evidence.[62] Both "extremes" distrusted the Charter as moving the nation closer to their respective bogeymen of a naked or sacred public square. However, it was just such groups whose activities had prompted the Charter's creation.

The Williamsburg Charter and other religious organizations' activities celebrating the Constitution thus demonstrate the distinction between community and society that exists in contemporary America. Public affirmation of political norms does not necessarily imply agreement or social solidarity, but may be used to shield communal beliefs and practices from involvement in the public sphere. As Cuddihy observes, the American understanding of civility is ultimately a social fiction, because "[i]n a regime of civility, everybody doesn't love everybody. Everybody doesn't even respect everybody. Everybody 'shows respect for' everybody. Social equality, like legal equality, is 'formal,' not 'real.'"[63] When groups such as the NCCJ and the Williamsburg Charter Foundation used the Constitution's Bicentennial as an opportunity to promote racial and religious tolerance, they did not summon any heightened sense of communal solidarity—only civility. This was fitting for a legal document primarily concerned with the procedures of representative government, which requires at least a moderate degree of civility for deliberation and negotiation. Yet, it also illustrates the limits of the Constitution in serving as a source for more substantive beliefs that could unite Americans.

Intermediate Institutions as Legitimating Institutions

In contrast to the Williamsburg Charter Foundation's fragile attempt to describe a constitutional community, the constitutional tradition may be more easily expressed in liberal, voluntaristic forms of association. The type of bond found in voluntary associations is quite different from the communal identity of organizations based upon a common religious commitment or ethnic origin. Such voluntaristic forms of association often mimic democratic procedures of decision-making and incorporate into their activities procedures of self-governance used in the institutions of the larger society. Rituals involving allegiance to the state find a place in civic organizations because they affirm that the sociality and agreement which members experience in their common activities. Voluntary associations often provide Americans with a forum in which to *practice* democracy, in both senses.[64] Citizens may practice at representative democracy by electing, and being elected as, association officers, and they may use their meetings to practice democracy by participating in discussions about civic matters.

As much as voluntary associations promote democratic practices and ideals, the practice of democracy in such groups is more akin to the simulation of democratic practices and substitute for authentic self-governance. Ceremonial occasions, such as the Constitution's Bicentennial, are particularly likely to include simulations of democratic institutions and decisions. Such programs, like the adult education program sponsored by the federal Commission on the Bicentennial, served aims other than deliberation and decision-making. The slogan of the Commission's program "The Constitution . . . Let's Talk About It" carried on the theme of deliberation, while a promotional poster informed readers that "the program lets people begin again—to grasp these important principles and apply them to contemporary issues," and proclaimed that the program "is democracy in action."[65] Yet, "The Constitution . . . Let's Talk About It" was not "democracy in action," but was instead an educational program designed to promote basic literacy among adults.[66]

The opportunity for sociable exchanges on topics of political and historic interest may simulate the experience of participatory democracy and leave people feeling empowered, but it is not self-government. In his *Democracy in America*, Alexis de Tocqueville observed that, "Town meetings are to liberty what primary schools are to science; they bring it within the people's reach, they teach men how to use and how to enjoy it."[67] Tocqueville understood that direct democracy made participants better citizens, but he did not confuse education with democracy as do many advocates of small group participatory politics. Booth Fowler argues that part of the idea of community in modern America is "that direct participatory politics will increase human esteem, [this] assumes the model person is active, energetic, self-confident, articulate, public—rather like the self-image of many intellectuals."[68] Indeed, the local community has served as a model of public discussion for intellectual societies since Benjamin Franklin founded his Junto, a group of young men who discussed literature.[69] Small-scale discussion of public issues also underlay such American movements of intellectual self-development as the Lyceum movement of the early nineteenth century and the late nineteenth century Chatauqua study circles.[70]

The connection between political participation and the realization of human potential is not the particular province of liberal, constitutional regimes; the link has been made by such diverse theorists as John Stuart Mill and Karl Marx.[71] William Graebner has labeled such programs which combine features of social action, education, and ideological self-justification as "democratic social engineering." Graebner argues that the governance of such organizations as senior citizens clubs and student councils is structured so that participants can make only minor decisions with largely symbolic consequences; more important decisions are made by other institutional authorities. Participatory decision-making in such small groups may thus symbolize democratic and consensual values while depriving the group of the sovereign (or semi-sovereign) powers which are necessary for democratic decision-making. The debate and decisions of the groups confirm the basic acceptability of current arrangements without the possibility that they will challenge those arrangements.[72]

Small groups have been used as tools for gaining the cooperation of such constituencies as farmers, through university extension services, and consumers, through the Carter-era National Energy Forums.[73] William Graebner describes this process of legitimation as having two different stages:

> In the first stage, the doctrine of consent was applied to the larger entity of "society"; that is, society itself was conceptualized as the critical mechanism of order and stability. In the second stage, the locus of consent was shifted from society to the family and other small groups, social microcosms that functioned, in a way, as surrogates for the whole society.[74]

When consent is confused with education, popular sovereignty is confused with deliberation. David Boggs, writing in a monograph entitled *Adult Civic Education,* assures us that "[d]eciding and acting are forms of participation. Increasing participation in the democratic process and using such participation as a catalyst for learning are desirable outcomes of adult civic education."[75] Boggs envisions educational agencies contributing to the creation of public dialogue about local zoning changes or municipal policies, yet he never questions whether it is appropriate for such agencies to involve themselves in the political process. And, for all his interest in using public discussion to create more active citizens, Boggs loses track of a primary feature of American political institutions, that participants in public debate do not "decide and act." Even in local government (with the exception of a few small New England towns), the decisions will be made by the people's representatives.

Proponents of adult civic education through participatory democracy often appear skeptical of the idea of representation, and the constitutional tradition itself. Such a skepticism is revealed in several of the programs which have used the Constitution as a concrete connection between democratic processes of deliberation and civic education. One group, the Jefferson Foundation, has developed a program of "Jefferson Meetings" that have been held in a number of communities in recent years.[76] The Meetings' evocation of Thomas Jefferson draw upon both his interest in public education and his skepticism toward the permanence of constitutions.[77] The Meetings also evoke the Founding period through the idea that citizens were capable of fundamentally restructuring American society. As the Jefferson Foundation's executive director argued:

> Americans find themselves in a situation very much like that of Hamilton, Madison, Mason and other delegates to the 1787 convention. They must ask what values live through the Constitution, whether those values are both agreeable and effectively pursued, and whether proposed amendments would help bring about desirable change.[78]

Participants more realistically also find themselves in Jefferson's situation in 1787, when he was serving as Ambassador in Paris—far away from where fundamental decisions were being made. The Meetings were entirely without concrete consequences for the participants or the polity, as the United States has no institutional mechanism for constitutional change through direct democracy.

The Jefferson Meetings' format is itself a model of "instant community." Organizers are encouraged to use the meetings to cross organizational boundaries within their area, involving both individuals and a variety of groups in the program. After publicizing the event, the organizers select the participants, who are described in the guidelines for the Meetings as "delegates," preserving some notion of representation for the community. Delegates spend most of their time in "issues committees" where they debate such topics as the presidential election process, executive power, the length of legislative terms, judicial independence, the veto, representative versus direct democracy, and the financing of political campaigns.[79] Political issues of local concern were seemingly excluded from these essentially local assemblies in favor of consideration of the fundamental structure of the distant national government.

Such abstract questions, removed from daily politics, were the focus of other discussion programs. Programs addressed either current controversies within constitutional law, such as pornography and affirmative action, or whether the "town" should vote to "ratify" the Constitution in either its original form, its amended form, or a form modified by the group. Political discussions involving the restructuring of the constitutional system only become important when people start to take them seriously and wish to extend them beyond the basements of churches or meeting rooms in the local public library. In contrast, the federal Commission on the Bicentennial, while recognizing "Convention II," a group that ran programs where high school students deliberated over the necessity of reforming the Constitution, emphasized that the "recognition is given for the student discussion only and does not convey, and must not imply, Commission support of a real Constitutional Convention II."[80] Similarly, when discussing a mock Constitutional Convention staged with the winners of the National Bicentennial Writing Competition, Burger declared that the Commission had sponsored such a re-enactment "to ensure that no special interest group would be staging a re-enactment of the Convention."[81] The format of such meetings involved debates over the shape of the Constitution or its ratification, an agenda which served nostalgic impulses by placing participants in the Federal period, and implying that all fundamental political issues had been settled at that time.

This nostalgic impulse is also served through the symbol of the town meeting, which has served American politics as a symbol of lost community.[82] That "town meetings" may today be convened within any size of municipality—or even through the medium of national television—illustrates the power of Americans' longing for the mythical community of the past where face-to-face interaction led to consensus, and where everyone could speak and be heard. This form of small-scale democracy has been sympathetically described by Jane Mansbridge as consisting of "equal respect, face-to-face contact, common interest, and consensus" and "nothing but the natural conditions that prevail among friends."[83] However, in her study of small towns with such forms of self-governance, Mansbridge discovered that people worked things out because, short of moving from the community, they had no alternative. The capacity of town meetings to function depends upon the degree to which they are enmeshed within a closed social environment requiring consensus. Indeed, towns with a particularly high level of conflict may develop alternative mechanisms for resolving those conflicts, so that the town meeting can continue to function.[84] Because they require citizens to come to a working consensus on the practical issues over which they have power, actual town meetings bear little resemblance to forms of voluntary community which may hold citizen fora on issues such as whether the Supreme Court should strike down local anti-obscenity laws, over which they have no power and the implications of which they can easily escape.

Although they appropriated the method and form of direct democracy, the simulated town meetings sponsored during the Constitution's Bicentennial lacked the most important characteristic of actual town meetings, the ability to make binding decisions. Instead they focused on symbolic issues, such as whether the Constitution should have been ratified, or how the Bill of Rights should be interpreted by the courts. Actual town meetings are inevitably dominated by such prosaic items as the budget for road maintenance, but the decisions made have an impact on local citizens' lives. In the idealized town meetings of the Bicentennial, where citizens decided whether the Electoral College is a good thing, the idea of participation became more ceremonial in nature, and less tied to democratic decision-making and self-governance.[85] Perhaps it is this sense of sociality and decision-making that makes participants view such symbolic fora as more appealing substitutes for participation in the "real" political process by voting or working on a political campaign.

The transformation of American society from a small-scale republic to a mass democracy has been accompanied by changes in the concept of association. Rather than local deliberative bodies, intermediate associations have often become national organizations using publications, direct mail, and national programs. Voluntary associations have been transformed from what C. Wright Mills called a public, in which discussion is the predominant form of communication, into a "media market," in which the dissemination of information is the dominant form of discourse.[86] Mass marketing techniques may be used to simulate forms of voluntary community. Such was the intent behind the attempt by the Commission's private partner in corporate fundraising, the Foundation for the U.S. Constitution, to involve individual citizens by establishing a Society for the U.S. Constitution. Just as the Foundation had fallen short in its goals for corporate fundraising, the Society was also doomed to failure. Private interest in the Constitution appears to have been short-lived; membership fees declined by almost half from 1988–89 to 1989–90, and the success of the Society's magazine, Constitution, appears to have been equally limited. There was also little for members of the Society to do; the only thing that they had in common was the magazine and the souvenir items that came with membership.[87]

The state bicentennial commissions were more successful attempts to provide the celebration with a populist facade. The state commissions had three complementary purposes. First, they served as vehicles to secure state funding of bicentennial activities. However, their second function, to acknowledge the states' status as semi-sovereign political units, was of greater importance. As political subsystems, the states maintain political parties and civic organizations justifying their legitimacy, as well as state-level networks of civic, legal, and educational activists who would further spread the good word in ways that states as merely administrative regions could not.[88] Thirdly, state bicentennial commissions allowed for the development of programming bureaucracies outside of the federal government to symbolize the balance of power between Washington and the states. Such a strategy is common in federal programs which use federal funding and guidelines to encourage states to participate, allowing the national bureaucracy to expand its area of influence while keeping its own staff and size from expanding at the same rate.

Finally, the federal Commission offered programs directly to local communities. This followed from an ideological impulse to bring the celebration as close to "the people" as possible. This role was originally developed by the Commission on the Sesquicentennial of the Constitution during the New Deal.[89] Like the Sesquicentennial Commission, the Commission on the Bicentennial urged municipalities and other self-governing institutions, such as college campuses, to designate bicentennial commissions. With the addition of large scale direct-mail techniques, this provided a large network for the dissemination of materials and programs. In many ways, the Commission's work was best encapsulated in the resource guides prepared and distributed periodically to bicentennial communities, participating organizations, and interested persons. In the resource guide prepared for the final year for the celebration, the year celebrating "The Bill of Rights and Beyond," the Commission offered readers the addresses of organizations involved in the Bicentennial, lists of audio-visual materials, posters, commemorative items, music, plays, educational materials, and a bibliography of books about the Constitution and Bill of Rights. The guide suggested how individuals or organizations could create their own celebration or exhibition, and even included clip art figures for use in flyers or pamphlets.[90]

If the Constitution's Bicentennial was an attempt to overcome the alienation of popular sovereignty, the programs sponsored by local communities and private organizations played an important symbolic function of returning the celebration to the people. While civic commemorations may seem to be a natural element of community life, the use of local ceremonies to legitimate larger polities is particular to modern nation-states.[91] Such local celebrations are, however, not entirely local in origins, but have been encouraged by the federal government during twentieth century commemorations, beginning as early as the bicentennial of George Washington's birth in 1932, and culminating in the success of the American Revolution Bicentennial in 1976. Local celebrations were a major component of the Constitution's Bicentennial. The Commission hoped to emphasize the popular roots of the American system of governance, and to demonstrate that national institutions are still rooted in the popular will. The involvement of civic associations and local communities helped to further equate the Constitution with the other institutions that mediate American political relationships. Unlike advertising or popular media, and to a greater degree than commerce and education, images of face-to-face community and voluntary association have a continuing mythological appeal within American political culture. Local celebrations and involvement by voluntary associations joined both the medium and message of citizen participation to represent community support for the Constitution.

Within democratic theory, participation is not important as an educational aid or because it contributes to the realization of human potential, but because participatory government provides citizens with a direct voice in affairs that affect them. Participation in voluntary associations cannot be equated with participatory government because such associations lack the principal attribute of government, power. As Robert Bellah argues, the substitution of voluntary association for more formal methods of mediation makes participatory politics in America "discontinuous, oriented to single issues, opportunistic, and therefore easily coopted, local, and anti-institutional."[92] Bellah observes that such an orientation is self-defeating for those who believe that local, grass roots movements can empower people and reconstruct democracy because such local groups cannot contest the power of large-scale institutions without themselves building "counterinstitutions."[93] As Robert Dahl and Edward Tufte make the argument, a citizen may have "more opportunity . . . to participate effectively in decisions" in small democracies. However, in larger democracies citizens

are provided with methods "to participate . . . in the decisions of a political system large enough to control all or most
of the major aspects of their situation that can be controlled."[94] Americans' proclivities for the processes and symbols of small-scale democracy may imperil their ability to
benefit from the power of a central government—even the
limited forms of federal power created through the Constitution. As the institutions with real power over people's lives
become more distant, symbolic participation may replace
participatory decision-making and provide citizens with a
feeling of self-governance. Such fora simulate participatory,
"town meeting" democracy in the same sense that Disney-
land simulates an American small town. They are more con-
vincingly democratic than the "real thing."

Symbolic Community and Popular Sovereignty

Many of the participatory activities organized as part
of the Constitution's Bicentennial were more symbolic of a
general ethic of community than a specific commitment to
the principles of the U.S. Constitution. Indeed, a number of
the community projects endorsed by the Commission on
the Bicentennial had little to do with the Constitution or
simply used a constitutional theme in a manner that made
little difference in the activity being sponsored. The Bicentennial cookbook sponsored by the National Grange was
one such project that lacked a clear commitment to constitutionalism, as was the "Appalachian Regional Commission Quilt Competition" that used a constitutional theme
in its contest to "foster awareness, knowledge, and appreciation of the United States Constitution."[95] But such activities were thoroughly appropriate in the eyes of the
Commission if they brought the Constitution into daily life
and American culture because they brought communities
together. The "Living Legacy" project, which encouraged
the planting of "Constitution Gardens" to commemorate
the Bicentennial, involved individuals, voluntary associa-

tions, and municipal governments as active participants in the national celebration. The national organizations which cosponsored the "Living Legacy" program with the Commission had little specific connection to constitutionalism, or related activities as political action or civic commemoration, but largely consisted of gardening groups and groups serving elderly and disabled individuals. Although flora has nothing *per se* to do with the Constitution, the Living Legacy project provided ordinary Americans with a way to express their personal connection to the "living Constitution."[96] However, simply through their association with other members of their organization, members of such groups are more likely than unaffiliated citizens to engage in both community activities and political discussion.[97]

While the Living Legacy program suited those participating organizations which were looking for a low-cost, preplanned activity to offer to members, the program was a way for the Commission to publicize the Bicentennial, and to portray the celebration as a grass roots affair. Multiplying the sheer number and variety of events encouraged participation from those who might be apolitical or not particularly interested in community affairs. A representative political system has as one of its advantages that people have other things to do besides participate in public affairs. By transforming gardening or other hobbies into commemorative events, the Commission and its associated groups were able to transform what were otherwise private activities into public events. Such events provided them with more visible successes, but it also took advantage of an insight as old as Aristotle, that humans are essentially social creatures.[98] An important element of American citizenship is the collective identity which the Constitution has helped to create.[99]

Collective identities define personal identities in terms of larger social relations. In contrast to other forms of social mediation, small groups have been associated with immediacy and deliberation among equal parties. Thus, while modern communications have solved some of the logistical problems of popular deliberation, we still retain the language of small-scale society in reporting "public discussion" and referring to citizens' "voice" or ideological "debates," and "describ[ing] a politician as 'taking his case to the people.'"[100] In recent years, such phenomena as the "electronic town meeting" have been used by political candidates to symbolically erase the social distance between themselves and "the people." While political candidates and organizations have used such mediated "face-to-face" encounters have become part of mass politics, small associations still make a particular contribution to the process of legitimation because they provide attractive opportunities for individuals to perform their roles as active citizens. Tocqueville declared that democracies create a different type of loyalty from that of monarchies or aristocracies because "[t]he reflecting patriotism of a republic" does not come from citizens' familiarity and comfort with one's history and surroundings, but results from citizens' involvement in creating the institutions, laws, and customs of the country.[101] Patriotism reflects citizens' pride in themselves as those who built it and have maintained the nation.[102]

Patriotism and democracy reinforce each other, for self-imposed laws are better than those imposed by others.[103] As George Fletcher expresses it, "In acting loyally, the self acts in harmony with its personal history. One recognizes who one is."[104] Affirmation of social and political principles as one's own makes them part of oneself; affirming such principles as part of a group is an important step in creating a collective identity. These acts of self-recognition may occur in the voting booth or it may come through participation in civic commemorations or other rituals. Many new citizens find the act of naturalization an emotional experience, and take great pride in their knowledge of, and fidelity to, the principles of constitutionalism.[105] Experiences in which one finds oneself in accord with the community build patriotic loyalty and a bond that is constitutive of citizenship.

The idea of consent is so strong in American political culture that Americans often choose their own forms of community.[106] Americans' preference for voluntary forms of community reflects their view of themselves as autonomous political beings capable of separating ourselves from our immediate surroundings—a view which is radically incompatible with a rich sense of civic history. If consent based on "natural reason," rather than our embeddedness in the particular history, that historical self is particularly weak. However, if citizens cannot help but consent to those political obligations because they share a common identity, then the theory of consent is a false front which disguises the multiplicity of identities by emphasizing a few common political principles over fundamental disagreements about the meaning of many other principles. As Don Herzog argues, "Talk of consent allows us to sidestep evaluation of the substantive merits of people's choices . . . A society as pluralist as ours isn't about to agree on the merits of a host of unconventional life plans. But we can agree that people have voluntarily chosen them."[107] Community, in the more voluntaristic forms in the United States, symbolizes normative agreement among fellow citizens only to extent that the Constitution's ratification symbolized agreement in the state conventions in 1787 and 1788 while often discussing very different documents. For, even if Americans view the Constitution as a symbol of the deliberation, decision, and consensus of two hundred years ago, it was not, and our capacity to agree today is no greater.

CHAPTER SIX

The Constitution in Educational Policy

In a 1987 hearing before a Senate Committee, former Chief Justice Warren Burger worried aloud that, according to a national survey, students "could not tell the difference between the Declaration of Independence and the Constitution," and found it even more "appalling" that many students believed that Karl Marx's phrase, "from each according to his talents and abilities, and to each according to his needs," was part of the Constitution.[1] Burger was seemingly as alarmed about students' familiarity with Marx as he was concerned with their lack of familiarity with the Constitution; such confusion was as dangerous as simple ignorance. As a response to this crisis in American public life, Burger called for the Constitution's Bicentennial to serve as "a history and civics lesson for all of us."[2] Such calls for improved civic education are an abiding characteristic of American political rhetoric. Yet they seem remarkably fruitless. As another concerned witness had remarked before yet another Senate committee, although "virtually every State in the Nation mandates the study of American history and civics . . . recent studies have documented that the public has only a feeble understanding of their heritage and only a feeble understanding of what the Constitution is about."[3]

Jeremiads decrying public ignorance of the Constitution have long been a staple of American politics. Michael

Kammen's *A Machine That Would Go of Itself,* a cultural history of American constitutionalism, is largely a chronicle of perceived public ignorance in American constitutional discourse, and was written as a inquiry into "the consequences of our curious blend of reverence and ignorance" of the Constitution.[4] Elites have called for programs of improved civic education to combat such varied ills as the disunion of the Civil War and poor hygiene. Professional associations, such as the American Political Science Association and the American Historical Association, began to take an interest in civic education at the turn of the twentieth century, and battles between social scientists and historians over the content of civic education were integral to the politics of Progressive Era education. During the 1920s, conservative political groups promoted the Constitution as a bulwark against Bolshevism and the influence of recent immigrants, often doing so through the legislation of requirements that public schools teach students about the Constitution.[5] In one example of such a plea, the Better American Federation called for the requirement that "every school and college student in American not only learn the *Preamble* to the Constitution so that they could repeat verbatim at any time or any place, but . . . know its *meaning* so well that when they repeat it they would recall the entire philosophy of the American government."[6]

Such concern about public knowledge of the Constitution assumes that citizens must understand the document for the American political system to function properly. While treated as a simple truth, it is not clear that individuals must understand the Constitution to be good citizens. Indeed, this assumption is ironic because the Constitution is the legal mechanism by which Americans have transferred their sovereign powers to a representative government, thereby making public knowledge of its contents less important than public knowledge of the political system in a pure democracy. A further irony lies in the way in which elite alarm over public ignorance about the Constitution differs from concern over ignorance of other facets of the political system that might have an effect on the daily lives of citizens: the structure of the Federal Reserve Board, the rule-making procedures of administrative agencies, or even the names of their elected representatives. While expecting citizens to understand the administrative rule-making process, which affects their everyday lives in important ways, might seem unrealistic and unnecessarily demanding, elites regularly appear shocked that citizens are less than knowledgeable about the Constitution and its complicated provisions. What requires explanation is not public ignorance about the Constitution, but why elites expect citizens to know anything about it.

The answer to this question is largely found in the way in which elite calls for increased attention to civic education, and the rhetoric of educational crisis, depend on the myth of a "golden age" of energetic civic participation when the citizenry shared an enthusiasm for governance and the nation's history. The idea that there was ever a period when every American was knowledgeable about the nation's history and government is simply wrong. In 1943, in the midst of the patriotism that accompanied World War II, only sixteen percent of college students could identify Thomas Jefferson, whose birth two hundred years before was being celebrated; more than twice as many of the young scholars believed that Jefferson had discovered electricity.[7] The study prompted the education editor of *The New York Times* to exclaim that there was a need for "a rebirth in the teaching of American history and Americanism."[8] A 1942 study of students' knowledge of American history turned in similarly poor results; when the survey was revived in 1976, the results were roughly the same.[9]

While Warren Burger was declaring that the most recent national study of student knowledge of civics, history, and social studies had shown "an alarming trend toward constitutional illiteracy in the 1980s,"[10] the report showed no significant decline. In fact, students from disadvantaged backgrounds and middle school students actually had significantly improved scores.[11] Nor was the perception of a crisis in education particularly widespread, public opinion polls conducted in 1987 found that more people believed that the schools and student achievement had improved than believed that it had declined; this belief in improving public education was strongest among parents of children in the public schools.[12] And a 1985 survey of attitudes about public education showed that parents became more positive in their responses when asked about their own community's schools and most positive when asked about their children's school.[13]

Criticism of American public schools, especially the announcement of crises in civic education, has two major sources. The first is publication of statistics demonstrating student ignorance without historical perspective on previous levels of knowledge. This leads to a presumption of educational decline which may occur casually, such as when, during a congressional hearing, Warren Burger asserted that although he "was not able to check the facts," he believed that "the rate of literacy was higher in 1787 than it is today."[14] Burger's assertion that the rate of literacy was higher in federalist America than contemporary America, even if restricted to white males, as women and African-Americans were much less likely to be literate, was wildly wrong; all historical evidence points to the conclusion that literacy rates are dramatically higher in contemporary America than in any previous period.[15] Indeed, recent national studies show that only five percent of Americans between the ages of 18 and 24 are functionally illiterate.[16] Such jeremiads are not unique to the United States; in recent years, public schools in virtually every Western industrialized country have been "under a concerted attack to justify themselves in terms of mythical values of 'excellence' that they are accused of no longer conveying."[17] The assumption that literacy was once the norm, and that illiteracy is a novel condition, recurs in the rhetoric of educational crises.

The second reason for the announcement of educational crises derives from an elite concern about citizen alienation from political institutions and the perception of social crises, which are translated into educational crises. When a "National Task Force on Citizenship Education" reported in

1977 that it had found "that the nation's young people have scant knowledge about the responsibilities of citizenship or how to become involved in government," the Task Force's "concerns" regarding citizenship education extended far beyond the realm of education:

> the erosion of the values and attitudes of young people, the serious and continuing pressures on family life, the rising rate of juvenile crime and the increasing violence of crimes committed by teenagers, and the general alienation of people from their institutions.[18]

The declaration of educational crises substitutes for the announcement of other social crises, and the schools' shortcomings become symbolic of the "erosion of shared political values in American society" and citizens' lack of "a commitment to participate in the making of political decisions."[19] Statistics illustrating student ignorance of the political system are equated with a lack of concern about politics and an unwillingness to abide by the law. However, such causation is hardly self-evident.[20] Many individuals drive cars without the slightest understanding of an internal combustion engine.

The educational system is held responsible for bad citizenship not because of its own failures, but because it is a possible solution. As Joseph Gusfield argues, the perception of public problems in America is often constructed so that the public institution perceived to be capable of solving that problem becomes "responsible" for that problem, regardless of whether it had any role in creating it.[21] Gusfield's argument is well-illustrated by the way in which public education has become the scapegoat for many of society's ills, while also being viewed as the cure for far more. The public school has become the social agency of first resort because, as John Dewey wrote, it has "a steadying and integrating office" through which it helps students to understand their roles in a complex, modern society.[22] This function has become ever more important as society has become more complex and diverse, and one would be fairly amazed if any set of institutions could succeed at what has been asked of the public schools. Over the past fifty years, the traditional subjects gathered under the rubric of "civic education"—history, geography, and government—have been joined by such approaches as law-related, consumer, economic, global, environmental, gun safety, and free enterprise education. Additional courses teach "adolescent behavior and psychology, marriage and family problems, vocational interests, and personal values" as part of "citizenship education"—further demonstrating that "civic education" has lost any sense of definition, except as a potential solution to a social problem.[23] Indeed, as James Banner writes, "Civic education threatens to become . . . the vessel which bears all of our expectations and that, bearing them, shatters."[24]

Criticism of schools provides a vehicle for social criticism that focuses on aggregates of individuals rather than the social structure. According to Richard Pratte, the central assumption behind civic education "is that one improves society by improving citizens and not vice versa."[25] Civic education poses no particular challenge to existing political or economic arrangements, because its proponents assume that governmental and economic institutions are largely successful, while asserting that it is the schools' fault if students are apathetic or ignorant. Where a social critic might find student alienation a rational response to a lack of opportunities for economic success or political reform, the diviner of educational crises sees a failure to teach students to appreciate the political system. The American tendency to attribute success or failure to individuals suggests that "society . . . is benign; no doubt it has problems, but it is basically sound."[26] The enterprise of civic education, and constitutional education in particular, implies that it is the citizens, not the political system, that have to be remade.

The Function of Civic Education

While he portrayed the entire Bicentennial of the Constitution as a "civics and history lesson," Warren Burger had a special emotional attachment to one particular lesson, the "National Historical-Pictorial Map Contest," in which students drew maps noting the history of the Federal period. When Burger spoke about the map contest, he sometimes reminisced about the prizewinning map of England he had drawn in Ms. Edna Moore's high school class in St. Paul, Minnesota. Recalling how drawing the map had "embedded" the events and geography of English history in his mind, Burger spoke of how such maps helped students to remember dates and events by providing them with a setting.[27] The map contest also had an important ideological objective: reviving the old civics curriculum that had stressed the combination of geography and history, two subjects which Burger thought inseparable. In further support of the program, Burger argued that teachers "have recognized that teaching social science in a broad way, with no specific focus on either history or geography, is not the way to do it."[28]

For Burger, the "National Historical-Pictorial Map Contest" was more than a test of students' knowledge of historical geography or a nostalgic recollection of his youth, it was a critique of many twentieth century theories of civics education. While progressive educators, such as John Dewey, had also proposed that history be combined with geography, they saw the study of geography as being something close to what is today labeled "ecology." Dewey and other progressives strongly opposed the predominance of political history, calling for the increased teaching of intellectual, social, economic, and natural history in the schools.[29] Contrasted with Dewey's ecological approach, Burger's emphasis on history and geography was rooted in a nineteenth century conception of civic education which taught students that civic duties were moral obligations, and treated the Constitution as a sacred object unaffected by ordinary politics.[30] Nineteenth century textbooks often described the Constitution as the crowning achievement of human endeavor, and the word "Constitution" was "usually preceded by the epithet 'our glorious.'"[31] Many of these textbooks' treatments of the Constitution were inadequate, mystifying, or simply wrong.[32] In early texts, the governmental structure was treated as essentially static and the "[g]rowth of the Constitution by statute, judicial decision, and usage was largely ignored"[33]; school textbooks only began to discuss the actual structure of governmental agencies or political parties in the twentieth century.[34]

The progressive educators of the 1890s through 1930s replaced the Constitution and history with "social studies" as the organizing framework for civic education, and such classes as "social problems" and "problems in democracy" asked students to take a more policy-oriented approach to government. Educators using the "new social studies" presented students with a vision of America that lacked a unified tradition, emphasizing "social problems" which required students to view society in terms of controversy instead of consensus.[35] But, while the Progressive call for relevance asked students to pay more attention to politics and policy, it also shifted attention from actors and institutions at the national level to the local level,[36] arguing that "[c]ivics should concern itself less with constitutional questions and remote governmental functions and should direct attention to social agencies close at hand and to the informal activities of daily life that regard and seek the common good."[37] Progressive theories of education were compatible with the expanded use of social science and the "new social history" in the 1960s, which replaced political history with the study of "women, blacks, workers, ethnic groups, and so forth."[38] The progressive concept of civic education focused on citizens' understanding of their fellows and daily politics, and was less concerned with the values underlying the constitutional system and national identity.

Such approaches favor a progressive political agenda, while conservatives have been more interested in cultivating positive student attitudes toward the existing institutional order. As John J. Patrick has argued, "In American schools, there has been tension between those who would view political education of the masses as primarily socialization to the status quo, and those who would try to teach as many youngsters as possible to think for themselves."[39] Conservative criticism of the progressive approach is well-illustrated in a report issued by the National Endowment for the Humanities that argued that America's "cultural memory" is declining and that "the culprit is 'process'—the belief that we can teach our children *how* to think without troubling them to learn anything worth thinking about."[40] A return to specific texts, such as the Constitution, follows from such an approach.

The conservative account of civic education assumes that there is a single set of things worth knowing, while progressive theories of civic education have preferred process over content in part because of its belief that civic education is a symbol of a community's values, which are not easily defined. However, process-based approaches may also be profoundly conservative. Adopting a substantive definition of civic literacy may become politically dangerous when there is no well-defined consensus, and most administrators and teachers have adopted strategies that are designed to minimize public outrage. Attempting to insulate education from what they see as political distractions, education professionals are likely to teach history instead of contemporary politics, adopt a curriculum that is more symbolic of citizenship or political involvement than practical and participatory, and advocate vague guidelines allowing local administrators enough latitude to accommodate local sensitivities.[41] While parents and the public rate the teaching of citizenship as less important than the teaching of skills needed to succeed in the job market, they are quite concerned with the content of civic education. As Richard Pratte phrases it, "The community has never had much use for civic education *per se;* it is interested in the control of civic education, not the phenomenon itself."[42]

Civic education is as much about reassuring elites and parents that the future generation has been properly socialized as educating future citizens. This explains why a politically illiterate public supports patriotic displays, like the Pledge of Allegiance, in the schools and requires that schools teach students about the Constitution without monitoring such efforts. Civic education is a largely symbolic set of policies whose purpose is to reassure citizens that their concerns are being taken seriously, even if there is little that the state can do to solve the problem. Civic education thus partakes of much of the same dynamic which guaranteed that, even in such periods of widespread lawlessness such as Prohibition, citizens would continue "to support the passage of laws to eradicate behavior which appears to be ineradicable" because such legislation was not simply about ending the behavior but also assured citizens that political authority lay behind their own moral consensus.[43]

Although public school curricula are often controversial, the Constitution is not. Most states mandate that the Constitution be taught in the schools. However, students may not learn much about the Constitution because, while its study is often mandated, there is little enforcement by state authorities. When Henry Arnold Bennett surveyed the teaching of the Constitution during the early 1930s, he found that, although forty-three states then had statutes in effect requiring the teaching of the Constitution, "very few" state educational bureaucracies had effectively pursued the statutes' "purpose of elevating the Constitution to a place in the curricula essentially coordinate with the conventional social sciences."[44] The situation was little different in 1979 when the American Bar Association reported that forty-five states required the teaching of the Constitution in public schools, but that sanctions were applied only if no course was offered, and there was little monitoring of courses' content.[45] Bennett's conclusion, that state laws requiring instruction about the Constitution were ineffective because classroom teachers had not been properly "convinced of the desirability of developing a new attitude towards the Constitution,"[46] poses the question of what would renew interest in using the Constitution in classroom instruction.

The opportunities for national reform of civic education are quite limited. Although the national government has financed local educational efforts since before the Constitution was ratified,[47] national educational policy is improbable because it involves so many different actors. The federal government, states, and local school boards all make educational policy, and at the federal level, educational programs are administered by such disparate agencies as the National Endowment for the Humanities and the Law Enforcement Assistance Agency, in addition to the Department of Education. At the same time, school administrators, researchers, teachers' unions, corporations and foundations have their own policy agendas, the publishers of textbooks, curricula, and testing materials play important roles in determining the content of lessons,[48] and local school boards, in all their variety, remain the ultimate institutional decision-makers.[49]

Ultimately, those dedicated to raising the profile of constitutionalism in the schools must convince teachers of the Constitution's importance and make them comfortable with the subject. Retraining teachers is essential to the success of any reform of civics curriculum because teachers may hesitate to adopt new approaches and thus effectively "veto" new curricula.[50] Moreover, retraining teachers may be seen as part of the work of repairing the past mistakes made by the educational system. Warren Burger advocated such retraining as part of his reaction against progressive theories of education.[51] So that teachers would continue to focus more heavily on the Constitution in civic education after the Bicentennial, Congress created a federal agency, the James Madison Memorial Fellowship Foundation, to fund graduate study of the history of the Constitution for high school civics teachers. While conceived as a foundation in which federal dollars would match private contributions, the Madison Fellowships were funded almost entirely through taxpayer dollars because of the lack of demonstrable public support in the form of private donations.[52]

The lack of a national school system or educational policy means that educators who wish to increase the attention paid to the Constitution in American classrooms must effectively flood the market with curricula and materials for teaching constitutionalism. During the Bicentennial, for example, the federal Commission overwhelmed both teachers and students with programs and materials in an attempt to convince them that the Constitution was important and interesting. The campaign more closely resembled advertising than a well-conceived theory of instruction. The most important programs were those which would garner positive publicity for the use of the Constitution in civic education programs, and particularly such educational programs that would emphasize affective ties to the Constitution, dramatizing the commitment of the larger community to the Constitution and its values.

Visible Constitutionalism

While the hard work of teaching and learning takes place behind classroom walls, the perpetuation of constitutional norms can also be publically staged through visible manifestations of civic education that symbolize devotion to the document as much as they encourage learning about it. Mandating the teaching of the Constitution with little effective monitoring of local programs or commitment of resources illustrates the process of symbolic politics, by which elites adopt policies that visibly commit the state to improving some element of civic life without acting to ensure that such an improvement takes place.[53] Such mandates are less of a public presence than the contests and reenactments of historical events, essay contests, dramatic presentations, and other public programs that have been regular features of American political culture since the early part of this century.[54] Such competitions and displays provide both opportunities for their sponsors to display their commitment to the socialization of the young, and occasions in which youth and others can demonstrate their ability and desire to participate in the common culture.

During civic commemorations, visible educational programs, such as essay contests, may become so popular that their sheer number can confuse school administrators and compete for support.[55] Just as importantly, such programs create winners who visibly symbolize the achievements of the educational system and whose personal success stories attest to the effectiveness of government agencies and civic organizations in improving the next generation's citizenship skills. American schooling may thus be simultaneously criticized for its failure at an institutional level, while earning praise for the achievements of individuals. Such a focus on individual achievement concurrent with the criticism of educational institutions leads to an ironic depiction of citizenship as a virtue that is more personal than social in its origins.[56]

During civic celebrations, examples of visible citizenship allow a vast number of organizations to share in displays of their civic leadership in educating the next generation. The Constitution's Bicentennial included many similar competitions. One essay contest for elementary school students sponsored by the U.S. Department of Education was publicized through the *Weekly Reader*, and the first set of selections was made by state educational agencies and the Council for American Private Education. The winning essays about the meaning of the Constitution were then printed in a booklet, *The Constitution's Children*, published by the Department, and the winning authors met President Reagan in a Rose Garden ceremony, providing all the participating organizations a high profile event to publicize.[57] Other organizations, including the Associations of American Chambers of Commerce in both Latin America and Japan, the Daughters of the American Revolution, and American Legion sponsored essay contests for schoolchildren,[58] and a contest for law students was sponsored by the West Publishing Company.[59]

The most expensive and complex of all of the essay contests during the Constitution's Bicentennial also involved the most public and extended possibilities for credit-claiming and spotlight sharing. The National Bicentennial Writing Competition cost an estimated $2 million and was cosponsored by the Commission on the Bicentennial and *USA Today*. Expenses included trips for the fifty-two state-level winners and their advisers to Washington, D.C. to be congratulated by President Reagan, a reenactment of the Constitutional Convention in Williamsburg, Virginia, and generous cash prizes.[60] The national winners also traveled to New York to appear on the "Good Morning, America" and "Today" television shows.[61] By showing off the young citizens in a variety of settings, and by showing them participating in the deliberative process through the reenactment of the Constitutional Convention in Williamsburg, the sponsors were able to present the image of a politically active generation willing to continue the work of the Framers.

Reenactments of the Constitutional Convention and ratification conventions were particularly popular during the Constitution's Bicentennial as ways to demonstrate that the current generation was politically engaged in a constructive fashion. Massachusetts students participated in a mock version of their state's ratification debate funded by the federal Commission, as did students in Delaware and Nevada.[62] The Jefferson Foundation promoted its "Jefferson Meetings," in which "delegates" debated the current desirability of features of the Constitution, as an appropriate classroom exercise.[63] Such programs were a way to simulate student involvement in the community without actual community involvement. Another program during the Constitution's Bicentennial designed to show how students could apply constitutional norms to the larger society was sponsored by the Polaroid Corporation, which donated cameras decorated with the bicentennial logo to public and private schools, where they were to be used by students "to photograph objects or scenes that represent the Constitution, freedom of the press, freedom of religion, freedom of speech, etc."[64]

However, the most visible single program organized by the federal Commission on the Bicentennial, in conjunction with private organizations, was the "Celebration of Citizenship" held in Washington, D.C. on September 16, 1987. Celebration of Citizenship was a joint project of the Commission and the American Newspaper Publishers Foundation (ANPA), which originated the idea as a "universal pledge of allegiance," a title which more closely mirrored the program's message of uncritical loyalty.[65] Indeed, Celebration of Citizenship reflected the different agendas and interests of many different organizations with an interest in a widely visible demonstration of support for the Constitution. Before the Commission and the ANPA were finished, Celebration of Citizenship was a national event broadcast with donated time on ABC and sponsored by Xerox and RJR Nabisco.[66]

Warren Burger promoted the day as a "national teach-in" about the Constitution, appropriating a term from the counterculture of the 1960s to signal that schools should not conduct business as usual, while the *Washington Post* described Celebration of Citizenship as "[p]art civics lesson, part pep rally and part patriotic talent show."[67] The program contained standard patriotic elements, such as the performance by the U.S. Army Band of the "Star-Spangled Banner" and "America the Beautiful," intermixed with educational moments that focused on the goals of the Constitution, and made no mention of the development of constitutional doctrine beyond the Constitutional Convention.[68] Warren Burger painted a picture of a country disunited under the Articles of Confederation, and then read the Preamble. Senate Majority Leader Robert Byrd spoke, characteristically perhaps, about how the Constitution was the result of a series of legislative compromises that smoothed over the differences between the large and small states, and Speaker of the House Jim Wright, who would soon be forced to resign from his post because of scandal, prophetically told students that "Nobody here is above the law. Most of all, those who govern us have a duty to respect it." Chief Justice William Rehnquist weighed in with a lesson about the checks and balances embodied within the Constitution. While the President, Congress, and the Supreme Court were all physically present for the Celebration of Citizenship, their representatives' merely explained their functions within the constitutional framework with little commentary about the day-to-day political process.

The program's purpose of providing a visual model for citizenship culminated with the introduction of President

Reagan by two students. One was the winner of the 1987 National Spelling Bee, the other was an honor student from Washington, D.C. who had auditioned for the occasion.[69] Viewers were invited to join President Reagan in the recitation of the Pledge of Allegiance. This simultaneous affirmation of national unity was at the heart of the program,[70] but was also quite ironic. Although the federal Commission on the Bicentennial was running advertisements with the message "The President Doesn't Take an Oath to Defend the American Flag or the Statue of Liberty," its centerpiece program culminated in the president leading the nation in a Pledge of Allegiance "to the flag." The content of Celebration of Citizenship was less oriented toward the Constitution than students' membership within civil society. Host Ted Koppel assured viewers that "the ceremony here today wasn't meant to be a birthday party," but rather was "an invitation to all of us to get involved." Koppel's cohost, Floretta McKenzie, Superintendent of Schools for the District of Columbia, told students how they could become better citizens: "Get involved. Volunteer. The people who wrote the Constitution did, and look at what they accomplished."[71] This "national reaffirmation of the Constitution" thus conflated constitutionalism with voluntarism and private action. The Framers, remade as apolitical "volunteers," provided a model for citizenship that privileged voluntary private action, not engaged political activism.

Citizenship education may also be made visible in ways that would warm the heart of any federal bureaucrat. Making civic education part of the federal educational policy has subjected civic education programs to the same bureaucratic imperatives faced by programs in other policy areas, including the necessity of demonstrating the value of the program to congressional representatives and quantitative program evaluations. The largest and best funded program designed to respond to the "crisis" in civic education, the National Bicentennial Competition, was designed to cater to just those political necessities. Administered by the Center for Civic Education (CCE), which employed a professional lobbying firm and maintained a governmental relations office in Washington, the National Bicentennial Competition was as much designed to maintain political support as to teach students about the Constitution. The director of CCE spent so much time lobbying in Washington for support that Warren Burger commented he "is virtually almost a member of the Commission. We work that closely."[72] Unlike most programs created during the Constitution's Bicentennial, the National Bicentennial Competition promises to live well into the future.[73]

The National Bicentennial Competition was seemingly designed to ensure congressional support. After using CCE's *We the People* series of textbooks to learn about the Constitution, high school students could elect to compete. Students first took multiple choice examinations; afterwards, members of each competing classroom participated as "witnesses" in a simulated congressional hearing, presenting prepared statements and being questioned by judges, attorneys, and community leaders. Involving community leaders, especially congressional representatives, resulted in positive publicity, and community leaders generally received a positive impression of both the school and the program from their experience of working with motivated students.[74] The competition was also structured to produce a winner within each congressional district, ensuring that every member of Congress would have the opportunity to take credit for this educational opportunity and congratulate his or her civically-minded young constituents.[75] Winners at the state level could expect similar treatment from Senators, and traveled to Washington to compete in the national finals. District coordinators also traveled to Washington, and were encouraged to meet with congressional representatives, provide their representatives with appropriate inserts for the *Congressional Record*, and publicize their meeting through photographs and press releases.[76] In the ultimate session of the national finals, members of the Senate Committee on the Judiciary questioned the contestants; the winners traveled to White House to receive their awards.[77]

The National Bicentennial Competition's role as a high-visibility program by which Congress, the Administration, and the federal Commission on the Bicentennial could address the problem of constitutional illiteracy makes it a textbook example of symbolic politics, in which programs are chosen for their ability to deliver the message that something is being done to solve a particular problem.[78] Pictures of local winners could be used to demonstrate the program's value to local residents—the students embodying the contemporary equivalent of civic virtue, perfectly illustrating Sheldon Wolin's observation that "[m]eritocracy is republican elitism in the age of the Educational Testing Service."[79] Moreover, these symbolic results could be delivered at relatively low cost. Instead of investing enough money to underwrite the entire national program, the federal money put into education was to play "a catalytic role" in creating a program that could then be sold to the participating states or school districts.[80] It was doubly important that the program show results in order to sell its books, materials, and program services to educational bureaucracies across the country.[81]

As part of CCE's documentation of the program's effectiveness, the results of competitors' test scores were compared against those of college students who took the same test. Such results help to justify continued public funding, as CCE could use these results to demonstrate that its programs yielded tangible benefits.[82] One study commissioned by CCE found that those students who had used the curriculum outperformed students who had not on the multiple choice test used in the National Bicentennial Competition, and that even "students at a major west coast urban university" did not score as well on the test as participating high school students.[83] On their own terms, the "We the People" curriculum and the National Bicentennial Competition were quite effective. Yet, those terms may be the problem. As a program that combined instruction and testing, the National Bicentennial Competition was particularly open to the criticism that it encouraged "teaching to the test," especially given its emphasis on measurable achievement. This criticism has particular resonance in the case of the Competition because the test asked students questions in language similar to that used in the text.[84]

Perhaps the best measurement of the way in which visible constitutionalism may dominate civic education was delivered in the form of an unscientific survey of teachers conducted during the Bicentennial.[85] When asked about the programs with which they were most familiar, elementary and middle school teachers mentioned the National Historical-Pictorial Map Contest, while the National Bicentennial Competition had the greatest awareness among secondary school teachers. The emphasis on contests may indicate that exercises which created clear winners and opportunities for communicating the successes of the educational system in teaching about the political system were particularly likely to be adopted. Yet, while the National Historical-Pictorial Map Contest had the greatest awareness at the primary grade levels and the highest rate of usage among those who were familiar with it, it had the lowest rating for its "perceived usefulness . . . in helping students learn about the Constitution." The National Bicentennial Competition had a far better rating for its usefulness in teaching,[86] however, its popularity may have been affected by CCE's extensive publicity on its behalf. And, ultimately, both programs were as much about symbolizing the capacity of individual students to appreciate the American past as about developing their abilities to be active or critical citizens.

The Constitution as a Symbol in Civic Education

During the "Celebration of Citizenship" broadcast from the Capitol, Senate Majority Leader Robert Byrd told students across the nation that the Constitution was the result of "a compromise. Power would be divided and shared." Continuing his theme, Senator Byrd declared that "Even the Congress is divided . . . It is a compromise that

works. This is what we do in the Congress. We compromise. We look for positive solutions that work for all Americans."[87] In his brief civics lesson, Senator Byrd expressed
a more sophisticated view of constitutional dynamics than
most textbooks, viewing the political structure established
through the Constitution as one of compromise and shared
powers in addition to the familiar "separation of powers"
and "checks and balances" to which he also paid tribute.

Traditional instruction about the Constitution still suf-
fers because governmental institutions and the formal legislative process have been emphasized to the exclusion of
descriptions of the actual politics of interests and influence.[88] As Bernard Crick has argued, teaching constitutionalism without teaching about contemporary politics or
policy is much like teaching language by introducing gram-
mar first, and only later adding substantive content.[89] If
American schools have abandoned the nineteenth century
glorification of the Constitution, they have replaced ha-
giographies of the Framers with a mechanistic understanding of the Constitution as a Newtonian system whose three
separate branches and checks and balances keep it running
in place.[90] Analysts of recent texts have found that a preference for depicting governmental institutions as static leads
to bad history and bad political science. Thus textbooks have
ignored developments in federalism since the Civil War,[91]
and have depicted the separation of powers as resulting in
a system in which the three branches are distinct and self-
contained, with little allowance for the way that power may
shift between them.[92]

Reflecting their own prejudices, analysts of secondary
school textbooks have found that the texts either privilege
political science or history. While one analyst of high school
civics textbooks found them to explain the creation of the
separation of powers as both simple and inevitable,[93] an analyst of high school history texts found them to describe the
creation of the document without mentioning the political
philosophy of the time, "to the point where the final document appears merely a product of interest-group compro-

mises, a masterpiece of political tinkering."[94] These differing accounts result from the way in which political science and history divide up the territory of civics into two distinct disciplines. Because government courses examine the Constitution in order to understand contemporary political institutions, the principles behind institutional agreement and conflict are emphasized, while history textbooks, just as naturally, focus on the historical motives and tactics of particular individuals.

Poor textbooks and a fear of controversy by educational administrators also pose problems for teaching politics in the schools. Yet, the amorphous nature of a constitutional system remains a far greater problem than the deficiencies of the educational system. Research on youth attitudes toward democracy has shown that students tend to conflate the notion of democracy with its practice in the United States, and "associate [democracy] primarily with the exercise of their personal freedoms and secondarily with representative government."[95] While such findings may be seen as evidence of the schools' failure, they also indicate the difficulties students have understanding the abstract principles of constitutionalism, preferring to identify democracy in the more concrete form of the system with which they are most familiar, just as, at an even lower level of abstraction, young children personify the American political system in the form of George Washington.[96]

That students identify democracy with the United States government, and young children associate the American political system with George Washington, attests to the improbability of teaching abstract thought through rote and example. "Back to basics" movements are unlikely to improve students capacity to think abstractly.[97] A revival of geography and history, such as Warren Burger advocated during the Constitution's Bicentennial, might improve students' knowledge of the Constitution by providing them with more concrete signposts. However, it would not improve their understanding of the abstract principles underlying the constitutional system and citizens' myriad relationships with the state. More importantly, neither rote learning nor the teaching of abstract principles or cognitive processes will accomplish the underlying mission of civic education, the development of active citizens.

Identifying the necessary skills for citizenship is an essential step in assessing civic education, including education about the Constitution. The primary justification for civic education within a liberal democracy—the creation of citizens who can perform such "functions" as voting, petitioning their representatives, and obeying the law as part of a democratic system—is itself anti-democratic in both its theoretical principles and practical implications.[98] A functionalist theory of society evaluates every individual, activity, or norm by how he, she or it contributes to the functioning of the social system. Within such a functionalist theory, education is the primary institutional mechanism that contributes to the perpetuation of the constitutional system and increased public knowledge of governmental structure and history. The functionalist approach to civic education thus focuses on integrating students within social institutions, providing them with the skills to perform such tasks as voting and reading the newspaper, while also developing normative orientations that make their performance of these tasks more likely. The development of "National Standards for Civics and Government" by the Center for Civic Education and the National Council for the Social Studies, in a project funded by the federal Department of Education and the Pew Charitable Trusts, indicates the degree to which functionalism has shaped civic education in the United States.[99] This vision of civic education and citizenship does not contain any meaningful reason that the civically literate, standardized citizens of the future should care about politics, nor does such a vision tell us what to do with the "civically illiterate" or "civically incompetent." Illiteracy has a distinctive cultural significance, and the illiterate are stigmatized because they lack the capacity to function properly in society or the polity.[100] The idea that a person must have certain skills in order to "function" in society presumes that the social system is superordinate, and that individuals must be shaped in order to accommodate its demands.

During one congressional hearing, Warren Burger argued that basic literacy was needed because the Commission on the Bicentennial and others involved in civic education could not reach illiterate students through written materials.[101] The Commission's concern about reaching illiterate students was characteristic of the concern that the illiterate are not properly integrated into society.[102] In many instances, illiterates have been excluded from a community largely defined by literacy, and the capacity to participate in many communal activities, including elections, has been conditioned on literacy.[103] However, even illiteracy did not leave one outside of the range of the Commission's efforts to educate; one of the Commission's many advertising campaigns brought the celebration to those who could not read through television advertisements that urged viewers to call a telephone number for a packet of materials, including pocket-sized Constitutions, as part of a larger program to encourage literacy.[104]

The necessity of literacy is closely related to the degree to which social integration is fostered by print, rather than speech. While there are important reasons that citizens should know and care about their government, the desire for Americans to have an unmediated encounter with the Constitution has to be assessed against the history of past literacy campaigns. Large-scale literacy campaigns have been closely tied to attempts by elites, and particularly central state authorities, to develop a political or moral consensus and create a distinctive national identity.[105] The great literacy campaigns of eighteenth century New England and Sweden, for instance, were undertaken to further Protestant religious observance by allowing congregants to read Bibles, prayers, and catechisms, thus symbolically promoting piety and orderliness.[106] Alternatively, the revolution in literacy which followed Luther's Protestant revolt against Rome resulted as much from tradesmen's desire to integrate into the evolving market economies as from any new em-

phasis on the text of the Bible.[107] And literacy may be especially important in the type of liberal democracy that is built
on market norms. As Edward Stevens writes, nineteenth
century literacy campaigns were themselves legitimated by
the constitutionalist ideals of consent and contract: the citizens were assumed "to have access to information relevant
to their consent."[108]

Contemporary notions of literacy are far removed from
older, more limited conceptions of literacy which focused on
the capacity to read a few texts, such as the Bible or prayer
book, which were generally memorized. Reading new material was considered a special effort, and, because of the
scarcity of material and the slower pace of life, books were
often read aloud in the home or in other social settings.[109]
Contemporary notions of literacy are incompatible with a
common core of a few crucial texts, which, in the older conception of literacy, provided a basis for cultural, as well as
political, solidarity. In contrast, modern media may require
more education, in the case of such demanding new media
as computers, or less education, as in the case of more accessible media, such as television. In either case, the cultural implications do not lead to greater appreciation of a
few, central texts, but lead participants to pursue even more
diverse interests. Just as the ability to read a Bible does not
necessarily lead to Bible reading as a preferred literary pas-
time, "constitutional literacy" is not particularly likely to
lead to civic virtue.

For students to appreciate constitutionalism as both
theory and practice, they must internalize the practice of
politics. Merely teaching about political institutions and
practices does not lead to students' development of political
consciousness if they do not learn to regard activities beyond
school or work to be important contributions to the community. Students must develop, in Eric Gorham's words, "the
capacity to love politics and engage actively in it."[110] The development of affective ties to the larger community, both local and national, is an important part of civic education
which is impossible to conceive in the restricted terms of

"civic literacy." To train citizens to become "civically compe-
tent" or "civically literate" is hardly respectful of citizens' capacity to govern themselves, for such designations are
primarily markers of elite prescriptions for citizen self-
development. Educational programs centered on the Constitution can be particularly problematic because of their
frequent assumption that students will better absorb the
principles of American constitutionalism from late eighteenth century texts rather than in the continuing debates
of the newspapers, television debates, or radio talk shows.
Socializing students to develop a strong understanding of
contemporary political issues is a more direct solution to the
problem that underlies the "crisis" in civic education, the
perception of youth alienation from political institutions,
than an education which repeatedly invokes the largely
symbolic presence of historical texts.

As Richard Pratte diagnoses the problem, "The distin-
guishing aspect of the present civic education crisis . . . is
precisely the breakdown of the crucial link between the citizen and the community."[111] The symbolic nature of civic education, and its crises, reveals how Americans regard the
schools as institutions that develop links between future citizens and the polity. Civic commemorations such as the Constitution's Bicentennial provide opportunities for elites to
instruct the public through educational activities inside,
and outside, the schools, to depict themselves as concerned
about larger social disintegration, and to symbolize that
concern through visible events, such as essay contests, that
convey the message that citizens could succeed as individuals and that the constitutional system is serving the needs
of the public. If people do not participate in the political
process because of poor education, then they have only
themselves or the schools to blame. The alternative is that
the constitutional system has little to offer them for their
participation.

Of course, American constitutionalism is not about participatory democracy. The more sophisticated understanding
that "illiteracy was endemic at the time the Constitution was

ratified and remains so today"[112] should restore our faith
that representative democracy takes the practice of everyday governance out of the hands of the larger public and allows the nation to muddle through. Representative
democracy is preferable to direct democracy in part because
of the public's imperfections. To require that citizens are capable of acting as fully informed and deliberating decision-
makers is to treat them as legislators, and not as constituents.
Instead, representative democracy is better served when citizens understand both the limits placed on citizen participation by the American tradition of constitutionalism and the
limits of the educational system's capacity to inculcate citizenship. When, as James Banner writes, "We are told that
the decline in voter participation and the contempt in which
public authority is said to be held originated in incompe-
tence in the classroom,"[113] the role of education in creating
social dysfunction been exaggerated out of all proportion,
and the role of our constitutional system in distilling the
popular will has been forgotten.

Conclusion: Popular Sovereignty in a Representative Democracy

> *[T]he history of popular sovereignty . . . can be read as a history of the successive efforts of different generations to bring the facts into closer conformity with the fiction.*
>
> Edmund Morgan[1]

In 1987, the Bicentennial committee in Knoxville, Tennessee planned a gala ceremony celebrating the Constitution's anniversary; approximately one thousand people attended. The very next day, at the same site, a crowd of fifty thousand turned up for a barbecue competition.[2] In Philadelphia, We the People 200's "National Celebration" failed to attract corporate sponsorships and had limited success in drawing tourists to Philadelphia. The nationally televised *We the People 200: The Constitutional Gala* came in a distant third in the Nielsen ratings, behind a Bob Hope special and the movie *Mr. Mom.*[3] Following the success of the fund-raising drive for the restoration of the Statue of Liberty, the Constitution's Bicentennial was a disappointment. The Foundation for the Constitution failed to even approach its goals for raising corporate money for the celebration, the Society for the U.S. Constitution floundered for lack of public interest, and the James Madison Memorial Fellowship

Foundation raised only a fraction of the private funds required to begin offering scholarships to high school teachers. Throughout this book, I have suggested that the Constitution is too abstract and multidimensional to symbolize national unity. But the lack of public interest in the Constitution's Bicentennial may be explained in several different ways. Perhaps it resulted from a failure by the elites coordinating the celebration to create sufficient excitement in the general public. Or, it could be interpreted as proof, along with such evidence as low voter turnout and citizens' ignorance of the political system, that Americans are alienated from the political process because they are cynical or apathetic. This last theory was certainly held by many of those who planned the Constitution's Bicentennial and who continue to lobby for civic education and public history programs.

The idea that citizens are alienated from the political process certainly merits consideration. However, there is no reason that such alienation means that the Constitution, or the nation, are in jeopardy. While democratic theory demonstrates a strong preference for citizenship involvement, there is no requirement in constitutional theory that citizens be involved in self-government beyond the election of their representatives. One might easily argue that one of the most important attributes of the Constitution is the freedom it provides for citizens to engage in private pursuits. Warren Burger wrote of the glory of the Constitution as being demonstrated "out west of the Beltway" by American energy and prosperity and concluded that

> the unleashing of the infinite human power, latent in so many people, made it [sic] possible by this Constitution and this system of freedom had greater consequences—up to now at least—than the splitting of the atom in our time.[4]

Burger's argument echoed Paul Eidelberg's observation that "[f]or the Founders, the primary purpose of laws and institutions is to prevent evil. For the neo-moderns, the primary purpose of laws and institutions is to make men comfortable."[5] Indeed, the Framers' vision of civic virtue could be easily reconciled with modern prosperity, a view well-articulated by Progressive era political theorist Herbert Croly: "by virtue of the more comfortable and less trammeled lives which Americans were enabled to lead, they would constitute a better society and would become in general a worthier set of men."[6]

If the public is more interested in its own affairs and current events than the exploration of abstract political principles, this does not demonstrate indifference to, or alienation from, the political system. The bonds between citizen and nation-state may be better represented through more concrete symbols of national identity and state sovereignty, especially individuals.[7] The coronation of Queen Elizabeth II and the assassination of President John Kennedy were both moments where the populace of large, modern nations felt a general sense of connection and community, because these were events which involved real persons.[8] Yet such events are rarities, and, while national identity may be an important element in citizens' self-understanding, political activity is decidedly less fundamental to the lives of most citizens. Indeed, if the majority of citizens were politically active on a regular basis, such an intensity of interest might disrupt the stability of the government. As Sidney Verba observed in an essay on Kennedy assassination, "a deep emotional commitment to politics may be unstabilizing if it is constantly in the foreground, but it may also be unstabilizing if it is not in the background."[9]

As a symbol, the Constitution is a defining element in our national identity and still functions as a source of stability and identity for many Americans. This was demonstrated in the results of two 1987 polls. Sixty-one percent of those polled by the Hearst Organization supported calling a constitutional convention in 1987 to deal with "contemporary issues such as prayer in public schools, abortion, freedom of the press and other matters."[10] However, a Gallup Poll found that forty-four percent of respondents supported "basic changes or amendments," and when asked whether a constitutional convention should be called, only twenty-one percent stated that a convention was "needed to make changes" while seventy-two percent feared that a constitutional convention "might make things worse."[11] Thus, at least half of those who would change the Constitution to address current political controversies were unwilling to tolerate the level of uncertainty that might accompany such a convention. Support or opposition to changes in the Constitution may therefore be tied, in a paradoxical way, to popular trust in the government. While those who call for changes signal their frustration with the political system, many who would favor such changes are also sufficiently distrustful of the political process to pass on a convention that might make such changes.

One might even claim that an ethic of participatory democracy is incompatible with a Constitution that values representative democracy above direct democracy. While it is often ignored, a central element of the Framers' theory of limited government was the requirement that the people choose representatives who would prove to be among the wisest and most virtuous among them.[12] But the theory of limited government is as much about the potential for citizens to have a limited role in governance as it is about limiting the power of government over citizens' lives and activities. Indeed, much of the appeal of limited government derives from the degree to which it allows citizens to invest their energy into private activities while delegating their sovereign powers to representatives who, in the manner of all hired hands, do the necessary work while requiring a minimum of their clients' time.

The removal of government from the direct control by the popular sovereign does, however, result in the insistence on that sovereignty in the rhetoric of modern constitutionalism. This was well-expressed in Ronald Reagan's 1987 State of the Union address when he spoke of the American founding as "the first time in history" that "government, the people said, was not our master. It is our servant; its only power that which we, the people, allow it to have." In his speech, Reagan declared that "here in America, we, the people, are in charge," and identified "we the people" as "the kids on Christmas Day looking out from a frozen sentry post on the 38th parallel in Korea . . . farmers on tough times . . . volunteers at the hospital . . . a million mothers like Nelle Reagan."[13]

The individuals Reagan cited as symbolizing the American people were more easily imagined than the abstract principle of popular sovereignty, and embodied the practical values of the American polity. Reagan's list of soldiers who exemplified duty and service, farmers who manifested self-reliance and persistence, volunteers who symbolized caring and community, and mothers who embodied family and love, was an attempt to articulate the central values which in American society "establish the identity of individuals and bind them into a common universe."[14] Through his description of "we, the people," Reagan equated the Constitution with the larger symbolic universe of American identity that went well beyond the political institutions established through the document. Rather than praising the constitutional system of representative self-government, Reagan described an America where the people are always present and not merely represented.

Reagan's address, televised nationwide, illustrates how mediating institutions have become more powerful in their ability to represent forms of community within a mass society. Because modern practices involving the mass media are both "immediate to the individual and pervasive throughout the social system,"[15] mass society is able to involve individuals in large-scale, coordinated celebrations that simulate the experience of face-to-face community. The contemporary phenomenon of nationwide town meetings, where television's ability to represent political leaders and the public in a dialogue, "creates the illusion, if not the reality, of direct democracy."[16] Simulated forms of public deliberation, in which political leaders visit citizens in their living rooms and citizens have direct access to leaders, through such media as call-in radio and television talk shows, promise democracy

without representation. When the people can become immediate and present in national forms of political deliberation,
the nature of representation in a constitutional democracy
changes dramatically.

Only One Master Among Many

Assessing the real impact of constitutionalism as an
ideological and rhetorical system is difficult, if not impossible. Programs intended to educate the public about the
Constitution do not promise to create or better define a
fully developed ideology of constitutionalism, but instead
raise consciousness about an ideology presumed to be
shared by the majority of the public. But the presumption
that Americans both agree with and care about the Constitution are the least of the problems of turning constitutionalism into a central ideology. The problems of
remaking constitutionalism as a central element in popular political culture can be understood through an examination of the concept of ideology itself. As Melford Spiro
has outlined it, an ideology has five levels. The first level is
learning, the second level is understanding, and the third
level requires that people believe the concept to be right or
true. In the fourth level, people begin to incorporate the
concept into their daily lives, and finally, in the fifth level,
ideology motivates people in their actions.[17] As an ideology,
constitutionalism may function well in the first three levels of learning, understanding and belief. However, insofar
as people were supposed to order their lives according to
constitutional ideals or motivated to put them into action,
there are relatively few forms of civic involvement that extend beyond education and expressions of admiration for,
and loyalty to, the symbol to make constitutionalism a
part of their daily lives. During the Bicentennial, the federal Commission used an advertising slogan, "The Words
We Live By," which presumed that Americans had already
incorporated the Constitution into their everyday lives

without providing any concrete ways in which one might perform specifically constitutional activities.

Rather than leading to particular forms of constitutional politics, the ideological justification for increasing popular knowledge about the Constitution is the hope at such knowledge will lessen citizens' estrangement from the political system. Testifying before a congressional committee, Mark Cannon, the staff director of the federal Commission on the Bicentennial, argued that

> To teach about the Constitution as the set of rules by which government is organized and policy determined is to interest and empower people who might otherwise be alienated.[18]

Cannon's comments were part of a historic pattern of elite discourse about public interest and education about the Constitution. While ordinary citizens are important in discussions of the meaning of the Constitution, they serve, as Walter Berns observes, "mainly as objects of concern because of their presumed ignorance of the Constitution's structure and provisions."[19] For the elites who organized the Bicentennial, the larger purpose for the celebrations was to make visible a set of beliefs about the political system that they believed to be insufficiently shared among the larger public. Warren Burger's frequent description of the Bicentennial as a "history and civics lesson for the nation" placed those who planned bicentennial events in the privileged position of teaching the public about their own political responsibilities and patriotic feelings.

An additional irony attaches to the prospect of teaching constitutionalism as a subject distinct from the everyday normal politics. While many elites approve of teaching the Constitution as a primarily historical document or a document important for how it embodies lasting truths about human nature and the proper structure of government, such conceptions are profoundly anti-political, isolating the Constitution from the possibility of discussion, deliberation, and compromise which typifies a free society. Teaching or reading the Constitution as a simple thing leads to a form of political idolatry. As defined by historian of religion Jaroslav Pelikan, idolatry is distinguishable from iconography:

> An *idol* purports to be the embodiment of that which it represents, but it directs us to itself rather than beyond it-self . . . An authentic image, which came to be called *icon* . . . is what it represents; nevertheless it bids us look at it, but through it and beyond it, to that living reality of which it is an embodiment.[20]

So long as the Constitution functions as (in Pelikan's terminology) an idol or (in my own terminology) a fetish, it is unworthy of a long-standing and evolving tradition.[21] Only when the Constitution's meaning extends beyond its own boundaries to the nation, and the popular sovereign that it represents, is the constitutional tradition revealed. That tradition includes both extraconstitutional institutions, including the media, civic organizations and corporations, and those issues and ideas which divide Americans as much as those which unite Americans.

Worship of the Constitution is no substitute for citizenship, which occurs largely outside of the boundaries of constitutional politics. If civic virtue is to be reborn in contemporary America, it will first reappear in discussions in town halls over trash removal, and not in artificial discussions of such public issues as the Supreme Court's decisions on pornography, over which participants have no authority. Such discussions exist today as occasions for the ceremonial exercise of popular sovereignty through public deliberation. Yet, however popular in vision or execution, such deliberations can be only simulations of the actual process of political decision-making. In looking to 1787 for authenticity, modern Americans overlook the authentic constitutional controversies that have proliferated since even 1987. In that year, both the nomination hearings of Robert Bork and the Iran-Contra hearings raised important questions regarding the limits of governmental power, the proper distribution of power within the government, and the rights and responsibilities of both ordinary citizens and public officials. Since that time, serious debates over abortion, flag-burning, prayer at public school graduations, and other constitutional issues have been a regular feature of American political life. Yet, even these debates do not take the place of democratic self-governance, for they remain only discussions over a document in which the ultimate powers of self-government were alienated from the people over two hundred years ago.

If constitutionalism to become a more significant element in American political culture, Americans must make it their own through political action within a representative democracy, not civics classes or commemorative ceremonies. Sheldon Wolin writes that citizenship is a birthright that is transformed in every generation; "we inherit from our fathers, but we are not our fathers."[22] To be meaningful, tradition must become part of people's practice. The challenge of modern constitutionalism is to engage in the serious business of everyday politics, while recognizing the highly representational nature of the constitutional system and that there is more to the role of citizen than political activity. The constitutional tradition of limited and representative government is not furthered when popular sovereignty is celebrated through depictions of the statesmen of two hundreds years ago or self-portraits of "we the people." Instead, when Americans recognize how they are empowered by the limits of their own popular sovereignty, they will have made the Constitution their own.

Notes

A Note on Sources

The following abbreviations are used in the notes that follow. WTP refers to the records of We the People 200, stored in the archives of the City of Philadelphia. WTP Inc refers to records of We the People 200 Incorporated, also stored at the City of Philadelphia Archives. INHP refers to a series of binders kept in the archives of Independence National Historic Park. NA refers to the records of the Commission on the Bicentennial of the United States Constitution, stored at the National Archives in Washington, D.C. "CBC, *Final Report*" refers to the final report of the Commission of the Bicentennial of the United States Constitution, *We the People: A Final Report* (Washington, D.C. 1992).

Preface

1. "Introduction," in H. Varenne, ed., *Symbolizing America* (Lincoln: University of Nebraska Press, 1986), 1 (italics in original).

2. Merrill D. Peterson, *The Jefferson Image in the American Mind* (New York: Oxford University Press, 1960), vii.

3. Scott Lash, *Sociology of Postmodernism* (London: Routledge, 1990).

4. For examples of the mixture of politics and popular culture, see Robert L. Savage and Dan Nimmo, "Imagination, Politics,

and Popular Media: A Thematic Introduction," in R. L. Savage and D. Nimmo, eds., *Politics in Familiar Contexts: Projecting Politics Through Popular Media* (Norwood, NJ: Ablex, 1990), 2.

5. Robert A. Ferguson, "'We Do Ordain and Establish': The Constitution as Literary Text," *William and Mary Law Review* 29 (1987): 10–11.

6. For the idea of aura, see Walter Benjamin, "Art in the Age of Mechanical Reproduction," in Hannah Arendt, ed., *Illuminations*, trans. Harry Zohn (New York: Harcourt, Brace and World, 1968), 219–253.

7. Donald R. McCoy, *The National Archives* (Chapel Hill: University of North Carolina Press, 1978), 254-256; "Constitution, Declaration Stored in a Concrete Vault," *The Washington Post*, October 11, 1986, B2.

8. Tony Mauro, "Bill of Rights has not been Scuttled," *USA Today*, December 16, 1991, A13.

9. The other cosponsors were the American Bar Association, and the federal Commission on the Bicentennial of the United States Constitution. See testimony of Warren Burger, in House Committee on Appropriations, *Hearings: Departments of Commerce, Justice, and State, the Judiciary, and Related Agencies Appropriations for 1988,* 100th Cong., 1st Session, February 25, 1987, Pt. 1, 421–422.

10. We the People 200, Inc., accounting ledger "Accts. Receivable—Corp. Support," November 18, 1988, in Drawer 1, WTP INC.

11. May 25, 1987, Bonus Section "We the People."

12. "The Sour Taste of Good Intentions," *The New York Times*, September 27, 1987, sec. I, p. 50.

13. Seventy percent of those surveyed believed that the Constitution was effective in "making Americans think of themselves as one nation" compared with only forty-one percent of respondents who thought that the Constitution "treat[ed] all people equally," and fifty-three percent thought that the Constitution "establish[ed] a fair system of justice." Douglas Martin, "Views on Constitution: Promises Kept, Miles to Go," *The New York Times*, May 26, 1987, A20.

14. *The American Public's Knowledge of the U.S. Constitution: A National Survey of Public Awareness and Personal Opinion* (New York: Hearst Corporation, 1987).

15. A 1989 survey found that only thirty percent of the public could name even a single member of the Supreme Court. Indeed, less than one percent could name all nine members of the Court, while, by comparison, fifty-four percent could the name the judge on the popular television program, "The People's Court." Lee Epstein, et al., *The Supreme Court Compendium* (Washington, D.C.: CQ Press, 1994), 609.

16. Edward Corwin, "The Constitution as Instrument and as Symbol," in R. Loss, ed., *Corwin on the Constitution* 1 (Ithaca: Cornell University Press, 1981), 169 (italics in original).

17. Max Lerner, *Ideas for the Ice Age* (New York: Viking, 1941), 236.

18. Sanford Levinson, *Constitutional Faith* (Princeton, N.J.: Princeton University Press, 1988).

19. Michael Kammen, *A Machine That Would Go of Itself* (New York: Knopf, 1986).

20. See Henry J. Merry, *Montesquieu's System of Natural Government* (West Lafayette, IN: Purdue University Studies, 1970); Paul Merrill Spurlin, *Montesquieu in America, 1760–1801* (Baton Rouge: Louisiana State University Press, 1940).

21. Steven M. Dworetz, *The Unvarnished Doctrine: Locke, Liberalism and the American Revolution* (Durham: Duke University Press, 1990).

22. David E. Procter, *Enacting Political Culture: Rhetorical Transformations of Liberty Weekend* (New York: Praeger, 1991), 19.

23. As Ivan Karp writes, "[p]ublic culture provides some relatively formal settings for definitions and experiences of identities." "On Civil Society and Social Identity," in I. Karp, C. M. Kreamer, and S. D. Lavine, eds., *Museums and Communities: The Politics of Public Culture* (Washington, D.C.: Smithsonian Institution Press, 1992), 19.

24. Margaret Archer, *Culture and Agency* (Cambridge: Cambridge University Press, 1988). See also Anthony Giddens, *Central*

Problems in Social Theory (Berkeley: University of California Press, 1979), for a different perspective on the problem of analyzing both structure and action, and Michael Schudson on "interest theory vs. cultural theory," *Watergate in American Memory* (New York: Basic Books, 1992), 53–54.

25. See the comments of Michael Thompson, Richard Ellis, and Aaron Wildavsky, *Cultural Theory* (Boulder: Westview, 1990), 217–219.

26. Michael Schudson, "The Present in the Past versus the Past in the Present," *Communication* 11 (1989): 108–109.

27. See Michael Billig et al., *Ideological Dilemmas* (London: Sage, 1988), 28–29.

28. Clifford Geertz, "Ideology as a Cultural System," *The Interpretation of Cultures* (New York: Basic Books, 1973), 201–203, 210–213.

29. Edward Shils, *Center and Periphery* (Chicago: University of Chicago Press, 1975), x.

30. Alan Trachtenberg, *The Incorporation of America* (New York: Hill and Wang, 1982), 3.

Chapter One

1. See Kammen, *A Machine that Would Go of Itself,* xviii, 89–90, 127–151, 282–312.

2. For a confirming view, see Milton M. Klein, *The Constitution in the Public Imagination: The Lawrence F. Brewster Lecture in History* (Greenville, North Carolina: East Carolina University, 1987).

3. Michael Kammen, *Sovereignty and Liberty* (Madison: University of Wisconsin Press, 1988), 9.

4. For examples of such revolutionary iconography, see Michael Kammen, *A Season of Youth: The American Revolution and the Historical Imagination* (New York: Knopf, 1978).

5. Kammen, *A Machine That Would Go of Itself,* 303.

6. Wilbur Zelinsky, *Nation Into State: The Shifting Symbolic Foundations of American Nationalism* (Chapel Hill: University of North Carolina Press, 1987), 128.

7. Zelinsky, *Nation Into State,* 129–130.

8. The relative weakness of the Constitution in comparison to the Declaration existed in the nineteenth century as well. See Henry Gabriel, *The Course of American Democratic Thought* (New York: Ronald Press, 1956 (1940)), 99.

9. Kammen, *A Machine That Would Go of Itself,* 220–223, 385. The congressional resolution of February 29, 1952 is at 36 U.S.C. 153; Congress recognized the week starting September 17 as "Constitution Week" in 1956 (36 U.S.C. 159). See also Ronald Reagan, "Proclamation 5526—Citizenship Day and Constitution Week, 1986; September 17, 1986," in *Public Papers of the Presidents of the United States: Ronald Reagan: 1986* 2 (Washington, D.C.: Government Printing Office, 1989), 1200–1201.

10. A clause in an early agreement required that CBS pay up to half a million dollars, in addition to the already agreed upon figure of $2 million, for the television rights for both events if Congress authorized the federal holiday. Letter from Willard Rouse to Gary Smith and Dwight Hemion, February 13, 1987, Box 18, WTP INC. This was superceded by the firm figure of $2 million in the contract between Smith-Hemion and CBS dated April 17, 1987, Box 18, WTP INC.

11. For the congressional debate, see the *Congressional Record,* July 23, 1987, 133: H 6581–6598.

12. Kammen, *A Machine That Would Go of Itself,* 224.

13. Letter from Thomas Leahy, Executive Vice President of CBS/Broadcast Group, to Warren E. Burger, October 31, 1986, in, Records Relating to Commission History, 1981–1991, Box 6, NA; letter from Burger to Leahy, Nov. 6, 1986, Box 28 (B—4a), NA.

14. Such televised specials have been run in the past. See Kammen, *A Machine That Would Go of Itself,* 376–380.

15. Two short series of reports were especially noteworthy; PBS, traditionally a channel for educational programming,

broadcast a series produced with the cooperation of the American Bar Association and underwritten by the brokerage house Merrill Lynch; and the commercial network ABC broadcast a special report with news anchor Peter Jennings. Although the Bicentennial's promoters saw it as a five-year-long celebration, the programs were clustered just previous to the anniversary of the document's signing at the conclusion of the Constitutional Convention.

16. September 1987 was the month with the largest amount of television news time devoted to the Constitution's bicentennial, with a total of twenty-six minutes on all three networks. There was also little sustained coverage during those months leading up to the celebration. While the Statue of Liberty restoration and Liberty Weekend were regularly on network news shows for several months before the festivities, coverage of the Constitution's Bicentennial was sustained for no more than three days in a row, and in no month did stories about the bicentennial appear on any national commercial newscast on more than four separate days. Data assembled from *Television News Index and Abstracts,* (Nashville: Vanderbilt Television News Archives). In comparison to the scarce coverage of Constitution's bicentennial, David Procter estimated that there were over sixty hours of network and CNN coverage of Liberty Weekend. *Enacting Political Culture,* 25.

17. "Weekly Ratings Scorecard," *Variety,* September 23, 1987: 126.

18. Seventy-one percent knew that only a person born in the United States could be elected President, and sixty-seven percent knew that the President is not directly elected through the popular vote. See Hearst Corporation, *The American Public's Knowledge of the U.S. Constitution.*

19. Kammen, *A Machine That Would Go of Itself,* 23–24.

20. This meaning of the term had been revived in Britain by the time of Locke. Graham Maddox, "Constitution," in Terence Ball, James Farr, and Russell L. Hanson, eds., *Political Innovation and Conceptual Change* (Cambridge: Cambridge University Press, 1989), 51, 59.

21. Walter Bagehot, *The English Constitution* (Ithaca: Cornell University Press, 1966 (1867)), 82.

22. For the ways in which presidents become part of American political mythology, see Barry Schwartz, *George Washington: The Making of an American Symbol* (Ithaca: Cornell University Press, 1987).

23. Hearst Corporation, *The American Public's Knowledge of the U.S. Constitution: A National Survey of Public Awareness and Personal Opinion,* 16.

24. David I. Kertzer, *Ritual, Politics, and Power* (New Haven: Yale University Press, 1988), 19.

25. Alexis de Tocqueville, *Democracy in America,* ed. Phillips Bradley (New York: Vintage, 1945), I:72–73.

26. J. P. Nettl, "The State as a Conceptual Variable," *World Politics* 20 (1968): 561.

27. Tocqueville, *Democracy in America,* I:60.

28. Michael McGee, "In Search of 'the People': A Rhetorical Alternative," *Quarterly Journal of Speech* 61 (1975): 240.

29. Edmund S. Morgan, *Inventing the People* (New York: Norton, 1988), 153.

30. Michael Walzer, "On the Role of Symbolism in Political Thought," *Political Science Quarterly* 87 (1967): 194.

31. G. W. F. Hegel, *Hegel's Philosophy of Right,* trans. T. M. Knox (London: Oxford University Press, 1969), 182–183.

32. Shlomo Avineri, *Hegel's Theory of the Modern State* (Cambridge: Cambridge University Press, 1972), 187–188.

33. Edward Shils and Michael Young, "The Meaning of the Coronation," *Sociological Review* I (1953): 63–81.

34. Kertzer, *Ritual, Politics, and Power,* 11.

35. David Easton and Jack Dennis, *Children in the Political System* (New York: McGraw-Hill, 1969), 114–117, 138.

36. See, as the most familiar exercise in this area, Alexander Hamilton's *Federalist No. 70.*

37. John M. Murrin, "A Roof without Walls," in *Beyond Confederation: Origins of the Constitution and American National*

Identity, eds. R. Beeman, S. Botein, and E. C. Carter (Chapel Hill: University of North Carolina Press, 1987), 333.

38. Bagehot, *The English Constitution,* 82.

39. Albert Venn Dicey, *Introduction to the Study of the Constitution,* 8th ed. (1915; reprint Indianapolis: Liberty Press, 1982), xci.

40. "Introduction: Inventing Traditions," in Eric Hobsbawm and Terence Ranger, eds., *The Invention of Tradition* (Cambridge: Cambridge University Press, 1983), 12.

41. Emile Durkheim, "Individual and Collective Representations," *Sociology and Philosophy,* trans. by D. F. Pocock (New York: Free Press, 1974), 1–34; Durkheim, *The Elementary Forms of Religious Life,* trans. by J. W. Swain (New York: Free Press, 1915), 479–496

42. Richard M. Merelman, *Making Something of Ourselves: On Culture and Politics in the United States* (Berkeley: University of California Press, 1984).

43. Hegel, *Hegel's Philosophy of Right,* 292.

44. Otto Friedrich von Gierke, *Political Theories of the Middle Age,* trans. by F. W. Maitland (1900; reprint Cambridge: Cambridge University Press, 1951), 87.

45. Wilkins' piece is pictured in Commission on the Bicentennial of the United States Constitution, *We the People: Final Report* (Washington, D.C., 1992) *(hereafter, CBC, Final Report),* 99.

46. Anne Norton, "Transubstantiation: The Dialectic of Constitutional Authority," *University of Chicago Law Review* 55, no. 2 (1988): 459.

47. Quoted in Michael Warner, *The Letters of the Republic: Publication and the Public Sphere in Eighteenth—Century America* (Cambridge, MA: Harvard University Press, 1990), 105.

48. Cornerstone Marketing, "We the People—1987; Permanent Document; Preliminary Concept," March 27, 1986, Education: Office Files, Box 7, NA.

49. Britten Banners, Proposal, Box 61 (B-51), NA.

50. For a treatment of the issue of "masterless men," see Don Herzog, *Happy Slaves: A Critique of Consent Theory* (Chicago: University of Chicago Press, 1989).

51. Kammen, *Sovereignty and Liberty,* 12.

52. Judge Samuel Spencer, quoted in Michael Lienesch, "North Carolina: Preserving Rights," in M. A. Gillespie and M. Lienesch, eds., *Ratifying the Constitution* (Lawrence: University of Kansas Press, 1989), 358.

53. Warner, *The Letters of the Republic,* 106.

54. Gouvenor Morris did introduce such a plan, including a democratic House and a plutocratic Senate, during the Constitutional Convention, but it failed to gain sufficient support. Jennifer Nedelsky, *Private Property and the Limits of American Constitutionalism* (Chicago: University of Chicago Press, 1990), 79–86.

55. Louis Hartz, *The Liberal Tradition in America* (New York: Harcourt Brace Jovanovich, 1955); Tocqueville, *Democracy in America.*

56. Dick Howard, *The Birth of American Political Thought* (Minneapolis: University of Minnesota Press, 1989), 76.

57. Wood, *The Creation of the American Republic,* 604.

58. George Armstrong Kelly, "Hegel's America," *Philosophy & Public Affairs* 2, no. 1 (Fall 1972): 6.

59. Joseph Tussman, *Obligation and the Body Politic* (New York: Oxford University Press, 1960), 21.

60. 19 Howard 393 (1856) at 404.

61. As Richard Handler notes, "collectivities in Western social theory are imagined as though they are human individuals writ large." Richard Handler, "Is Identity a Useful Concept?" in John R. Gillis, ed., *Commemorations: The Politics of National Identity* (Princeton, NJ: Princeton University Press, 1994), 33.

62. William F. Harris II, *The Interpretable Constitution* (Baltimore: Johns Hopkins University Press, 1992), 73.

63. See Gordon S. Wood, *The Creation of the American Republic, 1776–1787* (New York: Norton, 1972 (1969)), 283.

64. Bruce Ackerman, *We the People: Foundations* (Cambridge, MA: Harvard University Press, 1991), 6–7.

65. For a detailed account of the Lockean theory of sovereignty, see Julie Mostov, *Power, Process, and Popular Sovereignty* (Philadelphia: Temple University Press, 1992), 52–72.

66. Thomas Paine, "The Rights of Man, Part Second," in Philip S. Foner, ed., *The Life and Major Writings of Thomas Paine* (Secaucus, NJ: Citadel Press, 1974), 375.

67. John Locke, *Second Treatise on Government,* C. B. McPherson, ed. (Indianapolis: Hackett, 1980), 52–53 (§ 95–99).

68. Dicey, *Introduction to the Study of the Law of the Constitution,* 26–29.

69. Mostov, *Power, Process, and Popular Sovereignty,* 51.

70. *Ibid.,* 50.

71. Kammen, *Sovereignty and Liberty,* 9.

72. Bertell Ollman, *Alienation* (New York: Cambridge University Press, 1971), 216.

73. Thus Blackstone writes,

> The king . . . is made a corporation to prevent, in general, the possibility of an *interregnum,* or vacancy of the throne, and to preserve the possessions of the crown entire; for immediately upon the demise of one king, his successor is . . . in full possession of the regal rights and dignity.

Commentaries on the Laws of England I, (1765; reprint, Chicago: University of Chicago Press, 1979), 458.

74. Jurisprudents had arrived at the concept of a perpetuity of both the whole body politic (head and members together) and the constituent members alone. The perpetuity of the "head" alone was of equally great importance, since the head would usually appear as the responsible part and its absence might render the body corporate incomplete or incapable of action.

Ernst Kantorowicz, *The King's Two Bodies* (Princeton: Princeton University Press, 1957), 314.

75. *Trustees of Dartmouth College v. Woodard,* 4 Wheaton 624, at 636 (1819).

76. Hendrik Hartog in his *Public Property and Private Power* (Chapel Hill: University of North Carolina Press, 1983), notes that corporations established prior to the new American state were attacked by republican politicians during the Federal period:

> A body with its continued existence protected from the will of the sovereign people contradicted cherished propositions that had guided the development of a republican political culture (p. 85).

77. F. W. Maitland, "Translator's Introduction," in Gierke, *Political Theories of the Middle Age,* ix.

78. Charles Taylor, *Hegel and Modern Society* (Cambridge: Cambridge University Press, 1979), 90–91.

79. For a history of the anthropological use of the term "fetish," see Sut Jhally, *The Codes of Advertising* (New York: St. Martin's, 1987), 53–56.

80. Roy Ellen, "Fetishism," *Man* 23, no. 2 (June 1988): 218–219.

81. Thus, for instance, Senator Strom Thurmond once declared "our most precious right" to be "the right to be governed *by* the Constitution." Sen. Thurmond did so while interrogating Abe Fortas on his nomination for Chief Justice, quoted in Bruce Allen Murphy, *Fortas* (New York: William Morrow, 1988), 454 (emphasis added).

82. Corwin, "The Constitution as Instrument and as Symbol," 169 (italics in original).

83. Lerner, *Ideas for the Ice Age,* 236.

84. Kammen, *A Machine That Would Go of Itself,* 17–20; see also Henry Steele Commager, *The American Mind* (New Haven: Yale University Press, 1950), 311–313.

85. Larry R. Baas, "The Constitution as Symbol," *American Politics Quarterly* 8, no. 2 (April 1980): 237–256.

86. *Ibid.,* 243.

87. "Common Sense" in P. Foner, ed., *The Life and Major Writings of Thomas Paine,* 29.

88. J. P. Nettl, "The State as a Conceptual Variable," *World Politics* 20 (1968): 574.

89. By using this term, I do not wish to refer to Sheldon Wolin's interesting use of the concept to draw attention to the contradictions between the political and economic institutions and cultural forms which govern American life. "The People's Two Bodies," *Democracy* 1, no. 1 (January 1981): 9–24.

90. *Reflections on the Revolution in France,* T. H. D. Mahoney, ed. (Indianapolis: Bobbs-Merrill, 1955 (orig. 1790)), 110.

91. *Ibid.*

92. Descriptions of the Gala are based on viewing videotape graciously provided by Tom Davies of Independence National Historic Park.

93. David J. Garrow, *Liberty and Sexuality* (New York: MacMillan, 1994), 668.

94. For the potential and pitfalls of the idea of representation as substitution, see Hanna Fenichel Pitkin, *The Concept of Representation* (Berkeley: University of California Press, 1967), 119–120.

95. See also Durkheim, "Individual and Collective Representations," 1–34; Durkheim, *The Elementary Forms of Religious Life,* 479–496.

96. Thus postmodernism can be defined as "a regime of signification whose fundamental structuring trait is 'de-differentiation.'" Lash, *Sociology of Postmodernism,* 5.

97. Music by Barry Manilow, lyrics by Bruce Sussman and Jack Feldman. Copyright 1990 by Careers-BMG Music Publishing, Inc. (BMI), Appoggiatura Music and Camp Songs. All rights reserved. Used by permission.

98. "We the People," music by Edd Kalehoff and lyrics by Victor Sonder. Copyright 1987 by Maxrex Music. All rights reserved. Used by permission.

99. The vocalists were Lee Greenwood, Marilyn McCoo, and John Schneider.

100. "We the People," music by Edd Kalehoff and lyrics by Victor Sonder. Copyright 1987 by Maxrex Music.

101. Donald Horne, *The Public Culture: The Triumph of Industrialism* (London: Pluto, 1986), 189 (italics in original).

102. *Time*, July 6, 1987.

103. *U.S. News and World Report*, April 27, 1987: cover and 3.

104. *Newsweek*, May 25, 1987.

Chapter Two

1. For a description of Burger's activities at Disney World, see Art Harris, "Hey Kids, It's Mr. Constitution," *The Washington Post*, October 4, 1986, B1, B6.

2. The dual goals of publicity and organization are described in a memo from Commission member Cornelia Kennedy to Chairman Burger, dated May 8, 1986, Records Relating to Commission History, 1981–1991, Box 3, NA. For a description of Disney's promotional campaign see Art Harris, "Disney Drawing Card," *The Washington Post*, October 6, 1986, B1.

3. Quoted in Ellen M. Kozak, "Disney World and the Constitution celebrate their joint birthdays," *Wisconsin Bar Bulletin* 59 (December 1986): 33; Patrick May, "Daniloff: Constitution Comforted Me in Jail," *Miami Herald*, October 4, 1986, 1A.

4. Carl Hiaasen, "A Star Guest Circumvented a Disney Hug," *Miami Herald*, October 8, 1986, 1B; Lloyd Grove, "Daniloff: Arduous Hour of the Hero," *The Washington Post*, October 9, 1986, C1.

5. The Commission specified that "where [the Commission's] members and the Constitution are concerned, due consideration and respect will be give to assure that nothing is done to trivialize this historic document or the work of the Commission." Letter from Mark Cannon to Tom Elrod of Disney, dated May 9, 1986, "Records Relating to Commission History, 1981–1991," Box 5, NA.

6. "Mickey Mouse, A Big Star," *San Jose Mercury News*, October 6, 1986, 4A.

7. See Procter, *Enacting Political Culture*.

8. See M. Kenneth Brody, *Sociological Theories of Symbolic Activity: A Case Study Application to the Bicentennial Observance* (Unpublished Ph.D. Thesis, University of Iowa, 1977).

9. Testimony of Warren Burger, House Committee on Appropriations, *Hearings: Departments of Commerce, Justice, and State, the Judiciary, and Related Agencies Appropriations for 1989,* 100th Cong., 2nd Sess., March 16, 1988, Pt. 5, 26.

10. Testimony of Mark Cannon, in House Committee on Appropriations, *Hearings: Departments of Commerce, Justice, and State, the Judiciary, and Related Agencies Appropriations for 1989,* 27.

11. House Committee on Appropriations, *Hearings: Departments of Commerce, Justice, and State, the Judiciary, and Related Agencies Appropriations for 1988,* 100th Cong., 1st Sess., February 16, 1987, Pt. 1, 400.

12. *Ibid.,* 404.

13. Stanley Kelley, *Professional Public Relations and Political Power* (Baltimore: Johns Hopkins Press, 1956), 230.

14. Benjamin Rush, "To Elias Boudinot? Observations on the Federal Procession in Philadelphia;" in L.H. Butterfield, ed., *The Letters of Benjamin Rush* 1 (Princeton: Princeton University Press, 1951), 472.

15. Francis Hopkinson, "An Account of the Grand Federal Procession," in *The Miscellaneous Essays and Occasional Writings 2* (Philadelphia: T. Dobson, 1792), 422 (emphasis in original).

16. *Democracy in America* I, 281.

17. *Democracy In America* I, 72–73.

18. Lawrence M. Friedman, *Total Justice* (Boston: Beacon Press, 1985), 45.

19. Theodore Lowi, *The End of Liberalism* (New York: Norton, 1978 (2nd Ed)), xi.

20. Frank Sorauf has argued that

In the nationalization of American culture local ways of life, local identification and pride, even local folkways, yield their place. Increasingly, the same political symbols, the same political issues and appeals, the same political personages dominate American politics.

Political Parties in the American System, (Boston: Little Brown, 1964), 35–36.

21. Alpheus T. Mason, "Business Organized as Power," *American Political Science Review* 44 (1950): 327–328.

22. As James Morone writes, "a century-long parade of special commissions fruitlessly touting more efficient government offers ironic testimony against the theory that elected officials control administrative chiefs who, in turn, hold subordinates to account." James Morone, *The Democratic Wish: Popular Participation and the Limits of American Government* (New York: Basic Books, 1990), 328.

23. *Statutes at Large* 97 (1983): 719.

24. *Public Citizen v. Commission on the Bicentennial of the United States Constitution,* 622 F. Supp.753 (1985), at 755.

25. Public Law 98–101 § 5(a),(b),(c), and (e)(1)(2), *Statutes at Large* 97 (1983): 720.

26. Public Law 98–101 § 5–6, *Statutes at Large* 100 (1986): 3064–3065.

27. House Committee on Appropriations, *Hearings: Departments of Commerce, Justice, and State, the Judiciary, and Related Agencies Appropriations for 1989,* Pt. 5, 8.

28. Testimony of Warren Burger, House Committee on Appropriations, *Hearings: Departments of Commerce, Justice and State, the Judiciary, and Related Agencies Appropriations for 1990,* 101st Cong. 1st Sess., March 16, 1988, Pt. 5, 153.

29. The original bill foresaw a budget that would start at $300,000 in 1983 and peak at $375,000 in 1988. Letter of Alice M. Rivlin to Strom Thurmond, Senate Committee on the Judiciary,

Bicentennial of the Constitution, 98th Cong. 1st Sess., 1983, S. Rept. 68, 45. Figuring a constant rate of increased expenditures for those six fiscal years, the total expenditures would be $2,362,500.

30. The exact figure was $83,859,200 from "Commission Budget Summary," in CBC, *Final Report,* 274.

31. Calculated by subtracting the amount counted as grants, $38,700,000, from total expenditures of $67,967,245. The exact operating costs without grants was thus $29,267,245. All figures calculated from "Commission Budget Summary," in CBC, *Final Report,* 274.

32. Public Law 99–549 § 8, *Statutes at Large* 100 (1986): 3065.

33. Public Law 102–181, *Statutes at Large* 97 (1991): 722.

34. Ronald Reagan, "Statement on the Meeting With Chairman Dwayne Andreas of the Foundation for the Commemoration of the United States Constitution; October 2, 1986," in *Public Papers of the Presidents of the United States: Ronald Reagan: 1986* II, (Washington, D.C.: Government Printing Office, 1989), 1318. In addition to Mr. Andreas, the Foundations' officers and trustees included the Chief Executive Officers of Time Inc., RJR Nabisco, American Express, and the Loews Corporation, former Atty. Gen. Griffin Bell, Mrs. Nelson A. Rockefeller, and Mrs. William P. Rogers, and attorneys Bernard Segal and Robert Strauss. Foundation for the United States Constitution, "Form 990, Return of Organization Exempt From Income Tax," 1987, 13 (attached to Foundation for the United States Constitution, Annual Financial Report (Charitable Organization) filed with New York State Department of State, 1988).

35. Irving Kristol, "On Corporate Capitalism in America," *The American Commonwealth—1976* (New York: Basic, 1976), 128–129.

36. Paul Starr, "The Meaning of Privatization," *Yale Law and Policy Review* 6 (1988): 11.

37. For an argument that looks at the dynamics of American constitutional law in just this light, see Gary Peller, "The Metaphysics of American Law," *California Law Review* 73 (1987): 1151–1290.

38. At the same time, reduced tax incentives for corporate giving and increased attention to profit margins discouraged firms from increasing their philanthropic activities. Edward J. Stendardi, Jr. "Corporate Philanthropy: The Redefinition of Enlightened Self-Interest," *The Social Science Journal* 25 (1992): 23–25.

39. Senate Committee on the Judiciary, *Hearing: Bicentennial of the Constitution,* 98th Cong. 1st Sess., March 1, 1983, 23.

40. A summary of private sector sponsorship of bicentennial events can be found in American Revolution Bicentennial Administration (hereafter ARBA), *The Bicentennial of the United States of America: A Final Report to the People* 2 (Washington, D.C.: Government Printing Office, 1977), 192–212.

41. Tom Konda and Lee Sigelman, "Ad-versarial Politics: Business, Political Advertising, and the 1980 Election," in R. L. Savage and D. Nimmo, *Politics in Familiar Contexts* (Norwood, NJ: Ablex, 1990), 102.

42. Karal Ann Marling, *George Washington Slept Here* (Cambridge, MA: Harvard University Press, 1988), 348–349.

43. Thus Chief Justice John Marshall once wrote:

[t]he objects for which a corporation is created are universally such as the government wishes to promote. They are deemed beneficial to the country; and this benefit constitutes the consideration, and, in most cases, the sole consideration of the grant.

In *Trustees of Dartmouth College v. Woodard,* 4 Wheaton 517 (1819), at 637.

44. Edwin M. Epstein, *The Corporation in American Politics* (Englewood Cliffs, NJ: Prentice-Hall, 1969), 295.

45. Memo to Finance Committee from Mark Cannon, September 10, 1986, found at "Records Relating to Commission History, 1981–1991," Box 5, NA.

46. Public Law 99–549, *Statutes at Large* 100 (1986): 3063.

47. The Foundation changed its name to the Foundation for the United States Constitution from the Foundation for the Commemoration of the United States Constitution in early 1988.

48. The federal Commission's general counsel signed the Foundation's incorporation papers. Joseph McGrath was one of three attorneys who signed the papers. Certificate of Incorporation and Articles of Incorporation, "Records Relating to Commission History," 1981–1991, Box 1, NA. McGrath still referred to the Foundation as "an entirely separate entity from the Commission." Report on the Foundation for the Commemoration of the United States Constitution, *ibid.*

49. Education: Office Files, Box 27, NA.

50. "Corporate Activities 1987–1991." "Records Relating to Commission History, 1981–1991," Box 3, NA.

51. Between March 31, 1986 and March 31, 1990, the Foundation received $4,686,348 in corporate donations. Foundation for the United States Constitution, Annual Financial Reports.

52. The only income that the Commission reported from outside sources that was not derived from the sale of commemorative items or interest was $75,223.07 listed as "Other/Miscellaneous." CBC, *Final Report,* 274.

53. Michael Useem, *The Inner Circle: Large Corporations and the Rise of Business Political Activity in the U.S. and U.K.* (New York: Oxford University Press, 1984), 125.

54. Edward Corwin, "The Constitution as Instrument and as Symbol," 168–179; Max Lerner, "The Constitution and Court as Symbols," 1290–1319.

55. For a summary of corporate involvement in the Bicentennial, see the Commission's internal report "Corporate Activities 1987–1991," in Records Relating to Commission History, 1981–1991, Box 3, NA.

56. Memorandum to the Commission from Mark Cannon, November 17, 1986, in "Records Relating to Media Events, 1985–1987," Box 2, NA.

57. Fred Stein, executive director of WTP Inc., quoted in Scott Flander, "Painting the Town with Red Ink," *Philadelphia Daily News,* February 17, 1987, 18.

58. Walter F. Naedele, "Salute to the Constitution gets Liberty fund-raiser," *The Philadelphia Inquirer,* July 16, 1986, 1B. Eric

Fettman and Roberta Brandes Gratz, "Rovsek Redux," *The Nation,* October 11, 1986, 333. "We the People 200 Sponsorship Opportunities," Box 54119, WTP.

59. Procter, *Enacting Political Culture,* 25.

60. Amended contracts between WTP Inc and Smith-Hemion Productions, February 13, 1987, Box 18, Binder 3, WTP Inc. The amount for this single day was one-fifth of what ABC had paid for the five-day-long Liberty Weekend celebration. Dan Nimmo and James Coombs, *Mediated Political Realities* (New York: Longman, 1990 (2nd ed.)), 31.

61. "We feel it is likely that major sponsors of CBS will also choose to sponsor a float in the parade." "We the People 200 Parade Marketing Plan Overview," June 1, 1987, Box 54111, WTP.

62. The amount was $925,000. WTP Inc., "Statement of Revenue & Expense: Grand Federal Procession, 1/7/87 thru 11/18/88," computer printout of November 18, 1988 found in Drawer 1, WTP Inc. Walter F. Naedele, "Reagan praises city efforts to honor the Constitution," *The Philadelphia Inquirer,* April 2, 1987, 18A. Even Chrysler Corporation, headed by former Statue of Liberty committee Chairman Lee Iaccoca, backed out at the last minute, leaving a $2 million hole in the celebration's finances. Walter F. Naedele, "Chrysler drops out of funding Constitution fete here," *The Philadelphia Inquirer,* March 26, 1987, 1B.

63. House Committee on Post Office and Civil Service, *Joint Hearing: Commission on Bicentennial of Constitution of United States,* 99th Cong. 1st Sess., December 5, 1985, 49.

64. Burger noted that the Foundation had not provided much support after 1987. Testimony of Warren Burger, House Committee on Appropriations, *Hearings: Departments of Commerce, Justice and State, the Judiciary, and Related Agencies Appropriations for 1990,* 101st Cong. 1st Sess., February 8, 1989, Pt. 5, 165.

65. Between April 1, 1987 and March 31, 1990, the Foundation relayed a total of $198,636, only 3.6% of its total revenues of $5,398,022. Foundation for the United States Constitution, Annual Financial Report (Charitable Organization) filed with New York State Department of State, 1988–1990. See also the

statement of Warren Burger, House Committee on Appropriations, *Hearings: Departments of Commerce, Justice and State, the Judiciary, and Related Agencies Appropriations for 1989*, 20–21.

66. Testimony of Warren Burger, House Committee on Appropriations, *Hearings: Departments of Commerce, Justice and State, the Judiciary, and Related Agencies Appropriations for 1989*, 31.

67. The Commission estimated that thirty million milk cartons carried such messages. CBC, *Final Report*, 118. Cartons on file with author. See also Ted McConnell, "1st Quarter Marketing Report," April 7, 1989, NA, Box 79, File: APR 29. The New Hampshire state commission promoted that state's role in the document's ratification on milk cartons as well. New Hampshire Bicentennial Commission on the United States Constitution, *New Hampshire: The State That Made Us a Nation*, (Portsmouth, N.H.: P.E. Randall, 1989), 47.

68. Theodore Levitt, *The Marketing Imagination* (New York: Free Press, 1986 (2nd ed.), 95.

69. As Theodore Levitt writes, "The less tangible the generic product, the more powerfully and persistently the judgment about it is shaped by the 'packaging'—how it's presented, who presents it, what's implied by metaphor, simile, symbol, and other surrogates for reality." Levitt, *The Marketing Imagination*, 98.

70. For the legislation authorizing the Commission to create and license a logo, see Public Law 98–101 §5(j), *Statutes at Large* 97 (1983): 721, and Public Law 99–549 §4, *Statutes at Large* 100 (1986): 3063–3064.

71. The logo was created by the Army's Institute of Heraldry. CBC, *Final Report*, 16.

72. The logo can be found at 45 CFR § 2001 (Appendix A) (1990) and CBC, *Final Report*, 16.

73. Kammen, *A Machine That Would Go of Itself,* 91.

74. Gabriel, *The Course of American Democratic Thought,* 96.

75. CBC, *Final Report,* 82.

76. Michael Schudson, *Advertising: The Uneasy Persuasion* (New York: Basic, 1984), 52.

77. A copy of the advertisement is in CBC, *Final Report,* 236.

78. Videotape on file with author.

79. Schudson, *Advertising: The Uneasy Persuasion,* 215.

80. Thus Paletz, Pearson, and Willis note that public service announcements frequently portray individuals rather than institutions or organizations as representations of social problems. David L. Paletz, Roberta E. Pearson, Donald L. Willis, *Politics in Public Service Advertising on Television,* (New York: Praeger, 1977), 80.

81. Associated Press, "Bicentennial Ads for Constitution," *The New York Times,* February 27, 1987, D18.

82. Advertising Council, Inc., Commemoration of the Bicentennial of the Constititution, Newspaper Kit (New York, 1987).

83. Levitt, *The Marketing Imagination,* 105.

84. See Schudson, *Advertising: The Uneasy Persuasion,* 51.

85. Ad Council, Bicentennial of the Constitution Campaign, Magazine Ads No. BC-2210–87 and BC-2212–87. The advertisements also appear at House Committee on Appropriations, *Hearings: Departments of Commerce, Justice, and State, the Judiciary, and Related Agencies Appropriations for 1988,* 450–452.

86. The Commission also selected the phone number (202) USA–1787 to symbolize its purpose.

87. Food Marketing Institute, "Help Celebrate the Bicentennial of the U.S. Constitution," *FMI Issues Bulletin,* June 1989: 6; Food Marketing Institute, "Supermarkets Combine Community Relations with History Lessons," *FMI Issues Bulletin,* June 1989: 4.

88. Paletz, Pearson, and Willis, *Politics in Public Service Advertising on Television,* 80–81.

89. An illustration of one such panel can be found at CBC, *Final Report,* 85.

90. *The Washington Post,* December 22, 1986, A25. One of the side panels is pictured in CBC, *Final Report,* 85. See also Records Relating to the Marketing and Advertising of Bicentennial Programs, Box 5, NA.

91. "Everyone Should Have a Copy of the Constitution," *The Washington Post,* December 28, 1986, D7.

92. The strip ran nationally in Sunday newspapers on February 22, 1987.

93. "Talk of the Town," *The New Yorker,* December 1, 1986: 29.

94. See Records Relating to the Marketing and Advertising of Bicentennial Programs, Box 5, NA.

95. "The Talk of the Town," *The New Yorker,* December 1, 1986: 29.

96. Place mats on file with author. Henry Allen, "Secrets of the Constitution," *The Washington Post,* April 20, 1987, B1. See also Irwin Molotsky, "Q&A: Warren E. Burger On Fixing the Constitution and Spilling Gravy All Over the Preamble," *The New York Times,* April 16, 1987, B8. In addition to those distributed in 1987, McDonald's also printed trayliners to commemorate the Bill of Rights bicentennial in 1991. Minutes of Commission Meeting, Sept. 14, 1991, in "Records Relating to Commission History, 1981–1991," Box 9, NA. See also CBC, *Final Report,* 84, 254.

97. Testimony of Warren Burger, Committee on Appropriations, *Hearings: Departments of Commerce, Justice, and State, the Judiciary, and Related Agencies Appropriations for 1988,* 409. Roy Rogers place mat at Box 11, NA. AHMA materials in Box 67, NA.

98. Grant McCracken, *Culture and Consumption* (Bloomington: Indiana University Press, 1988), 132.

99. Roy Rogers place mat at Box 11, NA.

100. Karl Marx, *Capital* I, S. Moore and E. Aveling, trans. (New York: International Publishers, 1967), 71–83. For an anthropological approach to this same issue, see Igor Kopytoff, "The Cultural Biography of Things," in A. Appadurai, *The Social Life of Things* (Cambridge: Cambridge University Press, 1986), 64–91.

101. "To be saleable for money . . . is to have something in common with a large number of exchangeable things that, taken together, partake of a single universe of comparable values." Kopytoff, "The Cultural Biography of Things," 69.

102. The Judiciary Committee emphasized its concern that a corporation might appropriate the logo and use it to promote "the official bicentennial widget." Senate Committee on the Judiciary, *Bicentennial of the Constitution,* 40.

103. *Code of Federal Regulations* 45 §2001.23(5)(b) (1990). By contrast, the Philadelphia promoters of WTP Inc. had minimal standards; the celebration's executive director ruled out official toilet seats. Fred Stein, quoted in Amy Wilentz, "The Pursuit of Tackiness," *Time,* February 9, 1987: 26.

104. Stephanie B. Goldberg, "The Selling of the Bicentennial," *ABA Journal,* September 1, 1987: 66. California Bicentennial Foundation for the U.S. Constitution, "Bicentennial Memorabilia" (Price list and order form), August, 1987, Box 73, NA.

105. William J. Bennett, "How Should Americans Celebrate the Bicentennial of the Constitution," *National Forum: The Phi Kappa Phi Journal* 64, no. 4 (Fall, 1984): 60.

106. Mary Douglas, *Purity and Danger* (London: Ark, 1984 (orig. 1966)), 35.

107. Curtis F. Brown thus identifies kitsch as going beyond schlock in its ability to cross boundaries and to sully otherwise sacred or venerable objects. He uses the similar example of the ashtray that beckons *"Come on, folks, stub out your cigarettes and cigars right into the upturned inspiring faces of our martyred New York State Senator, Robert F. Kennedy . . . and his brother, John F. Kennedy . . . thirty-fifth President of the United States of America." Star-Spangled Kitsch* (New York: Universe Books, 1975), 13–14 (emphasis in original).

108. Durkheim defined the sacred as "that which is *set apart,* that which is *separated.* What characterizes it is that it cannot, without losing its nature, be mixed with the profane." Durkheim, *Sociology and Philosophy,* 70.

109. See Merelman, *Making Something of Ourselves,* 146.

110. Schudson, *Advertising: The Uneasy Persuasion,* 225.

111. Even with promotional costs of over $500,000, the American Revolution Bicentennial Administration had a net profit from licensing of over $1 million in 1976. ARBA, *The Bicentennial of the United States of America* 2, 473.

112. Memorandum from Fred Stein, executive director, to the Executive Committee, July 8, 1985, Box 54120, WTP.

113. We the People 200, Inc., ledger labeled "Accts Receivable—Prom Sales," July 31, 1988, Drawer 1, WTP Inc.

114. Goldberg, "The Selling of the Constitution," 64.

115. The actual figure, $344,992.61, was calculated on net income of $471,399.75 minus interest income of $126,407.14. CBC, *Final Report,* 275.

116. Michel Foucault, *Discipline and Punish: The Birth of the Prison,* A. Sheridan, trans. (New York: Vintage, 1979).

117. Romain Laufer and Catherine Paradeise, *Marketing Democracy: Public Opinion and Media Formation in Democratic Societies* (New Brunswick, NJ: Transaction, 1990), 2.

118. See Edward L. Bernays, *Crystallizing Public Opinion* (New York: Boni and Liveright, 1923), 173.

119. Jhally, *The Codes of Advertising,* 72–73.

120. James Willard Hurst, *The Legitimacy of the Business Corporation in the Law of the United States, 1780–1970* (Charlottesville: University of Virginia, 1970), 59–60; see also Louis Hartz, *Economic Policy and Democratic Thought,* (Cambridge, MA: Harvard University Press, 1948), 71–72.

121. Hurst, *The Legitimacy of the Business Corporation,* 60.

122. Stephen Skowronek, *Building a New American State* (New York: Cambridge University Press, 1982).

123. However, as Edwin Epstein has argued, both bureaucracy and corporations have a problematic status in democratic political theory, which "provides no rationale to explain the political activities of fictional corporate 'persons' who are not accountable to any recognizable constituency." Epstein, *The Corporation in American Politics,* 145.

124. Hartz, *The Liberal Tradition in America,* 216.

125. Hartz, *Economic Policy and Democratic Thought,* 250.

126. *Ibid.,* 316.

127. Richard Eells, *Corporation Giving in a Free Society* (New York: Harper and Brothers, 1956), 90–91.

128. Commentators have declared that the American people prefer such a system of power divided between public and private actors. See, for example, E. E. Schattschneider, *The Semi-Sovereign People* (New York: Holt, Rinehart and Winston, 1960), 120–121.

129. The same idea that a decentralized, loosely coordinated celebration was more appropriate for a large, geographically and culturally varied nation-state was behind the scaling down of the original plan to celebrate the Bicentennial of the American Revolution. See Brody, *Sociological Theories of Symbolic Activity*, 89–90.

Chapter Three

1. California Bicentennial Foundation, "Constitution Class" (press release), Business Wire, September 8, 1987. Other festivities at the California Independence Hall included a ball and a naturalization ceremony. See "The Governors Ball: A Bicentennial Birthday Party" (program), in NA, Records Relating to State and Local Programs, 1986–1991, Box 1 (Alabama thru Louisiana), File: California. Richard Beene, "100 From Around Globe 'Honor US' By Taking Oaths," *The Los Angeles Times,* September 18, 1987, Pt 2, 1.

2. Zelinsky, *Nation Into State,* 214.

3. Always convinced that he was right, Ford declared that his copy would be better than the original. Edward Bernays, *Biography of an Idea* (New York: Simon and Schuster, 1965), 447.

4. Dean McCannell, *The Tourist* (New York: Schocken, 1976).

5. Analyzing another southern California amusement park, Jean Baudrilliard announces that

> Disneyland is there to conceal the fact that it is the "real" country, all of "real" America, which is Disneyland . . . Disneyland is presented as imaginary in order to make us believe that the rest is real, when in fact all of Los Angeles and the America surrounding it are no longer real, but of the order of the hyperreal and simulation.

Jean Baudrillard, *Simulations,* trans. P. Foss, P. Patton, and P. Beitchman (New York: Semiotext(e), 1983), 25.

6. McCannell, *The Tourist,* 3; Roger D. Abrahams, "An American Vocabulary of Celebrations," in A. Falassi, ed., *Time Out of Time* (Albuquerque: University of New Mexico Press, 1987), 177.

7. *The Presence of the Past: Essays on the State and the Constitution* (Baltimore: Johns Hopkins University Press, 1989), 2–3.

8. For a critique of the importance of struggle within the development of historical consciousness, see Daniel Boorstin, *The Genius of American Politics* (Chicago: University of Chicago Press, 1953), 33.

9. Michael Kammen, *Mystic Chords of Memory* (New York: Knopf, 1991), 351–370.

10. Umberto Eco, *Travels in Hyperreality,* trans. by W. Weaver (New York: Harcourt, Brace, and Jovanovich, 1986), 39.

11. Constance Grieff, *Independence* (Philadelphia: University of Pennsylvania Press, 1987), 77–162.

12. Hanna Fenichel Pitkin, *The Concept of Representation* (Berkeley: University of California Press, 1967), 8 (emphasis in original).

13. For a recent elaboration of this theory by one of its more important advocates, see Robert H. Bork, *The Tempting of America* (New York: Free Press, 1990).

14. *We the People: Foundations,* 34.

15. *We the People: Foundations,* 40–41.

16. Thurgood Marshall, "Reflections on the Bicentennial of the United States Constitution," *Harvard Law Review* 101 (1987): 5.

17. *Ibid.,* 4.

18. Ackerman, *We the People: Foundations,* 37.

19. Louis Marin, *Utopics: Spatial Play,* trans. by R.A. Vollrath (Atlantic Highlands, NJ: Humanities Press, 1984), 239.

20. James Michener, *Legacy* (New York: Random House, 1987), 149.

21. For the idea of political tradition as a birthright, see Sheldon Wolin, "Contract and Birthright," in H. C. Boyte and F. Reissman, eds., *The New Populism: The Politics of Empowerment* (Philadelphia: Temple University Press, 1986), 289.

22. Hobsbawm, "Introduction: Inventing Traditions," 4.

23. J. G. A. Pocock, "Modes of Political and Historical Time," in his *Virtue, Commerce, and History* (Cambridge: Cambridge University Press, 1985), 92.

24. J. G. A. Pocock, "Virtues, rights, and manners," in his *Virtue, Commerce, and History* (Cambridge: Cambridge University Press, 1985), 46.

25. U.S. Senate, Committee on the Judiciary, *Bicentennial of the Constitution,* Senate Report 97–535, (Washington, D.C.: GPO, 1982), 27. Public Law 98–101 specified that the Bicentennial focus on "the historical setting in which the Constitution was developed and ratified."*Statutes at Large* 97 (1983): 722.

26. Senate Committee on the Judiciary, *Bicentennial of the Constitution,* 42.

27. Judiciary Committee Chairman Strom Thurmond and Constitution Subcommittee Chairman Orrin Hatch, both key legislative supporters of the Bicentennial, were also ardent supporters of such a return to the principles of 1787. See, for example, Strom Thurmond, "The Bicentennial of the Constitution," *Marquette Law Review* 70 (1987): 375–380; Orrin G. Hatch and James MacGregor Burns, "Still Adequate for the Twentieth Century? A Debate," *Utah Law Review* 1987 (1987): 871–885.

28. Clifford Geertz, *Negara: The Theatre State in Nineteenth-Century Bali* (Princeton: Princeton University Press, 1980), 14.

29. Harold R. Isaacs, *Idols of the Tribe* (New York: Harper & Row, 1975), 117.

30. For the distinction between charisma and legal (or rational) forms of legitimacy, see Max Weber, *Economy and Society,* G. Roth and C. Wittich eds. (Berkeley: University of California, 1978), 215. For a comment on narratives of the routinization of charisma, see David Carr, *Time, Narrative and History* (Bloomington: Indiana University Press, 1986), 164.

31. See Edward Shils, "The Fortunes of Constitutional Government in the Political Development of the New States," in his *Center and Periphery*, (Chicago: University of Chicago Press, 1975) 458–459.

32. Douglas Adair, "Fame and the Founding Fathers," in his *Fame and the Founding Fathers*, T. Colburn, ed., (New York: Norton, 1974), 46.

33. Thus J. G. A. Pocock has argued,

> the charismatic figures who stand at the mythical beginnings of so many traditions . . . provide the inheritors of tradition with occasion to imagine politics and other activities as consisting of charismatic . . . instead of traditional action.

In Pocock, *Politics, Language and Time* (Chicago: University of Chicago, 1989), 243.

34. Walter F. Naedele, Mark Bowden, and Julia Cass, "In Philadelphia assembled, again," *The Philadelphia Inquirer,* July 17, 1987, 1-A. William K. Stevens, "Key to Nation is Celebrated on its 200th Birthday," *The New York Times,* July 18, 1987, A36.

35. Hans Gerth and C. Wright Mills, *Character and Social Structure* (New York: Harcourt, Brace and World, 1953), 276–277.

36. Max Lerner, "The Constitution and Court as Symbols," *Yale Law Journal* 46 (1937): 1299.

37. Anthony D. Smith, *The Ethnic Origins of Nations* (Oxford: Basil Blackwell, 1986), 192.

38. As Barry Schwartz writes, "Virtue does not speak for itself; to be known, it must be formulated in vivid, heroic images." *George Washington: The Making of an American Symbol,* 115.

39. Lincoln was seen as a decisive and strong leader, while Jefferson was closely associated with anti-statism; identification with a particular party was not as important as beliefs about a strong or weak state. Peter Karsten, *Patriot-Heroes in England and America* (Madison: University of Wisconsin Press, 1978), 100–109.

40. Daniel J. Boorstin, *The Americans: The National Experience* (New York: Random House, 1965), 367.

41. Testimony of Warren Burger, House Committee on Appropriations, *Hearings: Departments of Commerce, Justice, and State, the Judiciary, and Related Agencies Appropriations for 1989,* 100th Cong., 2nd Sess., March 16, 1988, Pt. 5, 26.

42. Edward S. Casey, *Remembering: A Phenomenological Study* (Bloomington: Indiana University Press, 1987), 226 (italics in original).

43. Schudson, *Watergate in American Memory,* 63.

44. Sixty-four percent were oriented to the past, 35.5% were present-oriented, and only 0.5% were future-oriented. Brody, *Sociological Theories of Symbolic Activity,* 104.

45. For the difference between official and vernacular history, see John Bodnar, *Remaking America: Public Memory, Commemoration, and Patriotism in the Twentieth Century* (Princeton, NJ: Princeton University Press, 1992), 14.

46. For a critique of this view, see Michael Foley, *Laws, Men, and Machines: Modern American Government and the Appeal of Newtonian Mechanics* (London: Routledge, 1990).

47. *The Federalist Papers,* C. Rossiter, ed. (New York: New American Library, 1961), no. 51, 322.

48. See Michael Lienesch, "The Constitutional Tradition," *Journal of Politics* 42 (1980): 2–30, for a history that views the Constitution as a system intended to restrain popular sovereignty in this way.

49. Alexander Bickel, *The Supreme Court and the Idea of Progress* (New Haven: Yale University Press, 1978).

50. Herbert Butterfield, *The Whig Interpretation of History* (London: G. Bell and Sons, 1959), 12.

51. For a description, see CBC, *Final Report,* 50–51. "Roads to Liberty" is further discussed in Chapter Four.

52. William J. Brennan, Jr., "Construing the Constitution," *University of California Davis Law Review* 19 (1985): 2.

53. Dicey, *Introduction to the Study of the Law of the Constitution,* cxxxvi-cxxxvii.

54. *Ibid.,* cxxxvii.

55. Quoted in Nadine Cohodas, "A Pioneer in the Halls of Justice," *The Washington Post,* January 24, 1993, X1.

56. Arjun Appadurai, "The Past as a Scarce Resource," *Man (N.S.)* 16 (1981): 216.

57. Robert A. Ferguson, "'We Do Ordain and Establish': The Constitution as Literary Text," *William and Mary Law Review* 29 (1987): 10–11.

58. For discussions of representation as agency and descriptive representation, see Pitkin, *The Concept of Representation,* 112–143 and 60–91, respectively.

59. Public Law 98–101, *Statutes at Large* 97 (1983): 722.

60. Senate Committee on the Judiciary, *Bicentennial of the Constitution,* 97th Cong., 2d Sess., 1982, S. Rept. 535, 33 (emphasis added).

61. See Memo from Mark Cannon, Sept. 5, 1986, "Records Relating to Commission History, 1981–1991," Box 6, NA. See also CBC, *Final Report,* 44–45.

62. *Ibid.*

63. During both the centennial of the Civil War and the bicentennial of Washington's birth, ethnic groups other than Anglo-Americans were each given a historical figure or two to be proud of, so as to include more groups in the celebrations. Bodnar, *Remaking America,* 216; Marling, *George Washington Slept Here,* 350.

64. Minutes of Commission Meeting, March 3, 1990 in "Records Relating to Commission History," Box 8, NA.

65. A consultant had been hired in 1988 to develop a plan and submitted a report in 1989. Memorandum to Commission from Jay N. Price, June 7, 1990, "Records Relating to Commission History," Box 8, NA.

66. Thus, Muir wrote:

> [m]ore than merely reinforcing the ideology of Venice, the ducal processions helped to create that ideology by serving as a conscious visible synthesis of the parts of society: each symbol or

person in the procession corresponded to a specific principle or institution; placed together and set in motion, they were the narrative outline for the myth of Venetian republicanism.

In E. Muir, *Civic Ritual in Renaissance Venice* (Princeton, NJ: Princeton University Press, 1981), 211.

67. *Sovereignty and Liberty,* 104–105.

68. An analysis of the We the People 200 parade's appropriation of the Constitution's textuality is contained in Chapter Four.

69. Susan G. Davis, *Parades and Power: Street Theatre in Nineteenth Century Philadelphia* (Berkeley: University of California Press, 1988),125.

70. For a full account of the 1788 procession, see Hopkinson, "An Account of the Grand Federal Procession." For a historical account of the federal processions and celebrations throughout the young nation, see Whitfield Bell, Jr., "The Federal Processions of 1788," *The New York Historical Society Quarterly* 46 (1962): 5–39.

71. For a full account of the 1887 procession, see A. Loudon Snowden, "Civic and Industrial Procession, September 15, 1887," in H. L. Carson, ed., *History of the Celebration of the One Hundredth Anniversary of the Promulgation of the Constitution of the United States* 2 (Philadelphia: J.B. Lippincott Company, 1889), 1–166.

72. One float in the section of the parade representing American Indians proclaimed "'Indians in the United States, 247,000; of school age, 46,877; in school, 12,316; leaving 34,561 growing up in ignorance and barbarism.' And on the end of the float, the words, 'We must educate.'" *Ibid.,* 41.

73. Guy Debord writes in his *Society of the Spectacle:* "The triumph of irreversible time is also its metamorphosis into the *time of things,* because the weapon of its victory was precisely the mass production of objects according to the laws of the commodity. The main product which economic development has transferred from luxurious scarcity to daily consumption is therefore *history.* (Detroit: Black & Red, 1983), Chap. V, § 142 (emphasis in original).

74. See John Bodnar's analysis of the great Centennial of 1876 in *Remaking America,* 30.

75. George H. Nadel, "Periodization," in D. L. Sills, ed., *International Encyclopedia of the Social Sciences* 11 (New York: MacMillan, 1968), 581.

76. Davis, *Parades and Power,* 123.

77. This portion of the We the People 200 parade is further described in Chapter Four.

78. Warner, *The Living and the Dead,* 124–128.

79. Daniel Boorstin, *Hidden History* (New York: Harper & Row, 1987), 154.

80. Michael Kammen, "History Is Our Heritage," in P. Gagnon, ed., *Historical Literacy* (New York: MacMillan, 1989), 145–146.

81. Dean MacCannell, "Staged Authenticity: Arrangements of Social Space in Tourist Settings," *American Journal of Sociology* 79 (1973): 589–603.

82. As Diane Barthel writes, "Preservation has become part of [the] myth-making process, as Americans began to construct ritualized presentations of their preindustrial past." Diane Barthel, "Historic Preservation: A Comparative Analysis," *Sociological Forum* 4 (1989): 101.

83. David Glassberg, *American Historical Pageantry: The Uses of Tradition in the Early Twentieth Century* (Chapel Hill: University of North Carolina Press, 1990) 43–67.

84. CBC, *Final Report,* 21–29.

85. Snowden, "Civic and Industrial Procession," 25 (also see accompanying photograph facing 24).

86. Julia Cass, "Fete Parade Promises Glitz Blitz," *The Philadelphia Inquirer,* September 6, 1987, B-2.

87. David Lowenthal, *The Past is a Foreign Country* (Cambridge: Cambridge University Press, 1985), 256.

88. The furniture was also among the most expensive items sold by the Commission. The Congress Hall secretary's desk cost $3,848 in mahogany while arm chairs were priced at just under $2,000. Commission on the Bicentennial of the United States Con-

stitution, *Commemorative Gifts Catalogue* (Washington, D.C.: Commission, n.d.).

89. Pitkin, *The Concept of Representation,* 8.

90. Kammen, *A Machine that Would Go of Itself,* 144–151.

91. The historians were the Commission's then deputy staff director, Herbert Atherton, and Chief Historian at Independence National Historic Park, David Dutcher. Biography of William A. Sommerfield, NA, Records Relating to Special Events, Box 7, File: G. Washington's April Journey 1989; 6/88–3/89. See also CBC, *Final Report,* 155–156.

92. See descriptions in CBC, *Final Report,* 92–99.

93. See descriptions in CBC, *Final Report,* 21–29, 216–230, and 184 respectively.

94. Kammen, *Mystic Chords of Memory,* 277–281, 422–425; Glassberg, *American Historical Pageantry.*

95. S. Freud, "A Disturbance of Memory on the Acropolis," in J. Strachey, ed., *Collected Papers* 5 (New York: Basic Books, 1959), 304.

96. *Ibid.,* 310.

97. Milton Singer, "On the Symbolic and Historic Structure of an American Identity," *Ethos* 5 (1977): 448–449.

98. "Introduction: Inventing Traditions," in Hobsbawm and Ranger, *The Invention of Tradition,* 2.

99. Hans-Georg Gadamer, *Truth and Method* (New York: Seabury Press, 1975), 333.

100. Carr, *Time, Narrative and History,* 167.

101. For instance, the seven-day-week in Jewish and Christian tradition is modeled on the Creation. Mircea Eliade, *The Myth of Eternal Return,* trans. W. R. Trask (Chicago: University of Chicago Press, 1954), 23, 129.

102. William M. Johnston, *Celebrations* (New Brunswick, NJ: Transaction, 1991), 31.

103. Stow Persons, "The Cyclical Theory of History in Eighteenth Century America," *American Quarterly* 6 (1954): 147–163.

104. Sacvan Bercovitch, *The American Jeremiad* (Madison: University of Wisconsin Press, 1978).

105. Bernard Bailyn, *The Ideological Origins of the American Revolution,* (Cambridge, MA: Harvard University Press, 1967), 6.

106. Daniel Boorstin, *The Image* (New York: Atheneum, 1975 (1961)), 250.

Chapter Four

1. For a historical examination of descriptions of the Constitution, see Kammen, *A Machine That Would Go of Itself.*

2. William H. Rehnquist, "The Notion of a Living Constitution," *Texas Law Review* 54 (1976): 693 (emphasis in original).

3. For a discussion of the historical comparisons between the U.S. and British constitutions, see Kammen, *A Machine That Would Go of Itself,* 156–184.

4. This meaning of the term had been revived in Britain by the time of Locke. Graham Maddox, "Constitution," in Terence Ball, James Farr, and Russell L. Hanson, eds., *Political Innovation and Conceptual Change* (Cambridge: Cambridge University Press, 1989), 51, 59.

5. Walter Bagehot comments that the monarchy "enables our real rulers to change without heedless people knowing it. The masses of Englishmen are not fit for elective government, if they knew how near they were to it, they would be surprised and almost tremble." Bagehot, *The English Constitution,* 97.

6. Harris, *The Interpretable Constitution,* ix–x.

7. Dicey, *Introduction to the Study of the Law of the Constitution,* cxxvii.

8. Warner, *The Letters of the Republic,* 102.

9. Jack Goody, *The Logic of Writing and the Organization of Society* (Cambridge: Cambridge University Press, 1986), 99.

10. William Lloyd Warner, *The Living and the Dead: A Study of the Symbolic Life of Americans* (New Haven: Yale University Press, 1959), 218.

11. S. Freud, "A Note upon the 'mystic writing-pad'," In *The Complete Psychological Works* 19, J. Strachey, ed. (London: Hogarth Press, 1961), 227.

12. Harris, *The Interpretable Constitution,* xiii.

13. Ed Reiter, "Designs are Released for Constitution Coins," *The New York Times,* April 12, 1987, A72.

14. Advertising Council, Inc., "Commemoration of the Bicentennial of the Constititution, Newspaper Kit" (New York, 1987).

15. Warner, *The Letters of the Republic,* 118.

16. Bumper sticker on file with author.

17. Norton, "Transubstantiation," 462.

18. McCoy, *The National Archives,* 254–256; "Constitution, Declaration Stored in a Concrete Vault," *The Washington Post,* October 11, 1986, B2.

19. "The Work of Art in the Age of Mechanical Reproduction," in *Illuminations,* 222.

20. Kammen, *A Machine That Would Go of Itself,* 73.

21. Benjamin, "The Work of Art in the Age of Mechanical Reproduction," 222.

22. *Ibid.,* 224.

23. *Ibid.,* 226.

24. Benjamin, "On Some Motifs in Baudelaire," in *Illuminations,* 190.

25. Jurgen Habermas comments that the aura

is the sign of magical world views in which the split between the sphere of the objectified, over which we have manipulative disposal, and the realm of the intersubjective, in which we encounter one another communicatively, has not yet been achieved.

Jurgen Habermas, "Walter Benjamin: Consciousness Raising or Rescuing Critique," in *On Walter Benjamin,* Gary Smith, ed. (Cambridge, MA: MIT Press, 1988), 107.

26. Benjamin, *Illuminations,* 223.

27. *Ibid.*

28. *Ibid.,* 223. For an account of Benjamin's thought in this area, see Richard Wolin, *Walter Benjamin: An Aesthetic of Redemption* (Berkeley: University of California Press, 1994), 184–191; see also Bernd Witte, *Walter Benjamin: An Intellectual Life,* J. Rolleston, trans. (Detroit: Wayne State University Press, 1991), 160–163.

29. Robin Ridless, *Ideology and Art: Theories of Mass Culture from Walter Benjamin to Umberto Eco* (New York: Peter Lang, 1984), xiv.

30. Elizabeth L. Eisenstein, *The Printing Press as an Agent of Change* I (London: Cambridge University Press, 1979), 81.

31. Levinson, *Constitutional Faith,* 29.

32. Cf. Stanley Fish, *Is There a Text in this Class?* (Cambridge, MA: Harvard University Press, 1980).

33. Eisenstein, *The Printing Press as an Agent of Change* I, 218.

34. Joseph Goldstein, *The Intelligible Constitution* (New York: Oxford University Press, 1992), 19.

35. Harris, *The Interpretable Constitution,* 111.

36. H. J. Chaytor, *From Script to Print: An Introduction to Medieval Vernacular Literature* (London: Sidgwick & Jackson, 1966 (orig. 1945)), 22.

37. Marshall McLuhan, *The Gutenberg Galaxy* (Toronto: University of Toronto Press, 1962), 236. This invention was crucial to the development of many other social movements besides modern nationalism. For a recent introduction to the literature on the connection between printing and Protestantism, see Carmen Luke, *Pedagogy, Printing, and Protestantism* (Albany: State University of New York, 1989).

38. McLuhan, *The Gutenberg Galaxy,* 236.

39. Benjamin, "The Work of Art in the Age of Mechanical Reproduction," 234

40. See, for example, Jean Bethke Elshtain, *Public Man, Private Woman* (Princeton, NJ: Princeton University Press, 1981).

41. Warner, *The Letters of the Republic,* 16

42. Leslie J. Limage, "Adult Literacy Policy in Industrialized Countries," in R. F. Arnove and H. J. Graff, eds., *National Literacy Campaigns: Historical and Comparative Perspectives* (New York: Plenum Press, 1987), 296.

43. Copy of circular for the week of August 2, 1989, on file with author. See also Food Marketing Institute, "Supermarkets Combine Community Relations with History Lessons," *FMI Issues Bulletin,* December 1990: 4.

44. See Edward L. Bernays, *The Engineering of Consent* (Norman: University of Oklahoma Press, 1952), 167, for the importance of keeping textual complexity within the grasp of the average American.

45. Jeanne S. Chall and Dorothy Henry, "Reading and Civic Literacy," in Sandra Stotsky, ed., *Connecting Civic Education and Language Education* (New York: Teachers College Press, 1991), 49.

46. *Ibid.,* 49–52.

47. *Ibid.,* 55.

48. "Cheney Considers Braille," *The New York Times,* February 13, 1987, Pt. I, 18.

49. Files containing the Constitution and many related documents, such as the Federalist Papers, may be found on a variety of Internet servers.

50. Frederick M. Muir, "In 1987, We the People get a 'User-Friendly' Constitution," *The Los Angeles Times,* August 24, 1987, Pt. 2, 1.

51. For a similar situation from the history of Protestantism, see Eisenstein, *The Printing Press as an Agent of Change* I, 343.

52. *Rights of Man* in Foner, *The Life and Major Writings of Thomas Paine,* 378.

53. Levinson, *Constitutional Faith,* 32.

54. Roger K. Newman, *Hugo Black: A Biography* (New York: Pantheon, 1994), 624.

55. "Burger's Goal," *The New York Times,* January 9, 1987, Pt. I, 16.

56. Burger, "Foreword," in CBC, *Final Report,* viii.

57. Max Horkheimer and Theodor W. Adorno, *Dialectic of Enlightenment,* John Cumming, trans. (New York: Continuum, 1987), 163.

58. Lee Soltow and Edward Stevens, *The Rise of Literacy and the Origins of the Common School in the United States* (Chicago: University of Chicago Press, 1981), 55.

59. Jefferson to Dr. James Mease, quoted in Kammen, *Mystic Chords of Memory,* 68.

60. Benjamin, *Illuminations,* 222.

61. "Centers, Kings and Charisma: Reflections on the Symbolics of Power," in *Local Knowledge: Further Essays in Interpretive Anthropology* (New York: Basic, 1983), 121–146.

62. Durkheim, *Sociology and Philosophy,* 70.

63. The original copies of these documents remain in their permanent "Shrine" at the National Archives.

64. Kammen, *Mystic Chords of Memory,* 572–581.

65. See Louis B. Wright, *Magna Carta and the Tradition of Liberty* (Washington, D.C.: American Revolution Bicentennial Administration, 1976); American Revolution Bicentennial Administration, *The Bicentennial of the United States of America: Final Report to the People* I, 259.

66. The tour was sponsored by American Express, and was endorsed by the Commission on the Bicentennial and funded through the Foundation for the Constitution. CBC, *Final Report,* 50–52. An account of the Magna Carta visit to Concord, NH is contained in New Hampshire Bicentennial Commission, *New Hampshire: The State That Made Us a Nation,* 52, 54–55; see also the statement of Warren Burger, House Committee on Appropriations, *Hearings: Departments of Commerce, Justice and State, the Judiciary, and Related Agencies Appropriations for 1989,* 100th Cong. 2nd Sess., March 16, 1988, Pt. 1, 20–21.

67. The H.M.S. *Rose* tour was funded by NYNEX corporation; see the description of the tour in CBC, *Final Report,* 219.

68. For a complete account of the Philip Morris campaign see Daniel Lessard Levin, "The Constitution in the Postmodern Marketplace: Philip Morris and the Bicentennial of the Bill of Rights," *The Legal Studies Forum* 20 (1996), 367–386.

69. The Freedom Train was sponsored by contributions from large corporations and was criticized by some for a conservative bias. Critics argued that documents concerning labor and civil rights had been given short shrift in the selection of materials. Kammen, *Mystic Chords of Memory,* 572–581.

70. See, for example, "Remarks at the White House Ceremony Opening the 'Roads to Liberty' Exhibit, March 11, 1987," *Public Papers of the Presidents: Ronald Reagan: 1987* I (Washington, D.C.: GPO, 1989), 235–236.

71. See Records Relating to Private Sector Programs, Box 3, NA.

72. Kammen, *A Machine That Would Go of Itself,* 285, and fig. 20 (between 262 and 263).

73. Walter F. Naedele, "Touring the U.S., 1215 Magna Carta adds Phila. Visit," *The Philadelphia Inquirer,* June 6, 1987, B4; see also Naedele, "With royal flourish, 1297 Magna Carta is welcomed to city," *The Philadelphia Inquirer,* May 2, 1987, A1.

74. James Pratt, "Jefferson exhibits coming to Nashville," *The Tennessean* (Nashville), September 12, 1987, 1A, 7A; Pratt, "State wins independence for freedom papers," *The Tennessean,* September 13, 1987, 1A, 8A.

75. CBC, *Final Report,* 259.

76. Geertz, "Centers, Kings and Charisma," 134–142.

77. Boorstin, *The Image,* 249.

78. David D. Hall, "The Uses of Literacy in New England, 1600–1850," in W. Joyce et al., eds. *Printing and Society in Early America* (Worcester, MA: American Antiquarian Society, 1983), 23.

79. Norton, "Transubstantiation," 461.

80. Harris, *The Interpretable Constitution* , xi.

81. Daniel Boorstin, *The Americans: The National Experience* (New York: Random House, 1965), 390.

82. See Jay Fliegelman, *Declaring Independence: Jefferson, Natural Language, and the Culture of Performance* (Stanford, CA: Stanford University Press, 1993), esp. 25–27.

83. Kammen, *A Machine That Would Go of Itself,* 127.

84. As Susan Davis writes, "Parades are public dramas of social relations, and in them performers define who can be a social actor and what subjects and ideas are available for communication and consideration." Davis, *Parades and Power,* 6. For another account of how processions signify positions of hierarchy and communal values, see Muir, *Civic Ritual in Renaissance Venice,* 185–211.

85. The Grand Federal Procession is described in greater detail in Chapter Three, while the Parade of America's People is briefly described in Chapter Two.

86. The use of the Preamble to organize the main body of the parade was Radio City's idea. Author interview with Fred Stein, former director of We the People 200, February 21, 1992.

87. For a historical treatment of the fetishism of the Constitution, see Kammen, *A Machine that Would Go of Itself,* 225–226, 248–251.

88. See Ferguson, "We Do Ordain and Establish," 10–11.

89. The states were represented according to the chronological order of their admission to the Union. A group of "Pony Express" riders on horseback symbolized one of the media which brought the nation together and the westward expansion.

90. The floats bearing the seals of both houses of Congress followed the cars containing members of Pennsylvania's congressional delegation, while the float bearing the Presidential Seal was surrounded by cadets from a local military academy who marched around a float bearing the presidential portraits.

91. The depiction of the judiciary as the pillar of the constitutional separation of powers served to perpetuate the ideal of an apolitical judiciary dedicated to the abstract principles of law in contrast to the more pragmatic and partisan "political branches."

92. Tocqueville, *Democracy in America* 1, Chap. XVI, 287. As Neil Postman argues:

> A society in which sacred knowledge is codified in complex pictographs to which few have access develops different religious sentiments and institutions from those of a society whose sacred knowledge is codified in an alphabet to which many have access.

N. Postman, *Teaching as a Conserving Activity* (New York: Delacorte, 1979), 42.

93. Burger, "Foreword," in CBC, *Final Report,* viii.

94. Videotape of CBS broadcast on file with author.

95. Ed Reiter, "Designs are Released for Constitution Coins," *The New York Times,* April 12, 1987, A72.

96. Jack Goody and Ian Watt, "The Consequences of Literacy," *Comparative Studies in Society and History* 5 (1963), 304–345.

97. Postman, *Teaching as a Conserving Activity,* 35.

98. On the Declaration, see Fliegelman, *Declaring Independence,* 65; on the Constitution, see Robert A. Ferguson, "'We Do Ordain and Establish'," 10–11.

Chapter Five

1. For a philosophical explanation and critique of the doctrine of original intent, see John Arthur, *Words that Bind* (Boulder: Westview, 1995), 7–43.

2. Robert H. Bork, *The Tempting of America* (New York: Free Press, 1990), 145.

3. Ackerman, *We the People: Foundations,* 263.

4. Nick Ravo, "Better Late Than Not at All: Town Ratifies Constitution," *The New York Times,* January 9, 1988, Pt I, 29; "U.S. Constitution Rejected," *The New York Times,* May 25, 1988, Pt. II, 2.

5. Ravo, "Better Late Than Not at All," 29.

6. The fountainhead of this tradition is James Madison's *Federalist No. 10.*

7. William Graebner, *The Engineering of Consent* (Madison: University of Wisconsin Press, 1987), 10.

8. Senate Committee on the Judiciary, *Bicentennial of the Constitution*, 98th Cong., 1st Sess., 1983, S. Rept. 68, 3 (emphasis added).

9. Gary Peller, "The Metaphysics of American Law," *California Law Review* 73 (1987): 1151–1290.

10. Thus, James Morone asserts that local communities and voluntary associations have long "offer[ed] Americans a counter to both liberalism and the state." Morone, *The Democratic Wish*, 73. Tocqueville thus wrote that political associations "constitute, as it were, a separate nation in the midst of the nation, a government within the government." *Democracy in America* I, 200. Also see Roger Boesche, *The Strange Liberalism of Alexis de Tocqueville* (Ithaca: Cornell University Press, 1987), 118–119.

11. Robert Nisbet, *The Quest for Community* (London: Oxford University Press, 1969 (orig. 1953)).

12. Kammen, *Sovereignty and Liberty*, 12.

13. Quoted in Dicey, *Introduction to the Study of the Law of the Constitution*, 37.

14. Richard B. Bernstein and Jerome Agel, *Amending America* (New York: Times Books, 1993), 176.

15. Wilson Carey McWilliams, "Afterword," in Michael A. Gillespie and Michael Lienesch, eds., *Ratifying the Constitution* (Lawrence: University of Kansas Press, 1989), 392.

16. For a discussion of the characteristics of liberalism and communitarianism, see, for example, Adrian Oldfield, *Citizenship and Community: Civic Republicanism and the Modern World* (London: Routledge, 1990), and Michael Sandel, "Introduction," *Liberalism and Its Critics* (New York: New York University Press, 1984).

17. Philip Abbot, *Seeking Many Inventions: The Idea of Community in America* (Knoxville: University of Tennessee Press, 1987), 164.

18. "[W]e become devoted to the people, places and ways that nurture us, and what is familiar and nurturing seems also natural

and right." John Schaar, *Legitimacy in the Modern State* (New Brunswick, NJ: Transaction, 1981), 287.

19. Michael Sandel, "Freedom of Conscience or Freedom of Choice?," in *Articles of Faith, Articles of Peace,* eds. James Davidson Hunter and Os Guiness (Washington, D.C.: Brookings, 1990), 76.

20. See J. David Greenstone, "The Transient and the Permanent in American Politics," in *Public Values & Private Power in American Politics,* Greenstone, ed., (Chicago: University of Chicago, 1982), 3–33.

21. As Robert Nisbet, an advocate of voluntary community, exults, "Crucial are the *voluntary* groups and associations. It is the element of the spontaneous, of untrammeled, unforced volition that is undoubtedly vital to creative relationships among individuals." *The Twilight of Authority* (New York: Oxford University Press, 1975), 270 (emphasis in original).

22. Abbott, *Seeking Many Inventions, passim.*

23. Peter L. Berger and Richard John Neuhaus, *To Empower People: The Role of Mediating Structures in Public Policy* (Washington, D.C.: American Enterprise Institute, 1977), 3.

24. Abbott, *Seeking Many Inventions,* 165.

25. A description of the Celebration of Citizenship can be found in Chapter 6.

26. See Peter Schuck and Rogers Smith, *Citizenship Without Consent* (New Haven: Yale University Press, 1985), 2 and *passim.*

27. Wolin, "Contract and Birthright," 289.

28. The studies also showed that aliens who become citizens were more likely to have ties in the community and be more aware of the larger community because they speak English, and that the naturalization rate increases with the amount of time that people have spent in the United States. Louis DeSipio, "Social Science Literature and the Naturalization Process," *International Migration Review* 21 (1987): 390–405; Alejandro Portes and Rafael Mozo, "The Political Adaptation of Cubans and Other Ethnic Minorities in the United States," *International Migration Review* 19 (1985): 35–63.

29. David G. Bromley and Bruce C. Busching, "Understanding the Structure of Contractual and Covenantal Social Relations," *Sociological Analysis* 49 (1988): 19S-21S.

30. See, for example, *Audrey Vokes v. Arthur Murray, Inc.,* Fla., 212 So.2d 906 (1968); see also Robert W. Gordon, "Unfreezing Legal Reality: Critical Approaches to Law," *Florida State University Law Review* 15 (1987): 195–220.

31. George C. Fletcher, *Loyalty* (New York: Oxford University Press, 1993), 68.

32. Tussman, *Obligation and the Body Politic,* 7–8.

33. See, for example, John Rawls, *A Theory of Justice* (Cambridge, MA: Harvard University Press, 1971), and Bruce Ackerman, *Social Justice in the Liberal State* (New Haven: Yale University Press, 1980). While Rawls simply constructs a theoretical "veil of ignorance," Ackerman maintains a tenuous link with reality by having the crew of a spaceship land on an uninhabited planet where they obey strict rules of political equality.

34. A transcript of the event is contained in the *Congressional Record,* 100th Cong. 1st Sess., 1987, Vol. 133, E 4175.

35. "Remarks at the 'We the People' Bicentennial Celebration in Philadelphia, Pennsylvania; September 17, 1987," in *Public Papers of the Presidents of the United States: Ronald Reagan: 1987* II, (Washington, D.C.: Government Printing Office, 1989), 1043.

36. Procter, *Enacting Political Culture.*

37. Stephen Macedo, *Liberal Virtues* (Oxford: Clarendon Press, 1990), 114.

38. Stephen Holmes, "Precommitment and the Paradox of Democracy," in *Constitutionalism and Democracy,* J. Elster and R. Slagstad, eds. (Cambridge: Cambridge University Press, 1988), 200–206, 217–218.

39. Levinson, *Constitutional Faith,* 107.

40. Ackerman, *We the People: Foundations,* 36–37.

41. Pamela Johnson Conover, Ivor M. Crewe, and Donald D. Searing, "The Nature of Citizenship in the United States and Eng-

land: Empirical Comments on Theoretical Themes," *Journal of Politics* 53 (1991): 823–24. See also Samuel P. Huntington, *American Politics: The Promise of Disharmony* (Cambridge, MA: Harvard University Press, 1981), 24–27; Gabriel A. Almond and Sidney Verba, *The Civic Culture* (Boston: Little, Brown, 1965), 64–65.

42. CBC, *Final Report,* 61.

43. National Conference of Christians and Jews *Official U.S. Constitution Sign-On Information & Documents* (New York: National Conference of Christians and Jews, 1987).

44. "National City is Leading Disciples' Nationwide Celebration of U.S. Constitution Bicentennial," *The National City Christian* 43 (Washington, D.C.), August 16–31, 1987: 1. Also CBC, *Final Report,* 83.

45. "The Williamsburg Charter" can be found in Hunter and Guiness, *Articles of Faith, Articles of Peace,* 127–145; newspaper accounts of the Foundation's activities can be found in John Dart, "Leaders of Differing Views Agree on Religion Clauses," *The Los Angeles Times,* June 25, 1988, Pt. 2, 6, and Laura Sessions Stepp, "An Affirmation of Religious Liberty," *The Washington Post,* June 25, 1988, A8.

46. "A Bicentennial Constitutional Sabbath," (Washington, D.C.: B'nai Brith Commission on Community Volunteer Services, n.d.), in Records Relating to the Marketing & Advertising of Bicentennial Programs, Box 9, NA.

47. Robert N. Bellah, "Civil Religion in America," *Daedalus* 96, No. 1 (1967): 1–21.

48. See Robert N. Bellah, *The Broken Covenant: American Civil Religion in Time of Trial* (New York: Seabury Press, 1975), esp. 36–60.

49. For further development of these issues, see Norton, "Transubstantiation: The Dialectic of Constitutional Authority," 458–472; and Gray, "The Constitution as Scripture."

50. Public Law 101–570, *Statutes at Large* 104 (1990): 2807.

51. CBC, *A Resource Guide for Religious Communities* (Washington, D.C.: The Commission, 1991), 6, 16–34.

52. See James Davison Hunter, *Culture Wars* (New York: Basic Books, 1991) for one description of these conflicts.

53. "Introduction," in Guiness and Hunter, eds., *Articles of Faith, Articles of Peace,* 12.

54. "The Williamsburg Charter," in Guiness and Hunter, eds., *Articles of Faith, Articles of Peace,* 135.

55. Ibid., 133–134.

56. The Williamsburg Charter Foundation developed and promoted a curriculum that integrated the study of religious history in the United States, closely connecting religious liberty with political liberty and ethnic diversity, into history and social studies courses. See Robert Marquand, "Schools and the fourth R," *The Christian Science Monitor,* November 14, 1988: 25; "Education; Group Promotes Study of Religion as Subject," *The New York Times,* October 26, 1988, B11; see also "Teaching Religious Toleration," (Editorial) *The Washington Post,* October 22, 1988, A22.

57. John Murray Cuddihy, *No Offense: Civil Religion and Protestant Taste* (New York: Seabury, 1978), 18–19.

58. *Ibid.,* 4.

59. "Williamsburg Charter," 136.

60. Cuddihy, *No Offense,* 23.

61. Laura Sessions Stepp, "An Affirmation of Religious Liberty," *The Washington Post,* June 25, 1988, A8; John Dart, "Leaders of Differing Views Agree on Religion Charter," *Los Angeles Times,* June 25, 1988, Pt. II,Washington Talk: The Bill of Rights; Has Religious Freedom Gone Sour?" *The New York Times,* December 29, 1987, B4.

62. "An End to Crusades," *The Economist,* July 2, 1988: 23 (U.S. edition). See also Ed Doerr, "The Williamsburg Charter," *The Humanist* 48, May/June, 1988: 37–38, and "The Williamsburg Charter II," *The Humanist* 48, July/August 1988: 37–38.

63. Cuddihy, *No Offense,* 210.

64. As John Schaar argues, "popular attachment to [political] institutions, together with agreement upon the ideals they embody, forms one of the essential elements of group unity." *Loyalty in America,* 20.

65. The poster is pictured in CBC, *Final Report,* 108.

66. Commission on the Bicentennial of the U.S. Constitution, *The Constitution . . . The Words We Live By: A Discussion Program: Supplemental Handbook for Tutors of New Readers* (Washington, D.C., n.d.).

67. Tocqueville, *Democracy in America* I, 63.

68. Robert Booth Fowler, *The Dance with Community* (Lawrence: University of Kansas Press, 1990), 44.

69. Benjamin Franklin, *The Autobiography and Other Writings* (New York: New American Library, 1961), 72–73, 197–200.

70. Leonard P. Oliver, *The Art of Citizenship: Public Issue Forums* (Dayton: Kettering Foundation, 1983), 7–8.

71. Donald W. Keim, "Participation in Contemporary Democratic Theories," in J. R. Pennock and J. W. Chapman, eds., *Participation in Politics: Nomos XVI* (New York: Lieber-Atherton, 1975), 16.

72. Graebner, *The Engineering of Consent,* 4–5.

73. Oliver, *The Art of Citizenship,* 8, 20–22.

74. Graebner, *The Engineering of Consent,* 10.

75. David L. Boggs, *Adult Civic Education* (Springfield, IL: Charles C. Thomas, 1991), 5.

76. An enthusiastic account of a Jefferson Meeting is reported by David Broder, "We the People," *The Washington Post,* December 1, 1985, C7.

77. Charles Bartlett, "Preface" in The Jefferson Foundation, *Rediscovering the Constitution* (Washington, D.C.: Congressional Quarterly, 1987), vii-viii.

78. Dick Merriman, "Teaching about Constitutional Issues and Values," *Social Education* 51 (September 1987): 348.

79. The Jefferson Foundation, *Rediscovering the Constitution,* esp. 178–186.

80. Letter from Mark Cannon to Martin F. Petraitis, III, January 29, 1987, in Education, Office Files, Box 6, NA.

81. Statement of Warren Burger, House Committee on Appropriations, *Hearings: Departments of Commerce, Justice and State,*

the Judiciary, and Related Agencies Appropriations for 1989, 100th Cong. 2nd Sess., March 16, 1988, 21.

82. Jane Mansbridge, *Beyond Adversary Democracy,* rev. ed. (Chicago: University of Chicago Press, 1983), vii-viii.

83. *Ibid.,* 9.

84. Abbott, *Seeking Many Inventions,* 143–144.

85. Sidney Verba and Norman H. Nie, *Participation in America* (Chicago: University of Chicago Press, 1972), 2–3.

86. C. Wright Mills, "Mass Society and Liberal Education," in *Power, Politics and People: The Collected Essays of C. Wright Mills.* Irving Louis Horowitz, ed. (London: Oxford, 1963), 355, 360.

87. In comparison to the $5.5 million raised through corporate contributions, membership fees to the Society for the U.S. Constitution raised only $114,005, and the fees fell in half from 1988–89 to 1989–1990. *Constitution* published five issues in 1988–89, published only three issues in 1989–90 and in 1990–91, and seems to have folded after publishing two issues in 1991–92. Foundation for the United States Constitution, Annual Financial Report (Charitable Organization) filed with New York State Department of State, 1988–1990.

88. Samuel Beer thus speaks of the states as important assets in the "mobilization of consent" for federal policies. Samuel H. Beer, "The Modernization of American Federalism," *Publius* 3, no. 2 (Fall, 1973): 85.

89. Kammen, *A Machine That Would Go of Itself,* 284–285.

90. Commission on the Bicentennial of the United States Constitution, *The Bill of Rights and Beyond: A Resource Guide* (Washington, D.C., 1991).

91. Thus, David I. Kertzer writes that "it was with the centralization of government that the problem of identifying local activities with higher level political organizations became especially important." Kertzer, *Ritual, Politics, and Power,* 22.

92. Robert N. Bellah, "Populism and Individualism," in *The New Populism: The Politics of Empowerment,* H.C. Boyte and F. Reissman, eds. (Philadelphia: Temple University Press, 1986), 101.

93. *Ibid.*, 103.

94. Robert Dahl and Edward Tufte, *Size and Democracy* (Stanford: Stanford University Press, 1973), 13. Even as strong an advocate of small scale democracy as Jane Mansbridge admits that the poor and vulnerable may be better protected in a larger polity. Mansbridge, *Beyond Adversary Democracy*, 280–281.

95. The cookbook was Project #86–067, see Memo from Mark Cannon to Commission, Sept. 5, 1986; the quilt competition was Project #86–086, see Memo from Mark Cannon to Commission, Sept. 3, 1986, both found at "Records Relating to Commission History, 1981–1991," Box 6, NA.

96. Memo from Cornelia Kennedy to Advisory Committee on Project Endorsement and Support, January 23, 1987 and attached memo from Mark Cannon, June 19, 1986, "Records Relating to Commission History," Box 6, NA. Information on the planning of the Living Legacy project can be found in Records Relating to Special Events, Boxes 12–15, NA. See also CBC, *Final Report*, 31–32.

97. Verba and Nie, *Participation in America*, 191. See also Sidney Verba, Norman H. Nie, and Jae-On Kim, *Participation and Political Equality* (Cambridge: Cambridge University Press, 1978), 100–106.

98. Aristotle, *The Politics of Aristotle*, E. Barker, ed. (New York: Oxford University Press, 1962), 5.

99. Norton, "Transubstantiation: The Dialectic of Constitutional Authority," 463.

100. Kelley, *Public Relations and Political Power*, 225. Similarly, Philip Abbott writes that, "Despite the uniqueness of the American experience and of modernity in general, our language of community has remained remarkably continuous with that of the past." Abbot, *Seeking Many Inventions*, 164.

101. Tocqueville, *Democracy in America* I, 252.

102. Thus Tocqueville writes that one cannot criticize America to Americans because "it is not only his country that is then attacked, it is himself." *Ibid.*, 253.

103. This understanding of participatory democracy as essentially linked to freedom may be identified with Jean-Jacques

Rousseau, who elaborates such a concept in *On the Social Contract.* See Keim, "Participation in Contemporary Democratic Theories," 9.

104. Fletcher, *Loyalty,* 25.

105. Robert R. Alvarez, "A Profile of the Citizenship Process Among Hispanics in the United States," *International Migration Review* 21 (1987): 330–332.

106. See Robert N. Bellah et al., *Habits of the Heart* (Berkeley: University of California Press, 1985).

107. Herzog, *Happy Slaves,* 222.

Chapter Six

1. Testimony of Warren Burger, in Senate Committee on Labor and Human Relations, *Hearing: Geography Education,* 100th Cong. 1st Sess., October 29, 1987, 7. Burger later incorrectly attributed the quote to Karl Marx's *Das Kapital.* CBC, *Final Report,* vi. The quote actually appears in *The Critique of the Gotha Program.*

2. Quoted in R. Freeman Butts, *In the First Person Singular* (San Francisco: Caddo Gap Press, 1992), 81.

3. Testimony of future member of the Commission on the Bicentennial, Betty Southard Murphy, in Senate Committee on the Judiciary, *Hearings: Bicentennial of the Constitution,* March 1, 1983, 28. Ms. Murphy was representing the American Bar Association at the time.

4. Kammen, *A Machine That Would Go of Itself,* 4–5.

5. Mary Jane Turner, "Civic Education in the United States," in *Political Education in Flux,* D. Heater and J.A. Gillespie, eds., (London: Sage, 1981), 52–53; Kammen, *A Machine That Would Go of Itself,* 232; Bessie Louise Pierce, *Public Opinion and the Teaching of History in the United States* (1926; reprint, New York, Da Capo Press, 1970), 184–194.

6. Woodworth Clum, "America is Calling," quoted in Pierce, *Public Opinion and the Teaching of History in the United States,* 194.

7. Peterson, *The Jefferson Image in the American Mind,* 433.

8. *Ibid.,* 433–434.

9. David Tyack and Larry Cuban, *Tinkering toward Utopia: A Century of Public School Reform* (Cambridge, MA: Harvard University Press, 1995), 36.

10. Cherie Burns, "The Constitution Goes to Schools," *Constitution* 2, no. 2 (Spring/Summer 1990): 26. The speakers referred to the National Assessment of Educational Progress.

11. National Assessment of Educational Progress, "Citizenship and Social Studies Achievement of Young Americans: 1981–82 Performance and Changes Between 1976 and 1982" (Denver: Education Commission of the States, 1983), 2–3, 26–27; National Center for Education Statistics, *Digest of Education Statistics 1991* (Washington, D.C.: Government Printing Office, 1991), Tables 121–122.

12. Alec M. Gallup and David L. Clark, "The 19th Annual Gallup Poll of the Public's Attitudes Toward the Public Schools," *The Gallup Report,* #264 (September 1987), 3. However, the public did feel that there was an increasing gap between the achievement of better students and below average students.

13. Tyack and Cuban, *Tinkering toward Utopia,* 31.

14. Testimony of Warren Burger, in Senate Committee on Labor and Human Relations, *Hearing: Literacy Corps Assistance Act of 1987,* 100th Cong. 1st Sess., April 22., 1987, 4.

15. Thus Anabel Powell Newman and Caroline Beverstock conclude a review of the literature with an "educated guess" that "more Americans are literate today than ever before." *Adult Literacy: Contexts and Challenges* (Newark, DE: International Reading Association, 1990), 62. Lee Soltow and Edward Stevens document a gradual rise in the rate of literacy among enlistees in the Army between 1799 and 1894, *The Rise of Literacy and the Common School in the United States,* 52–53. Similarly, while the Census Bureau did not inquire about literacy before the Civil War, there was steady rise in literacy rates between 1870 and 1970. U.S. Department of Commerce, Bureau of the Census, *Historical Statistics of the United States: Colonial Times to 1970* I (Washington, D.C.: Government Printing Office, 1975), 382 (Series H 664–668 and H 669–688).

16. See Daniel P. Resnick, "Historical Perspectives on Literacy and Schooling," *Daedalus* 119, no. 2 (Spring 1990): 16.

17. Leslie J. Limage, "Adult Literacy Policy in Industrialized Countries," in R. F. Arnove and H. J. Graff, eds. *National Literacy Campaigns: Historical and Comparative Perspective*, (New York: Plenum Press, 1987), 293–294.

18. B. Frank Brown, "Introduction," in National Task Force on Citizenship Education, *Education for Responsible Citizenship: The Report of the National Task Force on Citizenship Education* (New York: McGraw-Hill, 1977), 1.

19. Richard M. Battistoni, *Public Schooling and the Education of Democratic Citizens* (Jackson: University of Mississippi Press, 1985), 4.

20. This process mirrors that documented by Joseph Gusfield, in which blood alcohol levels were associated with impaired "drunk driving," although the amount of impairment is highly variable. Individuals are not necessarily impaired when they have a high blood alcohol level, and thus statistics showing the frequency of drivers with high blood alcohol levels should not be taken as definitive on the frequency of drunk driving. *The Culture of Public Problems* (Chicago: University of Chicago Press, 1981), 66.

21. *Ibid.*, 13–16.

22. Dewey, *Democracy and Education* (New York: Free Press, 1916), 22.

23. Turner, "Civic Education in the United States," 53; Richard C. Remy, "The Constitution in Citizen Education," *Social Education* 51 (February 1987): 332.

24. James M. Banner, Jr., "Thinking about Civic Education," in Alan H. Jones, ed., *Civic Learning for Teachers: Capstone for Educational Reform*, (Ann Arbor: Prakken Publications, 1985), 25.

25. Richard Pratte, *The Civic Imperative: Examining the Need for Civic Education* (New York: Teachers College Press, 1988), 10.

26. Michael Lewis, *The Culture of Inequality* (Amherst: University of Massachusetts Press, 1978), 43.

27. Kirk Stone, "Bicentennial Commission Busy with Exciting Projects," *Social Education* 53 (February 1989): 97; testimony of

Warren Burger, in Senate Committee on Labor and Human Relations, *Hearing: Geography Education,* 100th Cong. 1st Sess., October 29, 1987, 8. Pictures of winning maps are at CBC, *Final Report,* 103.

28. *Ibid.,* 6. Burger added that he would have compared history and geography to Siamese twins except "that Siamese twins sometimes have been believed effectively separated and survived." *Ibid.,* 10.

29. Thus Dewey declared:

> Economic history is more human, more democratic, and hence more liberalizing than political history. It deals not with the rise and fall of principalities and powers, but with the growth of the effective liberties, through the command of nature, of the common man for whom powers and principalities exist.

Dewey, *Democracy and Education,* 211, 215–216.

30. Before 1890, "when educators and others had occasion to speak of civic instruction, usually this was conceived and urged in terms of the Constitution." Henry Arnold Bennett, *The Constitution in School and College* (New York: Putnam, 1935), 26.

31. Ruth Miller Elson, *Guardians of Tradition* (Lincoln: University of Nebraska Press, 1964), 292. See also Bessie Louise Pierce, *Civic Attitudes in American School Textbooks* (Chicago: University of Chicago Press, 1930), 104–105.

32. Kammen, *A Machine That Would Go of Itself,* 4, 24.

33. Bennett, *The Constitution in School and College,* 63.

34. Morris Janowitz, *The Reconstruction of Citizenship: Education for Civic Consciousness* (Chicago: University of Chicago Press, 1983), 84, 91.

35. Turner, "Civic Education in the United States," 63.

36. Bennett, *The Constitution in School and College,* 33; Frances FitzGerald, *America Revised* (New York: Vintage, 1980), 174.

37. National Education Association, *Cardinal Principles of Secondary Education* (1918), quoted in Remy, "The Constitution in Citizen Education," 332.

38. Remy, "The Constitution in Citizen Education," 332.

39. John J. Patrick, "Political Socialization and Political Education in Schools," in S.A. Renshon, *Handbook of Political Socialization* (New York: Free Press, 1977), 190. Also Pratte, *The Civic Imperative*, 3.

40. National Endowment for the Humanities, *American Memory: A Report on the Humanities in the Nation's Schools* (Washington, D.C., 1987), 5 (emphasis in original).

41. Frederick M. Wirt, "The Uses of Blandness: State, Local, and Professional Roles in Citizenship Education," in *Teaching About American Federal Democracy*, S. L. Schechter, ed. (Philadelphia: Center for the Study of Federalism, 1984), 86.

42. Pratte, *The Civic Imperative*, 15.

43. Gusfield, *The Culture of Public Problems*, 183.

44. Bennett, *The Constitution in School and College*, 153.

45. Joel F. Henning et. al., *Mandate for Change: The Impact of Law on Educational Innovation* (Chicago: American Bar Association Special Committee on Youth Education for Citizenship, 1979), 36, 43–45.

46. Bennett, *The Constitution in School and College*, 154.

47. The Continental Congress dedicated part of every township to education, either as the site for a school, or to use to raise revenues to build institutions. Such provisions were made in both the land ordinances of 1785 and the Northwest Ordinance of 1787. Rush Welter, *Popular Education and Democratic Thought in America* (New York: Columbia University Press, 1962), 25.

48. This list of actors in educational policy is drawn from Joel H. Spring, *Conflict of Interests: The Politics of American Education* (New York: Longman, 1988).

49. All of this goes counter to the notion in American political culture that, as the Supreme Court expressed it, "[n]o single tradition in public education is stronger than local control." *Millikin v. Bradley,* 418 U.S. 717, at 741 (1974).

50. James P. Shaver, O. L. Davis, Jr. and Suzanne W. Helburn, "The Status of Social Studies Education: Impressions from Three NSF Studies," *Social Education* 43 (February 1979): 151.

51. Thus Burger testified that "an enormous percentage of the teachers, the younger element of teachers at grade and high school level are part of the generations where geography and history were being pushed aside in favor of social studies." Statement of Warren Burger, House Committee on Appropriations, *Hearings: Departments of Commerce, Justice and State, the Judiciary, and Related Agencies Appropriations for 1989*, 100th Cong. 2nd Sess., March 16, 1988, 25.

52. The Foundation was to begin its programs when it received $10 million in private funds, whereupon the federal government would appropriate $20 million to fully endow it. However, neither the Commission on the Bicentennial nor the private Foundation for the U.S. Constitution was successful in raising that kind of funding, particularly after 1987. Despite, and because of, the lack of demonstrable public support in the form of private donations, Congress directed that the Madison Fellowship Foundation be funded in its entirety through the United States Treasury. Congress dropped the requirement that the Foundation raise the $10 million in private contributions to qualify for federal funds, and then directed that surcharges from the sale of commemorative coins celebrating the Bicentennial of the Bill of Rights, which had been previously designated to reduce the federal deficit, be allocated to the Foundation "as funds contributed from private sources," enabling the Foundation to receive the full amount of the already-allocated federal matching grant. The coins "Amendment to James Madison Memorial Fellowship Act," Public Law 102–221, *Statutes at Large* 105 (1992): 1676. "White House Commemorative Coin Act," Public Law 102–281 § 507, *Statutes at Large* 106 (1992): 133.

53. See Murray Edelman, *The Symbolic Uses of Politics* (Urbana: University of Illinois Press, 1964).

54. Pierce, *Public Opinion and the Teaching of History in the United States*, 191–192.

55. Memorandum from Winston Wilkinson to Trudy Fry, November 6, 1986, in Education: Office Files, Box 7, NA.

56. For the American preference for the attribution of responsibility to individuals rather than institutions, see Merelman, *Making Something of Ourselves*, 20.

57. See *The Constitution's Children: A Collection of Essays by Schoolchildren to Commemorate the Bicentennial of the U.S. Constitution, 1787–1987* (Washington, D.C.: U.S. Department of Education, 1987). The book also includes foreword by William J. Bennett with a brief description of the contest, an introduction by Burger, and Reagan's remarks in the Rose Garden ceremony. Documents, including budgets and working papers, found in Education: Office Files, Box 7, NA.

58. Winners are listed in the Congressional Record at 134 Cong. Rec. S 8486, June 23, 1988 (100th Cong., 2nd Sess.) (Latin America) and 135 Cong. Rec. E 2253, June 27, 1989, (191st Cong., 1st Sess.) (Japan).

59. This contest was less successful, receiving only eighty-four entries, which were not of the highest quality. Although a law review in each federal judicial circuit had agreed to publish the winner for that circuit, at least two later refused because the essays did not meet their standards for publication. Letter "To Students in American Law Schools" from Lane Sunderland, dated March 1987; letter to Howard T. Markey from Levin H. Campbell, dated June 12, 1987; report entitled "Law School Essay Competitions [sic] Received" and dated May 18, 1987; letter from Adam Elsesser, Editor in Chief of *The Hastings Law Journal,* to Richard Dargan, November 5, 1987; Letter from William Anderson, President of *Minnesota Law Review,* to Richard Dargan, October 16, 1987. All in NA, Education: National Bicentennial Writing Competition, Box 2.

60. State winners received $1,000 in prize money; the national winners received $10,000. CBC, *Final Report,* 52–53. See also the statement of Warren Burger, in House Committee on Appropriations, *Hearings: Departments of Commerce, Justice and State, the Judiciary, and Related Agencies Appropriations for 1989,* 100th Cong. 2nd Sess., March 16, 1988, 21–22.

61. CBC, *Final Report,* 52.

62. "Students Taking Roles of 1787," *The New York Times,* November 8, 1987, Pt. I, 58; CBC, *Final Report,* 74.

63. The Jefferson Foundation, *Rediscovering the Constitution* (Washington, D.C.: Congressional Quarterly, 1987). This program is analyzed in further detail in Chapter 5.

64. See Records Relating to the Marketing and Advertising of Bicent. Programs, Box 8, NA.

65. See Minutes of Meeting, September 5, 1986, in Education: Project Files, Box 56, NA.

66. The commercial participation resulted despite ANPA's desire to keep the program free of commercialism. "Minutes, Meeting of Celebration of Citizenship Planning Group, Reston, Virginia—October 7, 1986," Education: Project Files, Box 50, NA. Although the federal Commission developed the program with educational and civic groups, all fund raising was conducted by the private Foundation for the Commemoration of the United States Constitution. However, the Foundation's activities remained "under the direction of the Marketing Division of the Commission." Letter from Terri Notari to Judy Hines, April 27, 1987, in Records Relating to Special Events, Box 2, NA. The thirteen national groups involved in educational issues who joined this coalition are listed at CBC, *Final Report,* 58.

67. Victoria Dawson, "Washington Celebrates Words to Live By," *The Washington Post,* September 17, 1987, A29.

68. A transcript of the event is contained in the *Congressional Record* 133, 100th Cong. 1st Sess., October 27, 1987, E 4175.

69. Victoria Dawson, "Young Achiever Calmly Faces Date with History," *The Washington Post,* September 16, 1987, B1.

70. The time for the broadcast was selected so that as many students as possible would be in class when it was broadcast live. Memorandum from Mark Cannon to Advisory Committee on Education Programs, September 2, 1986, Box 14 (A-3b), NA.

71. CBC, *Final Report,* 58.

72. Testimony of Warren Burger, House Committee on Appropriations, *Hearings: Departments of Commerce, Justice and State, the Judiciary, and Related Agencies Appropriations for 1990,* 101st Cong. 1st Sess., February 8, 1989, Pt 5, 162.

73. The National Endowment for the Humanities was designated to develop new civics curricula and administer a national competition for elementary and secondary school students interested in researching topics related to the Constitution. However,

this program, named the National Bicentennial Competition, was transferred to the new-born Commission on the Bicentennial before NEH had begun work on it. The competition was field tested using funds allocated by the Secretary of Education from his discretionary fund. Report of the Committee on Labor and Human Resources, 99th Congress 1st Session (Senate Report 99–125), August 1, 1985, pp. 8, 27; "Arts, Humanities, and Museums Amendments of 1985," Public Law 99–194, *Statutes at Large* 99 (1985): 1332, at 1346; Center for Civic Education, National Bicentennial Competition Progress Report, November 1985, found at "Records Relating to Commission History, 1981–1991," Box 4, NA. CCE used $100,000 in Department of Education funds.

74. Ruth Mitchell, *Testing for Learning: How New Approaches to Evaluation Can Improve American Schools* (New York: Free Press, 1992), 94.

75. For examples of CCE's efforts to draw this benefit to the attention of Congress, see the inserts following testimony by CCE Executive Charles Quigley, *Hearings: Departments of Commerce, Justice, and State, the Judiciary, and Related Agencies Appropriations for 1989,* Pt. 9, 421–447. The inserts include the National Bicentennial Competition's newsletter that lists winning schools and their congressional sponsors, and numerous newspaper or congressional newsletter articles detailing congressional involvement, or "sponsorship" of, in local competitions. In his testimony before Congress, Mr. Quigley asserted that 380 of the 435 members of the House and 80 of the 100 Senators had some involvement with the program, *Ibid.*, 409.

76. Memorandum from Chuck Quigley to State Coordinators. January 3, 1990, in NA, "Education" Center for Civic Education, Box 1, File: Center for Civic Education.

77. The program's format is described in CBC, *Final Report,* 35–37.

78. Edelman, *The Symbolic Uses of Politics.*

79. Wolin, *The Presence of the Past,* 49.

80. Written testimony of Charles Quigley, *Hearing: FY 89,* 419. In 1988, Quigley was expecting that just under $3 million in federal support would be supplanted by state and private monies

to raise a total $25 million for national implementation of the contest. *Hearing: FY 89,* 418. In 1986, Quigley forecast using federal support to "leverage on about a 10 to 1 basis, public-private sector support from state and local levels." *Hearings: FY 87,* 3.

81. According to CCE, participation rose from half a million students in its first year, 1987 to 3.5 million in the last year of the Bicentennial, 1991; CCE estimated that 1992 would raise the number to almost 5 million students. Of that number, only one-third are believed to have competed, while many of the others were most likely elementary and middle school students who were not eligible to compete. Unsigned fax from CCE to Herb [Atherton], March 3, 1992, in NA, "Education" Center for Civic Education, Box 1, File: Center for Civic Education.

82. See, for example, the statement entered into the *Congressional Record* by Rep. Robert Walker of Pennsylvania entitled, "Studies demonstrate instructional effectiveness of civics program teaching students about the Constitution," *Congressional Record* 136, 101st Cong. 2nd Sess., no. 140, October 17, 1990, E 3275.

83. *A Comparison of the Impact of the* We the People . . . *Curricular Materials on High School Students compared to University Students* (Pasadena, CA: Educational Testing Service, 1991), see esp. 1–7.

84. "Test on the History and Principles of the United States Constitution," (Calabasas, CA: Center for Civic Education, 1987). A copy can be found in Education, Center for Civic Education, Box 2, NA.

85. Unfortunately, the survey, conducted by the Gallup Organization for the Commission in December of 1991, is useless as a gauge of actual teacher interest because Gallup, at the Commission's request, used three mailing lists that the Commission had used for distributing materials, and thus excluded teachers who did not use the Commission's materials. *A Comparison of the Impact of the* We the People . . . *Curricular Materials on High School Students Compared to University Students* (Pasadena, CA: Educational Testing Service, 1991), 1–3.

86. Elaine H. Christiansen and Max D. Larsen, *Commission on the Bicentennial of the U.S. Constitution: National Survey of Teachers Regarding Use of Bicentennial Commission Programs and Publications* (Lincoln, NE: Gallup Organization, 1991).

87. "Celebration of Citizenship, September 16, 1987," *Congressional Record* 133, no. 169, Legislative Day of October 27, 1987, E 4175.

88. Howard Mehlinger, "The Crisis of Civic Education," in National Task Force on Citizenship Education, *Education for Responsible Citizenship: The Report of the National Task Force on Citizenship Education* (New York: McGraw-Hill, 1977), 71–72.

89. Bernard Crick, "The Introducing of Politics into Schools," in B. Crick and Derek Heater, eds., *Essays on Political Education* (London: Falmer, 1977), 16.

90. "The generative source of the mechanistic conception of American government that fuses the past and present so firmly together lies in the most obvious and most overlooked part of the American political system; that part which 'generations of schoolchildren have been taught' and which 'every schoolchild in America learns' as a matter of course—namely, the separation of powers." Michael Foley, *Laws, Men, and Machines: Modern American Government and the Appeal of Newtonian Mechanics* (London: Routledge, 1990), 50.

91. Ellis Katz, "Federalism in Secondary School American History and Government Textbooks," in S. L. Schechter, ed., *Teaching About American Federal Democrac,* (Philadelphia: Center for the Study of Federalism, 1984), 97

92. Foley, *Laws, Men and Machines,* 54–79.

93. *Ibid.,* 55.

94. FitzGerald, *America Revised,* 152. Ellis Katz agrees with FitzGerald, noting that government and civics texts present federalism as the result of the Connecticut compromise at the Constitution Convention without "theoretical justification beyond the politics of the times." Katz, "Federalism in Secondary School American History and Government Textbooks," 93.

95. Roberta S. Sigel, "Students' Comprehension of Democracy and its Application to Conflict Situations," *International Journal of Political Education* 2 (1979): 61.

96. Easton and Dennis, *Children in the Political System,* 114–117.

97. Daniel P. Resnick, "Historical Perspectives on Literacy and Schooling," *Daedalus* 119, no. 2 (Spring 1990): 17.

98. John A. Chilcott, "The Anthropological Perspective," in R.E. Gross and T.L. Dynneson, *Social Science Perspectives on Citizenship Education* (New York: Teachers College Press, 1990), 189.

99. Center for Civic Education,"National Standards for Civics and Government," (Calabasas, CA: The Center, 1994).

100. Soltow and Stevens, *The Rise of Literacy and the Common School,* 6–7. Harvey J. Graff, *The Literacy Myth: Literacy and Social Structure in the Nineteenth Century City* (New York: Academic Press, 1979), 53–54.

101. Testimony of Warren Burger, in Senate Committee on Labor and Human Relations, *Hearing: Literacy Corps Assistance Act of 1987,* 100th Cong. 1st Sess., April 22., 1987, 5.

102. Soltow and Stevens, *The Rise of Literacy and the Common School,* 6–7.

103. Robert F. Arnove and Harvey J. Graff, "Introduction," in *National Literacy Campaigns: Historical and Comparative Perspectives,* (New York: Plenum Press, 1987), 12.

104. CBC, *Final Report,* 118.

105. Arnove and Graff, "Introduction," 2, 25.

106. Harvey Graff, *The Labyrinths of Literacy* (London: Falmer Press, 1987), 34; Soltow and Stevens, *The Rise of Literacy and the Common School in the United States,* 55.

107. Gerald Strauss, *Luther's House of Learning: Indoctrination of the Young in the German Reformation* (Baltimore: Johns Hopkins Press, 1979), 195–196.

108. Edward Stevens, Jr., "The Anatomy of Mass Literacy in Nineteenth-Century United States," in Arnove and Graff, eds., *National Literacy Campaigns: Historical and Comparative Perspectives,* 105.

109. David D. Hall, "The Uses of Literacy in New England, 1600–1850," in W. Joyce, D. Hall, R. Brown, and J. Hench, eds., *Printing and Society in Early America* (Worcester, MA: American Antiquarian Society, 1983), 21–24.

110. Eric B. Gorham, *National Service, Citizenship, and Political Education* (Albany: State University of New York Press, 1992), 104–105.

111. Pratte, *The Civic Imperative,* 14.

112. Stephen R. Graubard, "Doing Badly and Feeling Confused," *Daedalus* 119, no. 2 (Spring 1990): 257.

113. James M. Banner, Jr., "Thinking about Civic Education," in Alan H. Jones, ed., *Civic Learning for Teachers: Capstone for Educational Reform,* (Ann Arbor: Prakken Publications, 1985), 25.

Conclusion

1. Morgan, *Inventing the People,* 152.

2. Klein, *The Constitution in the Public Imagination,* 11.

3. "Weekly Ratings Scorecard," *Variety,* September 23, 1987, 126.

4. Warren E. Burger, "Five Year Program Planned to Achieve Goals of the Bicentennial Commission," *Education* 107, No. 4 (Summer 1987), 347–348.

5. Paul Eidelberg, *The Philosophy of the Constitution,* (New York: Free Press, 1968), 248–249.

6. Croly, *The Promise of American Life* (Cambridge, MA: Harvard University Press, 1965 (1913)), 12.

7. For the classic formulation, see Bagehot, *The English Constitution;* for a more modern version of this argument, see Billig et al., *Ideological Dilemmas,* 38–39.

8. See Shils and Young, "The Meaning of the Coronation," and Paul B. Sheatsley and Jacob J. Feldman, "A National Survey on Public Reactions and Behavior," in Bradley S. Greenberg and Edwin B. Parker, eds., *The Kennedy Assassination and the American Public* (Stanford: Stanford University Press, 1965), 149–177.

9. Sidney Verba, "The Kennedy Assassination and the Nature of Political Commitment," in *The Kennedy Assassination and the American Public,* 360.

10. Hearst Corporation, *The American Public's Knowledge of the U.S. Constitution.*

11. Seven percent expressed no opinion. "Public Supports Constitution's Principles But Many See Need for Improvements," *The Gallup Report*, No. 266 (November 1987), 33.

12. James Madison, "Federalist No. 57," in Clinton Rossiter, ed., *The Federalist Papers* (New York: New American Library, 1961), 350–356.

13. "Address Before a Joint Session of Congress on the State of the Union," *Public Papers of the Presidents: Ronald Reagan, 1987* I (Washington, D.C: Government Printing Office, 1989), 60.

14. Liah Greenfeld and Michel Martin, "The Idea of the 'Center': An Introduction," in *Center: Ideas and Institutions* (Chicago: University of Chicago Press, 1988), ix.

15. Michael R. Real, *Mass-Mediated Culture* (Englewood Cliffs, N.J.: Prentice-Hall, 1977), x (emphasis deleted).

16. Douglass Cater, "The Role and Responsibility of Television in Civic Education," in National Taskforce on Citizenship Education, *Education for Responsible Citizenship* (New York: McGraw-Hill, 1977), 168.

17. Melford Spiro, "Buddhism and Economic Action in Burma," *American Anthropologist* 68 (1966), 1163.

18. Statement of Mark W. Cannon, House Committee on Post Office and Civil Service, *Joint Hearing: Commission on the Bicentennial of Constitution of United States,* 99th Cong. 1st Sess., December 5, 1985, 20.

19. Walter Berns, "The Constitution & Us" (review of Michael Kammen, *A Machine That Would Go of Itself*), *Commentary* 83 (February 1987), 68.

20. Taroslav Pelikan, *The Vindication of Tradition* (New Haven: Yale University Press, 1984), 55 (italics in original).

21. Pelikan argues that a "living tradition" can be identified by "its capacity to develop while still maintaining its identity and continuity." *Ibid.,* 58. I am indebted to Stephen Macedo's *Liberal Virtues,* 170, for calling my attention to Pelikan's argument in connection with constitutionalism.

22. Sheldon Wolin, "Contract and Birthright," 290.

Selected Bibliography

Abbot, Philip. *Seeking Many Inventions: The Idea of Community in America.* Knoxville: University of Tennessee Press, 1987.

Ackerman, Bruce. *We the People: Foundations.* Cambridge, MA: Harvard University Press, 1991.

Almond, Gabriel A., and Sidney Verba. *The Civic Culture.* Boston: Little, Brown, 1965.

American Revolution Bicentennial Administration, *The Bicentennial of the United States of America: A Final Report to the People.* 2 vols. Washington, D.C.: Government Printing Office, 1977.

Archer, Margaret. *Culture and Agency.* Cambridge: Cambridge University Press, 1988.

Arnove, Robert F., and Harvey J. Graff. *National Literacy Campaigns: Historical and Comparative Perspectives.* New York: Plenum Press, 1987.

Avineri, Shlomo. *Hegel's Theory of the Modern State.* Cambridge: Cambridge University Press, 1972.

Baas, Larry R. "The Constitution as Symbol." *American Politics Quarterly* 8, no. 2 (April 1980): 237–256.

Bagehot, Walter. *The English Constitution.* Ithaca: Cornell University Press, 1966 (orig. 1867).

Bailyn, Bernard. *The Ideological Origins of the American Revolution.* Cambridge, MA: Harvard University Press, 1967.

Ball, Terence, James Farr, and Russell L. Hanson, eds. *Political Innovation and Conceptual Change.* Cambridge: Cambridge University Press, 1989.

Banner, James M. Jr. "Thinking about Civic Education." In *Civic Learning for Teachers: Capstone for Educational Reform.* Edited by Alan H. Jones. Ann Arbor: Prakken Publications, 1985: 25–32.

Battistoni, Richard M. *Public Schooling and the Education of Democratic Citizens.* Jackson: University of Mississippi Press, 1985.

Baudrillard, Jean. *Simulations.* Translated by P. Foss, P. Patton, and P. Beitchman. New York: Semiotext(e), 1983.

Bell, Whitfield Jr. "The Federal Processions of 1788." *The New York Historical Society Quarterly* 46 (1962): 5–39.

Bellah, Robert N. *The Broken Covenant: American Civil Religion in Time of Trial.* New York: Seabury Press, 1975.

———. "Populism and Individualism." in *The New Populism: The Politics of Empowerment,* H. C. Boyte and F. Reissman, eds. Philadelphia: Temple University Press, 1986: 100–107.

Bellah, Robert N. et al. *Habits of the Heart.* Berkeley: University of California Press, 1985.

Benjamin, Walter. *Illuminations.* Edited by Hannah Arendt and translated by Harry Zohn. New York: Harcourt, Brace and World, 1968.

Bennett, Henry Arnold. *The Constitution in School and College.* New York: Putnam, 1935.

Bercovitch, Sacvan. *The American Jeremiad.* Madison: University of Wisconsin Press, 1978.

Berger Peter L., and Richard John Neuhaus. *To Empower People: The Role of Mediating Structures in Public Policy.* Washington, D.C.: American Enterprise Institute, 1977.

Bernays, Edward L. *The Engineering of Consent.* Norman: University of Oklahoma Press, 1952.

Bickel, Alexander. *The Supreme Court and the Idea of Progress.* New Haven: Yale University Press, 1978.

Billig, Michael, et al. *Ideological Dilemmas.* London: Sage, 1988.

Blackstone, William. *Commentaries on the Laws of England.* 4 vols. Oxford: Clarendon, 1765–1769; reprint, Chicago: University of Chicago Press, 1979.

Bodnar, John. *Remaking America: Public Memory, Commemoration, and Patriotism in the Twentieth Century.* Princeton, NJ: Princeton University Press, 1992.

Boorstin, Daniel. *The Americans: The National Experience.* New York: Random House, 1965.

———. *The Genius of American Politics.* Chicago: University of Chicago Press, 1953.

———. *The Image.* New York: Atheneum, 1975 (1961).

Bork, Robert H. *The Tempting of America.* New York: Free Press, 1990.

Brennan, Jr., William J. "Construing the Constitution." *University of California Davis Law Review* 19 (1985): 2–14.

Brody, M. Kenneth. *Sociological Theories of Symbolic Activity: A Case Study Application to the Bicentennial Observance.* Unpublished Ph.D. Thesis, University of Iowa, 1977.

Burke, Edmond. *Reflections on the Revolution in France.* Edited by T. H. D. Mahoney. Indianapolis: Bobbs-Merrill, 1955 (1790).

Butterfield, Herbert. *The Whig Interpretation of History.* London: G. Bell and Sons, 1959.

Carr, David. *Time, Narrative and History.* Bloomington: Indiana University Press, 1986.

Carson, H. L., ed. *History of the Celebration of the One Hundredth Anniversary of the Promulgation of the Constitution of the United States.* 2 vols. Philadelphia: J. B. Lippincott, 1889.

Commager, Henry Steele. *The American Mind.* New Haven: Yale University Press, 1950.

Commission on the Bicentennial of the United States Constitution, *We the People: Final Report* (Washington, D.C., 1992).

Conover, Pamela Johnson, Ivor M. Crewe, and Donald D. Searing. "The Nature of Citizenship in the United States and

England: Empirical Comments on Theoretical Themes." *Journal of Politics* 53 (1991): 800–832.

Corwin, Edward S. "The Constitution as Instrument and as Symbol." In *Corwin on the Constitution* I. Edited by R. Loss. Ithaca: Cornell University Press, 1981: 168–179.

———. "The Worship of the Constitution." In *Corwin on the Constitution* I. Edited by R. Loss. Ithaca: Cornell University Press, 1981: 47–55.

Crick, Bernard. "The Introducing of Politics into Schools." In *Essays on Political Education*. Edited by Bernard Crick and Derek Heater. London: Falmer, 1977: 5–20.

Croly, Herbert. *The Promise of American Life*. Edited by Arthur M. Schlesinger, Jr. Cambridge, MA: Harvard University Press, 1965 (1913).

Cuddihy, John Murray. *No Offense: Civil Religion and Protestant Taste*. New York: Seabury, 1978.

Dahl, Robert, and Edward Tufte, *Size and Democracy*. Stanford: Stanford University Press, 1973.

Davis, Susan G. *Parades and Power: Street Theatre in Nineteenth Century Philadelphia*. Berkeley: University of California Press, 1988 (1986).

Dewey, John. *Democracy and Education*. New York: Free Press, 1916.

Dicey, Albert Venn. *Introduction to the Study of the Constitution*. (Indianapolis: Liberty Fund, 1983 (orig. 1915).

Durkheim, Emile. *The Elementary Forms of Religious Life*. Translated by J. W. Swain. New York: Free Press, 1915.

———."Individual and Collective Representations." In *Sociology and Philosophy*. Translated by D. F. Pocock. New York: Free Press, 1974.

Easton, David, and Jack Dennis. *Children in the Political System*. New York: McGraw-Hill, 1969.

Eco, Umberto. *Travels in Hyperreality*. Translated by W. Weaver. New York: Harcourt, Brace, and Jovanovich, 1986.

Edelman, Murray. *The Symbolic Uses of Politics.* Urbana: University of Illinois Press, 1964.

Eidelberg, Paul. *The Philosophy of the Constitution.* New York: Free Press, 1968.

Eisenstein, Elizabeth L. *The Printing Press as an Agent of Change.* 2 vols. London: Cambridge University Press, 1979.

Eliade, Mircea. *The Myth of Eternal Return.* Translated by W. R. Trask. Chicago: University of Chicago Press, 1954.

Ellen, Roy. "Fetishism." *Man* 23, no. 2 (June, 1988): 213–235.

Elson, Ruth Miller. *Guardians of Tradition.* Lincoln: University of Nebraska Press, 1964.

Elster, Jon, and Rune Slagstad, eds. *Constitutionalism and Democracy.* Cambridge: Cambridge University Press, 1988.

Epstein, Edwin M. *The Corporation in American Politics.* Englewood Cliffs, NJ: Prentice-Hall, 1969.

Ferguson, Robert A. " 'We Do Ordain and Establish': The Constitution as Literary Text." *William and Mary Law Review* 29 (1987): 3–25.

Fish, Stanley. *Is There a Text in this Class?* Cambridge, MA: Harvard University Press, 1980.

FitzGerald, Frances. *America Revised.* New York: Vintage, 1980.

Fletcher, George C. *Loyalty.* New York: Oxford University Press, 1993.

Fliegelman, Jay. *Declaring Independence: Jefferson, Natural Language, and the Culture of Performance.* Stanford, CA: Stanford University Press, 1993.

Foley, Michael. *Laws, Men, and Machines: Modern American Government and the Appeal of Newtonian Mechanics.* London: Routledge, 1990.

Foner, Philip S., ed., *The Life and Major Writings of Thomas Paine.* Secaucus, NJ: Citadel Press, 1974.

Fowler, Robert Booth. *The Dance with Community.* Lawrence: University of Kansas Press, 1990.

Freud, Sigmund. "A Disturbance of Memory on the Acropolis," *Collected Papers* 5. Edited by J. Strachey. New York: Basic Books, 1959: 302–312.

———. "A Note upon the 'mystic writing-pad'." In *The Complete Psychological Works* 19. Edited and translated by J. Strachey. London: Hogarth Press, 1961: 227–232.

Gabriel, Henry. *The Course of American Democratic Thought.* New York: Ronald Press, 1956 (orig. 1940).

Geertz, Clifford. *The Interpretation of Cultures.* New York: Basic Books, 1973.

———. *Local Knowledge: Further Essays in Interpretive Anthropology.* New York: Basic, 1983.

———. *Negara: The Theatre State in Nineteenth-Century Bali.* Princeton, N.J.: Princeton University Press, 1980.

Gerth, Hans, and C. Wright Mills, *Character and Social Structure.* New York: Harcourt, Brace and World, 1953.

Gierke, Otto Friedrich von. *Political Theories of the Middle Age.* Translated by F. W. Maitland. Cambridge: Cambridge University Press, 1951 (orig. 1900).

Gillespie Michael A., and Michael Lienesch. eds. *Ratifying the Constitution* (Lawrence: University of Kansas Press, 1989.

Gillis, John R. ed. *Commemorations: The Politics of National Identity.* Princeton, NJ: Princeton University Press, 1994.

Glassberg, David. *American Historical Pageantry: the Uses of Tradition in the Early Twentieth Century.* Chapel Hill: University of North Carolina Press, 1990.

Goldstein, Joseph. *The Intelligible Constitution.* New York: Oxford University Press, 1992.

Goody, Jack. *The Logic of Writing and the Organization of Society.* Cambridge: Cambridge University Press, 1986.

Goddy, Jack, and Ian Watt, "The Consequences of Literacy," *Comparative Studies in Society and History* 5 (1963): 304–345.

Gorham, Eric B. *National Service, Citizenship, and Political Education.* Albany: State University of New York Press, 1992.

Graebner, William. *The Engineering of Consent*. Madison: University of Wisconsin Press, 1987.

Graff, Harvey J. *The Labyrinths of Literacy*. London: Falmer Press, 1987.

———.*The Literacy Myth: Literacy and Social Structure in the Nineteenth Century City*. New York: Academic Press, 1979.

Graubard, Stephen R. "Doing Badly and Feeling Confused." *Daedalus* 119, no. 2 (Spring 1990): 257–279.

Greenfeld, Liah, and Michel Martin. *Center: Ideas and Institutions*, Chicago: University of Chicago Press, 1988.

Greenstone, J. David, ed., *Public Values and Private Power in American Politics*. Chicago: University of Chicago, 1982.

Grey, Thomas C."The Constitution as Scripture." *Stanford Law Review* 37 (1984): 1–25.

Grieff, Constance. *Independence*. Philadelphia: University of Pennsylvania Press, 1987.

Gusfield, Joseph. *The Culture of Public Problems*. Chicago: University of Chicago Press, 1981.

Habermas, Jurgen. "Walter Benjamin: Consciousness Raising or Rescuing Critique." In *On Walter Benjamin*. Edited by Gary Smith. Cambridge, MA: MIT Press, 1988: 90–128.

Harris, William F. II, *The Interpretable Constitution*. Baltimore: Johns Hopkins University Press, 1992.

Hartog, Hendrik. *Public Property and Private Power*. Chapel Hill: University of North Carolina Press, 1983.

Hartz, Louis. *Economic Policy and Democratic Thought*. Cambridge, MA: Harvard University Press, 1948.

———. *The Liberal Tradition in America*. New York: Harcourt Brace and Jovanovich, 1955.

Hatch Orrin G., and James MacGregor Burns. "Still Adequate for the Twentieth Century? A Debate." *Utah Law Review* 1987 (1987): 871–885.

Hearst Corporation. *The American Public's Knowledge of the U.S. Constitution: A National Survey of Public Awareness and Personal Opinion*. New York: Hearst Corporation, 1987.

Hegel, G. W. F. *Hegel's Philosophy of Right*. Translated by T. M. Knox. London: Oxford University Press, 1969.

Herzog, Don. *Happy Slaves:A Critique of Consent Theory*. Chicago: University of Chicago Press, 1989.

Hinckley, Barbara. *The Symbolic Presidency*. New York: Routledge, 1990.

Hobsbawm, Eric, and Terence Ranger. eds. *The Invention of Tradition*. Cambridge: Cambridge University Press, 1983.

Hopkinson, Francis. *The Miscellaneous Essays and Occasional Writings*. 2 vols. Philadelphia: T. Dobson, 1792.

Horne, Donald. *The Public Culture: The Triumph of Industrialism*. London: Pluto, 1986.

Howard, Dick. *The Birth of American Political Thought*. Minneapolis: University of Minnesota Press, 1989.

Hunter, James Davidson, and Os Guiness, eds. *Articles of Faith, Articles of Peace*. Washington, D.C.: Brookings, 1990.

Huntington, Samuel P. *American Politics: The Promise of Disharmony*. Cambridge, MA: Harvard University Press, 1981.

Hurst, James Willard. *The Legitimacy of the Business Corporation in the Law of the United States, 1780–1970*. Charlottesville: University of Virginia, 1970.

Isaacs, Harold R. *Idols of the Tribe*. New York: Harper & Row, 1975.

Janowitz, Morris. *The Reconstruction of Citizenship: Education for Civic Consciousness*. Chicago: University of Chicago Press, 1983.

Jhally, Sut. *The Codes of Advertising*. New York: St. Martin's, 1987.

Johnston, William M. *Celebrations. New Brunswick, NJ*: Transaction, 1991.

Kammen, Michael. *A Machine That Would Go of Itself*. New York: Knopf, 1986.

———. *Mystic Chords of Memory*. New York: Knopf, 1991.

———. *A Season of Youth: The American Revolution and the Historical Imagination*. New York: Knopf, 1978.

———. *Sovereignty and Liberty: Constitutional Discourse in American Culture.* Madison: University of Wisconsin Press, 1988.

Kantorowicz, Ernst. *The King's Two Bodies.* Princeton: Princeton University Press, 1957.

Karsten, Peter. *Patriot-Heroes in England and America.* Madison: University of Wisconsin Press, 1978.

Katz, Ellis. "Federalism in Secondary School American History and Government Textbooks." In *Teaching About American Federal Democracy.* Edited by Stephen L. Schechter. Philadelphia: Center for the Study of Federalism, 1984, 91–98.

Kelly, George Armstrong. "Hegel's America." *Philosophy & Public Affairs* 2, no. 1 (Fall 1972): 3–36.

Kelley, Stanley. *Professional Public Relations and Political Power.* Baltimore: Johns Hopkins Press, 1956.

Kertzer, David I. *Ritual, Politics, and Power.* New Haven: Yale University Press, 1988.

Klein, Milton M. *The Constitution in the Public Imagination: The Lawrence F. Brewster Lecture in History.* Greenville, N.C.: East Carolina University, 1987.

Kopytoff, Igor. "The Cultural Biography of Things." In *The Social Life of Things.* Edited by A. Appadurai. Cambridge: Cambridge University Press, 1986: 64–91.

Lash, Scott. *Sociology of Postmodernism.* London: Routledge, 1990.

Lerner, Max. "The Constitution and Court as Symbols," *Yale Law Journal* 46 (1937): 1290–1319.

———. *Ideas for the Ice Age.* New York: Viking, 1941.

Levin, Daniel Lessard. "The Constitution in the Postmodern Marketplace: Philip Morris and the Bicentennial of the Bill of Rights." *The Legal Studies Forum* 20 (1996): 367–386.

Levinson, Sanford. *Constitutional Faith.* Princeton, N.J.: Princeton University Press, 1988.

Levitt, Theodore. *The Marketing Imagination,* 2nd ed. New York: Free Press, 1986 (2nd ed.).

Lienesch, Michael. "The Constitutional Tradition." *Journal of Politics* 42 (1980): 2–30.

Limage, Leslie J. "Adult Literacy Policy in Industrialized Countries." In *National Literacy Campaigns: Historical and Comparative Perspectives.* Edited by R. F. Arnove and H. J. Graff. New York: Plenum Press, 1987: 293–313.

Locke, John. *Second Treatise on Government.* Edited by C. B. McPherson. Indianapolis: Hackett, 1980 (1691).

Lowenthal, David. *The Past is a Foreign Country.* Cambridge: Cambridge University Press, 1985.

Lowi, Theodore. *The End of Liberalism.* New York: Norton, 1978 (2nd ed.).

Luke, Carmen. *Pedagogy, Printing, and Protestantism.* Albany: State University of New York, 1989.

Lunch, William M. *The Nationalization of American Politics.* Berkeley: University of California Press, 1987.

Macedo, Stephen. *Liberal Virtues.* Oxford: Clarendon Press, 1990.

Mansbridge, Jane. *Beyond Adversary Democracy,* rev. ed. Chicago: University of Chicago Press, 1983.

Marin, Louis. *Utopics: Spatial Play.* Translated by R. A. Vollrath. Atlantic Highlands, NJ: Humanities Press, 1984.

Marling, Karal Ann. *George Washington Slept Here.* Cambridge, MA: Harvard University Press, 1988.

Marshall, Thurgood. "Reflections on the Bicentennial of the United States Constitution." *Harvard Law Review* 101 (1987): 1–5.

McCannell, Dean. "Staged Authenticity: Arrangements of Social Space in Tourist Settings." *American Journal of Sociology* 79 (1973): 589–603.

———. *The Tourist.* New York: Schocken, 1976.

McCoy, Donald R. *The National Archives.* Chapel Hill: University of North Carolina Press, 1978.

McCracken, Grant. *Culture and Consumption.* Bloomington: Indiana University Press, 1988.

McGee, Michael. "In Search of 'the People': A Rhetorical Alternative." *Quarterly Journal of Speech* 61 (1975): 235–249.

McLuhan, Marshall. *The Gutenberg Galaxy.* Toronto: University of Toronto Press, 1962.

Merelman, Richard M. *Making Something of Ourselves: On Culture and Politics in the United States.* Berkeley: University of California Press, 1984.

———. *Partial Visions.* Madison: University of Wisconsin Press, 1991.

Mills, C. Wright. "Mass Society and Liberal Education." In *Power, Politics and People: The Collected Essays of C. Wright Mills.* Edited by Irving Louis Horowitz. London: Oxford, 1963: 353–373.

Michener, James. *Legacy.* New York: Random House, 1987.

Morgan, Edmund S. *Inventing the People.* New York: Norton, 1988.

Morone, James. *The Democratic Wish: Popular Participation and the Limits of American Government.* New York: Basic Books, 1990.

Mostov, Julie. *Power, Process, and Popular Sovereignty.* Philadelphia: Temple University Press, 1992.

Muir, Edward. *Civic Ritual in Renaissance Venice.* Princeton, NJ: Princeton University Press, 1981.

Murrin, John M. A "Roof without Walls." In *Beyond Confederation: Origins of the Constitution and American National Identity.* Edited by R. Beeman, S. Botein, and E. C. Carter. Chapel Hill: University of North Carolina Press, 1987: 333–348.

National Endowment for the Humanities. *American Memory: A Report on the Humanities in the Nation's Schools.* Washington, D.C. 1987.

National Task Force on Citizenship Education. *Education for Responsible Citizenship: the Report of the National Task Force on Citizenship Education.* New York: McGraw-Hill, 1977.

Nettl, J. P. "The State as a Conceptual Variable." *World Politics* 20 (1968): 559–592.

New Hampshire Bicentennial Commission on the United States Constitution. *New Hampshire: The State That Made Us a Nation.* Portsmouth, N.H.: P. E. Randall (for the Commission), 1989.

Nimmo, Dan and James Coombs. *Mediated Political Realities,* 2nd ed. New York: Longman, 1990.

Nisbet, Robert. *The Quest for Community.* London: Oxford University Press, 1969 (1953).

————. *The Twilight of Authority.* New York: Oxford University Press, 1975.

Norton, Anne. "Transubstantiation: The Dialectic of Constitutional Authority," *University of Chicago Law Review* 55 (1988): 458–472.

Oliver, Leonard P. *The Art of Citizenship: Public Issue Forums.* Dayton: Kettering Foundation, 1983.

Ollman, Bertell. *Alienation.* New York: Cambridge University Press, 1971.

Paletz, David L., Roberta E. Pearson, and Donald L. Willis. *Politics in Public Service Advertising on Television.* New York: Praeger, 1977.

Pelikan, Jaroslav. *The Vindication of Tradition.* New Haven: Yale University Press, 1984.

Peller, Gary. "The Metaphysics of American Law." *California Law Review* 73 (1987): 1151–1290.

Persons, Stow. "The Cyclical Theory of History in Eighteenth Century America." *American Quarterly* 6 (1954): 147–163.

Peterson, Merrill D. *The Jefferson Image in the American Mind.* New York: Oxford University Press, 1960.

Pierce, Bessie Louise. *Civic Attitudes in American School Textbooks.* Chicago: University of Chicago Press, 1930.

————. *Public Opinion and the Teaching of History in the United States.* New York: Da Capo Press, 1970 (1926).

Pitkin, Hanna Fenichel. *The Concept of Representation*. Berkeley: University of California Press, 1967.

Pocock, J. G. A. *Politics, Language and Time*. Chicago: University of Chicago, 1989.

————. *Virtue, Commerce, and History*. Cambridge: Cambridge University Press, 1985.

Postman, Neil. *Teaching as a Conserving Activity*. New York: Delacorte, 1979.

Pratte, Richard. *The Civic Imperative: Examining the Need for Civic Education*. New York: Teachers College Press, 1988.

Procter, David E. *Enacting Political Culture: Rhetorical Transformations of Liberty Weekend*. New York: Praeger, 1991.

Real, Michael R. *Mass-Mediated Culture*. Englewood Cliffs, N.J.: Prentice-Hall, 1977.

Rehnquist, William H. "The Notion of a Living Constitution." *Texas Law Review* 54 (1976): 693–706.

Remy, Richard C. "The Constitution in Citizen Education," *Social Education* 51 (February 1987): 331–336.

Resnick, Daniel P. "Historical Perspectives on Literacy and Schooling." *Daedalus* 119, no. 2 (Spring 1990): 15–32.

Rossiter, Clinton, ed. *The Federalist Papers*. New York: New American Library, 1961.

Savage, Robert L. and Dan Nimmo, eds., *Politics in Familiar Contexts: Projecting Politics Through Popular Media*. Norwood, NJ: Ablex, 1990.

Schaar, John. *Legitimacy in the Modern State*. New Brunswick, NJ: Transaction, 1981.

Schattschneider, E. E. *The Semi-Sovereign People*. New York, Holt, Rinehart and Winston, 1960.

Schuck, Peter and Rogers Smith. *Citizenship Without Consent*. New Haven: Yale University Press, 1985.

Schudson, Michael. *Advertising: The Uneasy Persuasion*. New York: Basic, 1984.

————. "The Present in the Past versus the Past in the Present," *Communication* 11 (1989): 105–113.

————. *Watergate in American Memory.* New York: Basic Books, 1992.

Schwartz, Barry. *George Washington: The Making of an American Symbol.* Ithaca: Cornell University Press, 1987.

Shaver, James P., O. L. Davis, Jr., and Suzanne W. Helburn. "The Status of Social Studies Education: Impressions from Three NSF Studies." *Social Education* 43 (February 1979): 150–153.

Shils, Edward. *Center and Periphery.* Chicago: University of Chicago Press, 1975.

Shils, Edward, and Michael Young. "The Meaning of the Coronation." *Sociological Review* I (1953): 63–81.

Singer, Milton. "On the Symbolic and Historic Structure of an American Identity." *Ethos* 5 (1977): 431–454.

Skowronek, Stephen. *Building a New American State.* New York: Cambridge University Press, 1982.

Soltow, Lee, and Edward Stevens, *The Rise of Literacy and the Origins of the Common School in the United States.* Chicago: University of Chicago Press, 1981.

Spiro, Melford. "Buddhism and Economic Action in Burma." *American Anthropologist* 68 (1966): 1163–1173.

Stendardi, Edward J. Jr. "Corporate Philanthropy: The Redefinition of Enlightened Self-Interest." *The Social Science Journal* 25 (1992): 21–30.

Stotsky, Sandra. ed. *Connecting Civic Education and Language Education.* New York: Teachers College Press, 1991.

Taylor, Charles. *Hegel and Modern Society.* Cambridge: Cambridge University Press, 1979.

Thompson, Michael, Richard Ellis, and Aaron Wildavsky. *Cultural Theory.* Boulder: Westview, 1990.

Thurmond, Strom. "The Bicentennial of the Constitution." *Marquette Law Review* 70 (1987): 375–380.

Tocqueville, Alexis de. *Democracy in America,* 2 vols. Edited by Phillips Bradley. New York: Vintage, 1945 (1835).

Turner, Mary Jane. "Civic Education in the United States." In *Political Education in Flux.* Edited by D. Heater and J. A. Gillespie. London: Sage, 1981: 49–80.

Tussman, Joseph. *Obligation and the Body Politic.* New York: Oxford University Press, 1960.

Tyack, David, and Larry Cuban. *Tinkering toward Utopia: A Century of Public School Reform.* Cambridge, MA: Harvard University Press, 1995.

Varenne, Herve, ed. *Symbolizing America.* Lincoln: University of Nebraska Press, 1986.

Verba, Sidney, and Norman H. Nie. *Participation in America.* Chicago: University of Chicago Press, 1972.

Walzer, Michael. "On the Role of Symbolism in Political Thought." *Political Science Quarterly* 87 (1967): 191–204.

Warner, Michael. *The Letters of the Republic: Publication and the Public Sphere in Eighteenth-Century America.* Cambridge, MA: Harvard University Press, 1990.

Warner, William Lloyd. *The Living and the Dead: A Study of the Symbolic Life of Americans.* New Haven: Yale University Press, 1959.

Weber, Max. *Economy and Society,* 2 vols. Edited by G. Roth and C. Wittich. 2 vols. Berkeley: University of California, 1978.

Welter, Rush. *Popular Education and Democratic Thought in America.* New York: Columbia University Press, 1962.

Wirt, Frederick M. "The Uses of Blandness: State, Local, and Professional Roles in Citizenship Education." In *Teaching About American Federal Democracy.* Edited by S. L. Schechter. Philadelphia: Center for the Study of Federalism, 1984: 79–89.

Wolin, Sheldon. "Contract and Birthright." In *The New Populism: The Politics of Empowerment.* Edited by H. C. Boyte and F. Reissman. Philadelphia: Temple University Press, 1986: 284–301.

———. "The People's Two Bodies." *Democracy* 1, no. 1 (January 1981): 9–24.

———. *The Presence of the Past: Essays on the State and the Constitution*. Baltimore: Johns Hopkins University Press, 1989.

Wood, Gordon S. *The Creation of the American Republic, 1776–1787*. New York: Norton, 1972 (1969).

Zelinsky, Wilbur. *Nation into State: The Shifting Symbolic Foundations of American Nationalism*. Chapel Hill: University of North Carolina Press, 1988.

Index